JUVENILE
LAW

JUVENILE LAW

Ochc record

Toni Marsh

THOMSON

DELMAR LEARNING Australia   Brazil   Canada   Mexico   Singapore   Spain   United Kingdom   United States

THOMSON
———✳———
DELMAR LEARNING

WEST LEGAL STUDIES
Juvenile Law
by Toni Marsh

Vice President, Career Education Strategic Business Unit:
Dawn Gerrain

Acquisitions Editor:
Shelley Esposito

Senior Product Manager:
Melissa Riveglia

Editorial Assistant:
Melissa A. Zasa

Director of Production:
Wendy A. Troeger

Content Project Manager:
Matthew J. Williams

Director of Marketing:
Wendy E. Mapstone

Marketing Channel Manager:
Gerard McAvey

Marketing Coordinator:
Jonathan Sheehan

Cover Design:
Dan Masucci

Cover Image:
Spike Mafford/Getty Images

Library of Congress Cataloging-in-Publication Data

Marsh, Toni.
   Juvenile law / Toni Marsh.
       p. cm.—(West legal studies)
   Includes bibliographical references and index.
   1. Juvenile justice, Administration of—United States. 2. Children—Legal status, laws, etc.—United States.
I. Title.
   KF9779.M37 2007
   345.73'08—dc22
                                      2006018689
ISBN: 1401840191

NOTICE TO THE READER

DEDICATION

To Jim, Anne, and Helen
con amore

CONTENTS

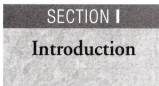

Chapter 4   INTERROGATION   41

Chapter 5   PRETRIAL DETENTION   65

Chapter 6	**DELINQUENCY HEARINGS**	**79**

Chapter 7   YOUTH COURT   100

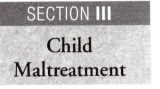

Chapter 9   **CHILD ABUSE AND NEGLECT**   **133**

Chapter 10 **ABUSE-NEGLECT-DEPENDENCY HEARINGS** **161**

Juvenile law is not easy and it is not simple because at the heart of every case is a hurt child. Legal standards can be vague and difficult to apply. Facts are slippery. Witnesses are unreliable. Cases go on forever, and nobody ever wins in a juvenile case. The nearest they come to a victory is when they limit the damage inflicted upon the child.

Juvenile law is physically draining. Practitioners are in court almost every day. They drive all over the city visiting children and families, interviewing witnesses, social workers, doctors, and teachers. They spend hours poring over case files, medical records, school records, and case law.

Juvenile law is emotionally draining. The stories are horrific. The things some children have had to endure in their short, innocent lives shouldn't happen to a thousand people in a thousand lifetimes.

Juvenile law is frustrating. Practitioners work for hours or days crafting solutions to problems only to have the parties reject them, or agree to them but fail to follow through. They labor to navigate a child through court or rehabilitation, only to run into him in the same court two weeks later for a different incident.

And juvenile law doesn't pay well.

So why do they do it? Why do lawyers and paralegals not only do, but love the toughest job in the law?

Because juvenile law matters.

Juvenile practitioners are the good guys. They have the most important job in the world. They represent the weakest, most vulnerable, most voiceless people on the planet—children. More often than not, the lawyers and paralegals who represent these children are the only positive, caring adults they have ever known.

PHILOSOPHICAL APPROACHES TO JUVENILE LAW

Some people believe that in abuse and neglect cases the family court must work to preserve and maintain the family unit at all costs. Others believe the court must protect children even if it means breaking up the family. Some believe that the parents' right to raise their children as they see fit is paramount and that if the court doesn't like it, too bad for the court. Others believe that a child's right not to be abused outweighs the parents' right to abuse.

Some observers believe that when a child breaks the law, it is the child who is the victim and that the delinquent act is evidence that society has failed the child. They believe the law should educate and rehabilitate juvenile offenders.

Others believe that it doesn't matter why juveniles break the law. All that matters is that they broke the law and they should, therefore, be punished. These observers believe delinquency law should be more criminalized and that the ultimate aim of the law should be to protect society and punish juvenile delinquents.

None of these ideas is right or wrong and all of them are right and wrong. There are as many answers as there are children, and like children, no two are the same.

Students, practitioners, and paralegals need to embrace the complexities inherent in juvenile law. The practice requires finesse, flexibility, creativity, empathy, and an open mind. It isn't enough to do everything correctly in a legal sense, although that is essential. Practitioners must also remain constantly aware of and sensitive to children and their families.

Throughout this text you will find difficult questions that have no right answers. These questions are intended to spark discussion and get students and teachers thinking. Ideally, you will finish this book with a keen understanding of how great and important a task it is to take on the care of children. You will also be aware of how much you can never know.

CHANGES IN JUVENILE LAW

Juvenile law has changed considerably over the years in response to events and shifts in public opinion. It is a volatile and emotional area that is particularly prone to reactive legislation.

The law of abuse-neglect-dependency has changed in two ways. First, some states and counties have revised their statutory schemes to reflect changed attitudes toward family reunification and children's vs. parents' rights. Some state laws now mandate that family reunification must be the ultimate goal of every abuse-neglect-dependency case and must remain so unless and until circumstances indicate that reunification is impossible. Other state legislatures mandate that county agencies and courts need not make efforts toward reunification if the parents have done such things as torture their children or grossly neglect them.

Second, in response to a spate of child abuse related tragedies involving the deaths of several children, many courts and county agencies have changed the way they conduct business. Courts have narrowed the list of practitioners allowed to try juvenile cases, and raised the standards relating to those practitioners. Among other things, they have mandated shorter time limits for bringing cases to trial and have demanded more investigation, follow up, and advocacy. Counties have decreased social worker caseloads and stepped up foster family recruitment, screening, and training.

Delinquency law has also changed. There has been a trend in recent years to favor transferring juve-niles to adult court under a wider set of circumstances and at younger ages. There has been more emphasis on punishment and retribution as societal goals and less on rehabilitation and reformation.

A BRIEF HISTORY OF THE JUVENILE COURT IN AMERICA

Throughout the 17th, 18th, and early 19th centuries there were no children in America in the eyes of American law. There were only miniature adults who were bound by the same laws and subject to the same criminal penalties as full grown adults. Those criminal penalties included hard labor, imprisonment, and death.[1]

Juveniles stood trial in adult courts, were bound by the same legal standards as adults, received the same penalties as adults, and went to the same prisons as adults, where they shared cells with adult prisoners. There was no separation between children and adults in prisons throughout the 18th and much of the 19th centuries.

In 1825, the Society for the Prevention of Juvenile Delinquency (originally named the Society for the Prevention of Pauperism) founded the New York House of Refuge, a detention facility designed solely for juveniles. Youths worked inside the facility, learned basic literacy skills, and received evangelical religious instruction. By the middle of the century, the House of Refuge was a model for reform institutions around the country.

---

[1] The Commonwealth of Massachusetts executed Thomas Graunger, a 16-year-old Plymouth boy, for the crime of bestiality in 1642. This was the first recorded execution of a juvenile in America. The state of Connecticut hanged 12-year-old Hannah Ocuish for murder in 1786. She was the youngest female the government has ever executed. The federal government of Arkansas executed 10-year-old Native American James Arcene for his involvement in a robbery and murder in 1885. He was the youngest person the American government has executed. The youngest juvenile to receive the death penalty in modern times was 14-year-old George Stinney, who received the death penalty in 1944 for the crime of murder.

The genesis for the House of Refuge and other juvenile institutions was in the belief held by a group of Americans, who came to be known as the "child savers," that delinquency was rooted in juveniles' lack of education and moral guidance. This group believed that society was responsible for juveniles and bore some of the blame for their delinquency. They advocated rehabilitation and education for juvenile delinquents.

Although there were separate juvenile detention facilities, there were no separate juvenile courts until the State of Illinois founded the nation's first juvenile court in 1899. The doctrine of *parens patriae,* or the state as parent, governed the operation of the Illinois court and those that followed. *Parens patriae,* prevalent throughout England, held that the state had the right and the duty to assume a parental role in juveniles' lives where their own parents failed to do so.

Parens patriae allowed juvenile courts to operate differently from the adult courts. Where adult courts required a probable violation of law before a prosecution could proceed, the juvenile courts could proceed on lesser grounds. Where the criminal courts were adversarial, the juvenile courts operated in communion with and for the benefit of juvenile defendants. Where the criminal courts had punishment, retribution, and deterrence as their goals, the juvenile courts had rehabilitation, education, and healing as their goals.

Operating under the *parens patriae* doctrine created a new set of problems, however, associated with the lack of standardized operating procedures—what is called "due process" in the criminal courts. The courts were meant to be informal and individualized, but they could be arbitrary and capricious at times. Juveniles often experienced worse treatment under the auspices of the paternalistic juvenile courts than they would have under the disinterested criminal courts.

Over time, the Supreme Court began to recognize and mandate certain constitutional protections for juveniles. The Supreme Court held in *Kent v. United States,* 383 U.S. 541 (1966), that juvenile defendants were entitled to hearings that measure up to the basic constitutional standards of due process. The Court continued through a series of cases to recognize more and greater constitutional protections for juveniles. Each case chipped away at *parens patriae* and built up constitutional protections around juveniles.

The court is still struggling to strike a balance among the competing interests of *parens patriae,* constitutional protections for juveniles, and the protection of society from delinquent juveniles. The most recent Supreme Court case to consider juvenile justice is *Roper v. Simmons,* No. 03-633 (argued October 13, 2004). In that case, the court decided by a 5–4 majority that it is unconstitutional to execute offenders for crimes they committed when they were juveniles. The *Roper* opinion was controversial and divisive, prompting angry and critical dissenting opinions.

Meanwhile, the states have been moving away from *parens patriae* and its purported goals of rehabilitation and education and back toward the more adult-like juvenile justice system of the 17th, 18th, and early 19th centuries. Since 1992, all but three states have enacted laws to make their juvenile justice systems more punitive. These state laws have increased the courts' ability to transfer juveniles to adult court, increased courts' sentencing options, and modified or removed traditional juvenile court confidentiality provisions.[2]

THE NEED FOR THIS TEXT

I wrote this book for two reasons. The first is to address vital issues concerning children in a reasonable, thorough, and intelligent manner. We need to face the problems that pervade our society and seek solutions for them. Many students of law—paralegals, college students, and law students—begin their educations with a desire to advocate for children. Somewhere along the line, they lose that desire because there is so

[2] Sickmund, M., & Snyder, H. M. (1999). Juvenile Offenders and Victims: 1999 National Report, OJJDP.

little in the system to encourage them to pursue child advocacy goals.

The second is that there are not enough juvenile law courses offered in the colleges and paralegal schools, and there is a dearth of good textbooks to use in those courses. Unlike the juvenile law textbooks currently available, which cover only one aspect of juvenile law, this book covers juvenile delinquency, child maltreatment, and other aspects of the laws that affect juveniles. I hope this book will encourage schools to offer more juvenile courses and I hope it will encourage more people to take on the challenges of juvenile law.

ORGANIZATION OF THE TEXT

This book comprises four sections. The first section is an introduction and overview. The second section covers delinquency and includes material on transfer to adult court, serious youth offenders, status offenses, the death penalty, and constitutional considerations surrounding detention, interrogation, and juvenile hearings.

The third section addresses child maltreatment. You will find the law governing temporary and permanent removal of children from their parents and efforts at reunification, including case plans, social services, and treatment programs available to children and parents in this section. There is also material on foster care, group homes, and other custodial arrangements.

Finally, there is a section on current issues. Here, I survey current topics such as youth gangs, parental notification of abortion and judicial bypass, emancipation, and marriage.

WHO SHOULD USE THIS BOOK

This book can serve as the text for a paralegal or legal assistant course on juvenile law or a college level course on juvenile law, criminal law, social work, or law enforcement.

PEDAGOGY

Each chapter contains:

Sidebars—These are boxed-text sections containing discussion of an interesting and illuminating matter that explains, complements, or enlarges upon issues in the text.

Illustrative Cases—These are highly condensed real cases that either illustrate a particular concept or are landmark cases.

Case Problems—These are problems based upon real cases. The answers and the citations to the actual cases appear in the instructor's manual.

Role-Play Problems—These are fictional cases or problems that teachers can use as in-class exercises. Each role-play problem has one or more roles that students can assume. Students should formulate arguments in support of their assigned positions, and advocate zealously for those positions.

Hypothetical Problems—These are also fictional problems designed to stimulate thought and discussion. Like the role-play problems, they are designed to illustrate important or subtle concepts in the chapter.

Ethical Concerns—These sections raise issues that have caused, or can potentially cause, ethical problems. They represent areas where practitioners are divided on the appropriate legal obligations or approaches to the law.

Discussion Questions—Instructors can use these questions to spark class discussions or as a basis for homework assignments.

Key Terms—These are terms that are new, unusual, or require explanation.

SUPPLEMENTAL TEACHING MATERIALS

• The **Instructor's Manual with Test Bank** is available online at www.westlegalstudies.com in the Instructor's Lounge under Resource. Written by the author of the text, the *Instructor's Manual* contains lecture outlines, teaching tips, suggested assignments, suggested testing, answers to the text questions, and a test bank.

• 🔵 **Online Companion**™—The Online Companion™ Web site can be found at www.westlegalstudies.com in the Resource section of the Web site. The Online Companion™ contains Power-Point presentations.

• **Web page**—Visit our Web site at www.westlegalstudies.com, where you will find valuable information specific to this book such as hot links and sample materials to download, as well as other West Legal Studies products.

• **Westlaw**®—West's online computerized legal research system offers students "hands-on" experience with a system commonly used in law offices. Qualified adopters can receive 10 free hours of Westlaw. Westlaw can be accessed with Macintosh and IBM PC and compatibles. A modem is required.

AUTHOR'S NOTE

I have omitted footnotes and citations in the cases, and heavily edited those cases without so indicating within the text. Readers wishing to read the full cases will find the citations in the text. I have used gender designations randomly.

Please note that Internet resources are of a time-sensitive nature and URL addresses may often be changed or deleted.

Contact us at westlegalstudies@delmar.com

ACKNOWLEDGMENTS

I would like to thank Shelley Esposito, Melissa Riveglia, Brian Banks, Sarah Duncan, and Pamela Fuller at Thomson Delmar Learning for their patience and generous assistance in bringing this book about. I would like also to express my sincere thanks to the many reviewers who offered their guidance in the development of this book.

Patricia Adongo
University of La Verne
La Verne, California

Mary Arnstein
Mt. Aloysius College
Cressen, Pennsylvania

Marilou Erb
Penn State–York and York College
Hanover, Pennsylvania

Craig Hemmens
Boise State University
Boise, Idaho

Melissa Howe
University of Paralegal Studies, LLC
Duncan, Oklahoma

David Meyer
University of Illinois College of Law
Champaign, Illinois

Kathryn Myers
St. Mary of the Woods College
St. Mary of the Woods, Indiana

Lisa O'Rear-Lassen
Cuyahoga Community College
Parma, Ohio

Kim Phifer-Starks
Tulane University College
Biloxi, Mississippi

Judith Sturgill
North Central State College
Mansfield, Ohio

Special thanks to the following people, who helped me in so many ways:

Officer William Annandono, Mayfield Village, Ohio
    Police Department
Ellen Erzen, Cuyahoga Community College
Anthony and Helen Frabotta
Gabrielle Frabotta
Morgan Hope
Gil and Lea Marsh
Midori Marsh
Mitsuko Marsh
Naomi Marsh
Probation Officer Ronald Penn, Lyndhurst, Ohio
    Municipal Court
Allie Petit
Susan Price and Karen Olivier Dunne, Cecil County
    Domestic Violence/Rape Crisis Center
Andrew Rivas, Esquire, Archdiocese of Washington,
    D.C.
Elizabeth Turqman, Esquire, BBG
Marla Wolfe, Esquire

Toni Marsh is a Washington, DC attorney who has been practicing juvenile law since 1991 and has taught at Georgetown University, Marymount University, and Cuyahoga Community College. She designed and directed the Paralegal Studies program at The University of North Carolina at Charlotte and is currently the Director of the Paralegal Studies Master's program at The George Washington University in Washington, DC.

SECTION I

Introduction

Chapter 1

JURISDICTION

OBJECTIVES

At the end of this chapter, the student should know:

- How age determines jurisdiction
- The minimum and maximum ages for juvenile court jurisdiction in the various states
- The parameters of the Indivisible Day Rule
- The subject matter over which juvenile courts have jurisdiction, such as delinquency, abuse-neglect-dependency, status offenses, serious youthful offenders, emancipation, judicial bypass, traffic offenses, and parentage actions

INTRODUCTION

Determining which cases a court will hear is a matter of determining the court's jurisdiction. Jurisdiction is the authority by which courts and judicial officers take charge of and decide cases.

Courts can have jurisdiction over cases by virtue of their subject matter or the properties of the people involved. Juvenile courts acquire jurisdiction over children by virtue of their age and the subject matter of the action.

AGE JURISDICTION

Age is a primary factor in juvenile actions. Some actions, such as delinquency actions, traffic offenses, and status offenses, have statutory minimum and maximum ages. Others, such as abuse-neglect-dependency actions and parental actions, have no minimum age but have a maximum age. Abuse-neglect-dependency actions involve children who have been victims of intentional, negligent, or innocent mistreatment, inattention, abandonment, or relinquishment.

EXHIBIT 1-1 Maximum Age for Juvenile Court Jurisdiction[1]

Age	State
15	Connecticut, New York, North Carolina
16	Georgia, Illinois, Louisiana, Massachusetts, Michigan, Missouri, New Hampshire, South Carolina, Texas, Wisconsin
17	Alabama, Alaska, Arizona, Arkansas, California, Colorado, Delaware, District of Columbia, Florida, Hawaii, Idaho, Indiana, Iowa, Kansas, Kentucky, Maine, Maryland, Minnesota, Mississippi, Montana, Nebraska, Nevada, New Jersey, New Mexico, North Dakota, Ohio, Oklahoma, Oregon, Pennsylvania, Rhode Island, South Dakota, Tennessee, Utah, Vermont, Virginia, Washington, West Virginia, Wyoming

[1]Source: Snyder, H. N. & Sickmund, M. (1999). *Juvenile Offenders and victims: 1999 National Report.* Washington, DC: Office of Juvenile Justice and Delinquency Prevention.

Maximum Age

jurisdiction

The authority by which courts and judicial officers take charge of and decide cases

Every state has a maximum age beyond which the juvenile court will not have **jurisdiction** over a person. This applies to all actions the juvenile court handles: abuse-neglect-dependency, delinquency, emancipation, marriage, and parental notification of abortion, parentage, and custody.

Exhibit 1-1 lists the maximum ages for the 50 states and the District of Columbia. Ages range from a maximum of 15 years old to a maximum of 17 years old, with the majority of states having a maximum age of 17 years old.

Most states define juveniles for jurisdictional purposes in delinquency actions as anyone under the age of 18. This means that the maximum age at which the state will **prosecute** a person as a delinquent is 17 years. If a person commits a crime on or after her eighteenth birthday the criminal court will have jurisdiction. Some states designate 15 or 16 years old as the maximum age for juvenile court jurisdiction.

prosecute

To file and follow through on criminal or delinquency charges against a person with the ultimate aim of gaining a conviction

North Carolina is an example of a state with a maximum age of 15 years. The applicable statutes define a "delinquent juvenile as any juvenile less than 16 years old but older than 6 years old" and mandate that the juvenile court has exclusive original jurisdiction over delinquent juveniles.

exclusive jurisdiction

The sole power to hear an action. Those courts possessing exclusive jurisdiction are the only courts empowered to hear cases falling within that jurisdiction

In some states both the juvenile court and the criminal court have **exclusive jurisdiction** over juveniles above a certain age who have committed certain offenses. This means that these courts are the courts in which juvenile actions begin. In these states the prosecutors decide in which forum they will prosecute the juvenile.

NORTH CAROLINA GENERAL STATUTES

§ 7B-1501. Definitions. In this Subchapter, unless the context clearly requires otherwise, the following words have the listed meanings.

(7) Delinquent juvenile.—Any juvenile who, while less than 16 years of age but at least 6 years of age, commits a crime or infraction under State law or under an ordinance of local government, including violation of the motor vehicle laws.

§ 7B-1601. Jurisdiction over delinquent juveniles. (a) The court has exclusive, original jurisdiction over any case involving a juvenile who is alleged to be delinquent. For purposes of determining jurisdiction, the age of the juvenile at the time of the alleged offense governs.

The **Indivisible Day Rule** states that the court will consider a person to have aged one year at midnight on that person's birthday regardless of the actual time of the person's birth. Most juvenile courts use this method to calculate a juvenile's age. So if a person was born at 8:00 p.m. on August 15, 1986, that person legally will turn 18 at 12:01 a.m. on August 15, 2004. If that person commits a crime at noon on August 15, 2004, the case will proceed in adult criminal court, not in juvenile court.

In cases where juveniles lie to the courts about their ages, most courts will treat them as juveniles once they discover their true ages. Some courts have held otherwise, reasoning that this allows juveniles to conceal their ages throughout a criminal proceeding and then reveal their ages if they do not like the result. Appellate courts have generally held on appeal that despite the possibility of such a charade, juvenile courts cannot waive their exclusive jurisdiction, nor can they confer jurisdiction where it does not exist.

Indivisible Day Rule
The rule that states that the court will consider a person to be a certain age at the start of the day on that person's birthday regardless of the person's actual time of birth

Minimum Age

Some states designate an age below which a child will be presumed to be incapable of **criminal intent.** Criminal intent is the affirmative desire to bring about an unlawful and malicious result through a specific action. For criminal intent to be present, the actor must have desired a certain result and must have intended to bring about that result. Exhibit 1-2 illustrates the minimum age at which a state will attribute criminal intent to a juvenile.

criminal intent
(or *mens rea,* "guilty mind") Desiring to do something illegal or malicious. Wanting to bring about a certain result and working to bring about that result

EXHIBIT 1-2 Minimum Age for Juvenile Court Delinquency Jurisdiction[2]

Age	State
6	North Carolina
7	Maryland, Massachusetts, New York
8	Arizona
9	Arkansas, Colorado, Kansas, Louisiana, Minnesota, Mississippi, Pennsylvania, South Dakota, Texas, Vermont, Wisconsin

[2]The other 35 states have no minimum age for jurisdiction.

SIDEBAR

VERY YOUNG KILLERS

Traditional English law held for centuries that children below the age of 8 were not accountable for their actions in any sense, and children below the age of 15 were capable of forming the requisite intent to be fully culpable for their actions. As the Minimum Age chart shows, the majority of American states still hold that very young children will not stand trial for their crimes.

But what does the system do when a very young child commits a horrendous act? In May 2005 a seven-year-old Florida boy took his sevenmonth-old sister, Jayza Laney Simms, out of her crib and lay her on a pile of blankets, where he proceeded to punch her, kick her, and beat her with a twoby-four until she was near death. He then went outside and told his parents the baby was bleeding. The parents rushed the baby to the emergency room, but she was dead by the time they arrived.

The boy told hospital and police personnel first that he accidentally dropped the baby on her head. Then he told them that another family member dropped her on her head and stepped on her. Finally, he admitted what he did. Seasoned detectives were shocked; they said they had never seen a young child display "so much violence and so little remorse," according to police spokeswoman Laura McElroy.

State authorities struggled for months over what to do with the boy. One commentator, Steve Drizin, assistant director of the Bluhm Legal Clinic at Northwestern School of Law, opined that the response should be one of compassion and understanding rather than punishment. Arthur Busch, a former Michigan state prosecutor who handled a case involving a six-year-old boy who shot a classmate to death, commented, "These are children who still believe in the tooth fairy and the Easter bunny and Santa Claus. Their view of

(continues)

reality is much different that [that] of adults." Busch went on to comment, "If we are a society which gives up on seven-year-olds, God help us."

After struggling with the issue for several months, prosecutors finally decided in July to charge the boy with aggravated manslaughter. Florida state attorney spokeswoman Pam Bondi said, "We thought that the juvenile system was the place for him, where he can get the help he needs."

The following September Circuit Judge Mark R. Wolfe ruled that the boy was not competent to stand trial. He based his decision upon the reports of court-appointed doctors, but he held out the possibility that the boy could receive training or counseling to help him better understand court proceedings.

SUBJECT MATTER JURISDICTION

The juvenile court has jurisdiction over most legal actions involving children. The exception would be in states where the family court or the domestic relations court has jurisdiction over parental actions and where the criminal court has original jurisdiction over certain crimes that juveniles over a certain age commit.

Subject matter jurisdiction is of two categories—acts upon children, and acts by children. Actions upon children include **abuse, neglect, and/or dependency** (a-n-d); establishment of paternity; adoption; custody; visitation; and child support. Actions by children include delinquency, including transfers to adult court; status offenses; abortion; and traffic offenses.

abuse-neglect-dependency actions
Actions involving a child who has been the victim of intentional, negligent, or innocent mistreatment, inattention, abandonment or relinquishment

Actions by Juveniles

There are two classes of actions that can affect juveniles and over which the juvenile court has jurisdiction: actions by juveniles, or actions in which juveniles engage, such as delinquency, emancipation, marriage, and abortion; and actions upon juveniles, or actions in which adults engage that affect juveniles, such as abuse, neglect, dependency, parentage, custody, child support, and other domestic matters.

Delinquency

Juvenile courts have exclusive original jurisdiction over **delinquency** actions subject to the age requirements outlined above. Most states define delinquency as a juvenile committing an act that would have been a crime if an adult had committed it. It is a noncriminal event. (*See* Chapter 2, Delinquency Overview.)

delinquency
Committing an act that would be a crime if an adult committed it

Serious Youthful Offenders

serious youthful offender statutes

A new category of delinquency statutes that allow blended sentences in delinquency cases that are serious but not serious enough to warrant transfer to criminal court

In those states that have **serious youthful offender statutes** the juvenile courts exercise jurisdiction over such actions. These statutes apply where a juvenile has committed an act that is too serious to warrant juvenile treatment but is not serious enough to warrant criminal court treatment. They also apply where the court's disposition in a juvenile case will extend beyond the period of the juvenile's minority. (See Chapter 8, Transfer to Adult Court.)

If a matter is very serious, the juvenile court can waive jurisdiction over the juvenile and transfer that jurisdiction to the adult criminal court. (See Chapter 8, Transfer to Adult Court.)

Status Offenses

Status offenses are offenses that are only punishable because of the juvenile status of the people who have committed them; they are not inherently criminal. They include curfew violation, truancy, marriage without parental permission, running away from home, and alcohol consumption.

Juvenile courts have jurisdiction over youths who have committed these offenses and can use any of the range of dispositional alternatives available to them upon an adjudication of status offender. (See Chapter 2, Delinquency Overview.)

Traffic Offenses

Juvenile traffic offenses are by far the most common actions that juvenile courts hear. There are traffic offenses that apply to all drivers and traffic offenses that apply strictly to juvenile drivers. Many criminal offenses include a suspension of driving privileges as part of their dispositions.

There is a distinction between offenses that are purely traffic offenses, such as exceeding the speed limit, and offenses that cross into criminal or delinquent behavior, such as vehicular homicide. If the statute that the juvenile violated is a criminal statute, most jurisdictions will authorize the state to prosecute the juvenile as a delinquent.

Parental Notification of Abortion and Judicial Bypass

judicial bypass

A court order authorizing a minor girl to obtain an abortion without having notified or obtained the permission of her parent or guardian

Parental notification of abortion statutes require minor girls to notify or obtain the consent of one or both of their parents before they can obtain abortions. The girl can circumvent the requirement in most of the states that have such statutes by obtaining a **judicial bypass.** A judicial bypass is a court order authorizing a minor girl to obtain an abortion without having notified or obtained the permission of her parent or guardian, if she can prove to the court that she is of sufficient maturity to make important decisions and that she will be subject to abuse or injury if she notifies her parents of her pregnancy. Juvenile courts have jurisdiction over judicial bypass actions. (See Chapter 12, Parental Notification of Abortion and Judicial Bypass.)

Emancipation

The juvenile court has jurisdiction over **emancipation** actions. Through emancipation, minors are granted the legal status of adults for purposes of housing, employment, contractual obligations, legal actions, and other activities. It frees the parents from any obligation to support or otherwise care for their children, and frees the children from the constraints of parental authority.

Emancipation can come about through the petition of the minors or the parents. The courts will grant emancipation where they determine the minor petitioners are financially, physically, and emotionally independent of their parents, and that emancipation would be in their best interests. (*See* Chapter 11, Emancipation.)

emancipation
The legal recognition that a child is mature enough to have the legal status of adult. Emancipation removes many of the legal disabilities attendant to minority

Actions upon Juveniles

This class of cases over which the juvenile court has jurisdiction comprises abuse-neglect-dependency actions, and in some states, all domestic actions, such as parentage, child support, custody, and visitation where the parents of the subject children have never been married.

Abuse-Neglect-Dependency

The juvenile court can assume jurisdiction over children if they have been subjected to abuse or neglect at the hands of parents or guardians. The court can also take jurisdiction over children it adjudges dependent.

Children are abused when they have suffered physical, sexual, or emotional harm. Most abuse statutes do not specify who inflicted the harm; it is sufficient for an adjudication of abuse that the court determines harm has occurred. Children are neglected when they receive less than adequate care in such areas as housing, diet, personal hygiene, education, or medical care. As in abuse, most neglect statutes focus on the neglect that has occurred and not on the person who is responsible for the neglect.

Children are dependent when the court must assume jurisdiction over them in order to provide them with necessary care through no fault of the parent or guardian. An adjudication of dependency is appropriate where a parent is severely physically or mentally disabled, deceased, imprisoned, or otherwise incapacitated. (*See* Chapter 9, Child Abuse and Neglect.)

The Ohio statute is an example of a statute granting the juvenile court jurisdiction over the panoply of matters outlined above.

OH ST § 2151.23 JURISDICTION OF JUVENILE COURT; ORDERS FOR CHILD SUPPORT

(A) The juvenile court has exclusive original jurisdiction under the Revised Code as follows:

(1) Concerning any child who on or about the date specified in the complaint, indictment, or information is alleged to have violated [the prohibition against illegal purchase, use or consumption of tobacco or tobacco products] or an order issued under that section or to be a juvenile traffic offender or a delinquent, unruly, abused, neglected, or dependent child and, based on and in relation to the allegation pertaining to the child, concerning the parent, guardian, or other person having care of a child who is alleged to be an unruly or delinquent child for being an habitual or chronic truant;

(10) To hear and determine applications for consent to marry . . .

(11) . . . to hear and determine a request for an order for the support of any child if the request is not ancillary to an action for divorce, dissolution of marriage, annulment, or legal separation, a criminal or civil action involving an allegation of domestic violence, or an action for support brought under Chapter 3115 of the Revised Code . . .

The following case illustrates the manner in which those courts that view abuse as a condition of the child rather than an action by a parent analyze this distinction.

People in Interest of P.D.S.
669 P.2d 627, (Colo.App.1983.)
KELLY, Judge

Respondent is the mother of P.D.S., an infant, who was found by the district court to be neglected or dependent under the Colorado Children's Code and whose physical custody was placed with the mother under a treatment plan. The sole issue on review is whether the district court must adjudicate the child neglected and dependent "as to" one parent only, where it has been stipulated that the child is neglected and dependent but that the other parent is blameless for the child's condition, and where, in return for this stipulation, the request to terminate parental rights was dismissed. We affirm.

Adjudications of neglect or dependency are not made "as to" the parents, but rather, relate only to the status of the child. The provisions of Colorado law define a neglected or dependent child, and make it plain that an adjudication of dependency or neglect is a determination of the status of the child and no more.

The other arguments in support of reversal are without merit.

Judgment affirmed.

CASE PROBLEMS

1. Coley was born at Emanuel Hospital in Portland on December 15, 1981, at 9:43 p.m. On December 15, 1996, the day of his 15th birthday, at around 2:30 p.m., armed with a firearm and aided by two friends, Coley robbed a victim. Based on that conduct, the state charged him with first- and second-degree robbery as an adult pursuant to the state law, which provides, in part:

> "Notwithstanding any other provision of law, when a person charged with [first- or second-degree robbery] is 15, 16 or 17 years of age at the time the offense is committed, and the offense is committed on or after April 1, 1995, * * * the person shall be prosecuted as an adult in criminal court."

Coley argued at trial that the criminal court lacked jurisdiction because the robbery occurred at 2:34 p.m., while he was not born until 9:43 p.m. on that date 15 years earlier. The criminal trial court rejected that argument, concluding that Coley was 15 at the time of the offense. After a bench trial, the court found Coley guilty and sentenced him as provided in the law.

Coley appealed on the grounds that the criminal trial court lacked jurisdiction under the law because he was not 15 years of age at the time he committed the offense. Petitioner particularly argued that the language of the law, and specifically the phrase "at the time the offense is committed," "should not be read so broadly to include any part of the day that offense is committed. The literal reading of the phrase '15, 16, or 17 years of age at the time the offense is committed' means, as applied in this case, that Petitioner was not yet 15 when he committed a crime."

Most simply stated, Coley argued that he was not 15 years of age until 9:43 p.m. on December 15, 1996, more than seven hours after he committed the robbery.

The post-conviction court agreed and ordered the Department of Corrections to release Coley. The court concluded that the law was ambiguous as to whether a person's age for purposes of that statute was to be assessed "precisely from the time of birth to the time of the offense, or from the day of birth to the day of the offense." Accordingly, the court entered a judgment granting Coley post-conviction relief on the grounds that the criminal trial court lacked jurisdiction.

The state appeals. What is the result?

2. Undercover police arrested a man after he attempted to sell narcotics to them. He told police his name was Alejandro Ceja-Prado and that he was 21 years old. He showed police identification that verified those facts.

A federal district attorney charged Ceja-Prado with conspiracy to distribute and possession with intent to distribute methamphetamine. Ceja-Prado pled to the charges. During the plea colloquy the district judge twice asked Ceja-Prado his age and consistent with the birthday that appeared on his identification

Ceja-Prado twice replied that he was twenty-one. At his sentencing hearing three months after his purported birthday the judge asked Ceja-Prado if he was 22 years old and he replied, "Yes." He received a sentence of 151 months in prison followed by three years of supervised probation.

Ceja-Prado filed a motion for remand. In his motion Ceja-Prado asserted for the first time that he is not Alejandro Ceja-Prado who was age 21 at the time of the crime but rather Javier Ceja-Prado who was only 16 years old at that time. He did not deny that he was the person who committed the acts for which he was convicted.

The defendant, a Mexican national who had entered the Untied States several years earlier, insisted that he is Javier and that he had been using his older brother Alejandro's identification papers in order to find work in this country. He contended that he did not disclose his true identity prior to the appeal because he feared the consequences of his use of false identification and he did not understand the special procedural protections afforded juveniles.

Will the appellate court remand Ceja-Prado's case for hearing on the issue of whether he is Alejandro or Javier and to determine his true age?

ROLE-PLAY PROBLEM

Ten-year-olds Robert Thompson and Jon Venables skipped school and spent the day at the mall shoplifting and harassing elderly people. They grew bored and decided to steal a baby. First, they tried to lure a four-year-old boy away from his mother, but stopped when the boy's mother noticed them.

Then they spotted two-year-old James, who was with his mother at the butcher shop. When the butcher misunderstood James's mother's order, she leaned closer to repeat it, looking away from James for just a moment.

"Come here, Baby. Come here, Baby," Jon and Robert whispered, and James went with them.

They led him outside to nearby railroad tracks where they sexually assaulted him, covered him in blue paint, stuck batteries in his mouth, kicked him, shook him, and beat him to death using bricks, rocks, and a large piece of metal they found.

In an effort to cover up what they had done, they laid James on the tracks where a train struck him and cut him in two. They hoped this would make it appear that the child had fallen accidentally onto the tracks and been killed.

Veteran policemen later testified that James's body was one of the most horribly brutalized they had ever seen.

Police soon found Jon and Robert, and under questioning each claimed that the other was the primary actor. Each claimed that he had attempted to stop the other but the other had been out of control. At some point Jon said, "I did kill him." Robert never made such an admission.

In the jurisdiction where these boys live, a child under the age of 10 cannot form the requisite intent to commit a crime. Both boys were a few weeks past 10.

Psychiatrists examined both boys and determined that they were sane, of above-average intelligence, and suffering no mental, physical, or emotional defects or diseases. Jon entertained rescue fantasies about the murder wherein he would save James from Robert. Robert did not discuss his feelings about the murder.

Psychiatric investigation revealed that both boys' fathers were aggressive alcoholics who brutally abused their wives and their children. The boys' mothers and siblings also abused them. At one point police had to stop an interview with Jon and his mother to allow her to calm down.

Both boys had failed a grade at school and were subjected to merciless teasing and bullying about it. They were outcasts. Robert played with dolls and endured ridicule for being girlish and playing with girls. Both boys moved often and frequently changed schools.

1. You work for the defense. What arguments will you proffer to defend your clients? What facts will you use to buttress your arguments?

2. You work for the prosecution. What arguments will you proffer to prosecute these clients? What facts will you use to buttress your arguments?

3. Is there anything more you would like to know to help you make your case to either defend or prosecute these juveniles?

4. Would your approach or your opinions change if the events had occurred a few weeks earlier and both boys had been nine years old?

HYPOTHETICAL PROBLEM

Sharon is six years old. One afternoon, after watching a Three Stooges marathon on television, she poked her fingers into both of her two-year-old sister, Linda's, eyes. Sharon pushed so hard that she actually put out Linda's eyes. She then picked up a broom and hit her sister over the head with it hard enough to cause slight subdural bleeding.

Sharon went into the basement, where her mother was doing laundry and laughingly told her mother what she had done. Her mother ran upstairs and found Linda unconscious and bleeding from the eyes.

Sharon told the hospital social worker that interviewed her that she got the idea to poke out her sister's eyes and hit her with a broom from watching the Three Stooges. The social worker asked Sharon whether she knew that she would hurt Linda, and Sharon said she did. The worker then asked Sharon whether she was sorry that Linda was hurt, and Sharon said she was not. Asked whether she would do it again, she replied that she would.

Sharon lives a state with no minimum age for juvenile court jurisdiction.

1. Should the state bring charges against Sharon?

2. What can a court action do for a child like Sharon?

3. Are there any non-legal actions or programs that could benefit Sharon?

ETHICAL CONCERNS

Prosecutors are supposed to bring charges against those who violate the law. They are not supposed to analyze the offenders' thoughts or motives, beyond the determination of whether they have the requisite criminal intent to commit a criminal act. In the case of very young children, however, prosecutors face the ethical dilemma of balancing their mission to prosecute against the legal, moral, and intellectual complexities involved with prosecuting those who may be incapable of criminal intent.

DISCUSSION QUESTIONS

1. Are very young children capable of evil?

2. Can they truly form the requisite criminal intent to merit prosecution?

3. Is there an age below which no child should ever face prosecution?

4. Can you ever draw a definite line in such cases?

5. What factors should a court consider when deciding whether to exert jurisdiction over a young child?

6. Is a 17-year-old too old for juvenile court jurisdiction?

7. Is it appropriate to have a separate court just for juveniles? Or would it be better to try all juveniles in the adult court?

KEY TERMS

abuse-neglect-dependency actions
criminal intent (or *mens rea*)
delinquency
emancipation
exclusive jurisdiction

Indivisible Day Rule
judicial bypass
jurisdiction
prosecute
serious youthful offender statutes

SECTION II

Delinquency

Chapter 2

DELINQUENCY OVERVIEW

OBJECTIVES

By the end of this chapter, the student should know:

- The terminology of the juvenile justice system
- How various jurisdictions define delinquency and the implications of those definitions
- How trying a juvenile delinquency case differs from trying an adult criminal case
- The meaning of *parens patriae* and how it informs the history and current status of the juvenile justices system
- The definition of a status offense, and how status offenses compare to delinquency
- The difference between procedural due process and substantive due process and how the concepts relate to juvenile justice
- The range of constitutional rights applicable to juveniles, as developed through the cases of *Kent, Gault,* and *Winship*
- The parameters of cross-examination
- The two approaches to juvenile justice

INTRODUCTION

Juvenile justice includes the judicial treatment of delinquency. Delinquency law is primarily the province of state laws, which have juvenile codes, juvenile rules, and juvenile courts. Federal delinquency law primarily concerns the allocation of funding and the setting of standards.

Delinquency is the juvenile term for criminal acts. Juveniles do not commit crimes. When a minor commits an act that would have been a crime if an adult had committed it, the juvenile court may adjudicate that minor a delinquent.

EXHIBIT 2-1 Juvenile Delinquency Statutes and Definitions

Criminal Term	Delinquency Term
Criminal	Delinquent
Crime	Delinquent act; Act that would have been a crime if an adult had committed it
Arrested	Taken into custody
Trial	Hearing; Adjudication; Disposition
Found guilty	Adjudicated delinquent
Sentence	Disposition
Indictment	Petition of delinquency
Jailed, imprisoned	Held in detention; Confinement; Secure confinement

Exhibit 2-1 shows the differences in the terminology of the juvenile justice system and the adult criminal system.

LEGAL DEFINITIONS OF DELINQUENCY

The State Code of Alabama is among the majority of state juvenile codes that generally define delinquency in terms of the juvenile's status rather than in criminal terms. It defines a delinquent child as "a child who has committed a delinquent act" and defines a delinquent act as "an act committed by a child that is designated a violation, misdemeanor, or offense under the law of this state or another state . . ."

[i]Other states, such as Colorado, define delinquency as a form of criminal conduct. Colorado's statute defines a juvenile delinquent as "a juvenile who has been found guilty of a delinquent act." This reflects a growing, though still minority, trend toward treating juveniles as adults in criminal matters, beginning with defining delinquency actions as criminal in nature.

The Federal Juvenile Delinquency Act mirrors the majority view of delinquency. 18 U.S.C. § 5031 defines an act of juvenile delinquency as any act that "would have been a crime if committed by an adult."

Juvenile offenses include any of the offenses for which states can prosecute adults as well as other lesser misdemeanors and a broad category of offenses called status offenses.

The following case, In re W.S.S., presents an interesting argument that focuses on the interplay between the delinquency statutes and their relationship to the underlying adult criminal statutes. The defense has argued that children cannot be convicted for a sexual offense since they cannot form the requisite sexual intent that adults can and must possess in order to be guilty of sexual offenses.

In re W.S.S.
266 Ga. 685, 470 S.E.
2d 429 (1996)

A delinquency petition was filed, alleging that W.S.S. "did an immoral and indecent act to (and in the presence of) [the victim], a child under the age of 14 years, attempt anal sodomy." OCGA § 16-6-4. At the conclusion of the hearing on the petition, the juvenile court stated that the law does not require "a finding that [W.S.S.] had the sexual intent or knowledge of an adult" and that "evidence has shown in this case that he had the requisite intent. . . ." W.S.S. appealed from the order adjudging him to be delinquent and, in an unreported opinion, the Court of Appeals affirmed. We granted certiorari to determine whether it was necessary to prove that W.S.S. had the intent or knowledge required to convict an adult and, if so, whether the evidence was sufficient to establish that intent or knowledge in this case.

The crime of aggravated child molestation is committed when a person performs an act of sodomy with a child under the age of 14 and does so "with the intent to arouse or satisfy the sexual desires of either the child or the person." OCGA § 16-6-4(a). Likewise, the attempt to commit an act of aggravated child molestation is a crime. OCGA § 16-4-1. However, at the time of the alleged conduct, W.S.S. was 11 years old. Therefore, he was not charged with the crime of attempted aggravated child molestation because, being under 13 years of age, he could not be considered or found guilty of any crime. OCGA § 16-3-1.

W.S.S. was charged with the delinquent act of attempted aggravated child molestation. In relevant part, OCGA § 15-11-2(6)(A) defines a "delinquent act" as "[a]n act designated a crime by the laws of this state. . . ." Thus, in order to find that W.S.S. committed the delinquent act with which he was charged, the juvenile court was not required to find him guilty of the crime of attempted aggravated child molestation. All that was necessary was that the juvenile court find from the evidence that W.S.S. had attempted an act of aggravated child molestation as defined by OCGA § 16-6-4.

At no point in the hearing did the juvenile court intimate that, contrary to OCGA § 16-6-4, it was authorized to adjudge W.S.S. to be delinquent without finding that he had the *intent* to arouse or satisfy the sexual desires of either the victim or himself. Rather, the juvenile court merely indicated that it was not required to find that W.S.S. "had the sexual intent or knowledge of an *adult*." (Emphasis supplied.) Whether W.S.S. had the sexual desire of an adult would be irrelevant, as all that OCGA § 16-6-4 requires is a proof of an intent to arouse or satisfy the sexual desire of either the child or the perpetrator. Thus, the focus is upon the sexual desires of the child or the perpetrator and not upon the sexual desires of some fictional child or adult. Accordingly, in order to show that W.S.S. was delinquent, all that needed to be shown was that he attempted to commit an act of sodomy with the intent to satisfy his own sexual desires.

Judgment affirmed.

SIDEBAR

TRYING A JUVENILE DELINQUENCY CASE

Because most states frame delinquency actions as noncriminal in nature, and because many states take a rehabilitative approach to delinquency actions, trying a delinquency case differs from trying a criminal case. In a delinquency action, both the prosecution and the defense can focus on matters extraneous to the actual crime or offense.

The prosecution may emphasize the juvenile's precarious or unstable family history in an effort to persuade the judge that there is a high probability the juvenile will offend again. The defense might use the same factors to demonstrate to the judge that the juvenile committed the offense as a result of factors beyond his own creation and should therefore receive the benefit of any doubts in his case. (*See* Chapter 6, Delinquency Hearings, for a detailed explanation of the hearing process.)

SIDEBAR

THE HISTORICAL DEVELOPMENT OF THE JUVENILE JUSTICE SYSTEM AND *PARENS PATRIAE*

parens patriae

Latin, "parent of the country." It is the power of the state to act on behalf of, or for the good of, its citizens, especially children

The current American juvenile justice system grew out of the English system of juvenile justice based upon the doctrine of **parens patriae.** *Parens patriae,* or the concept of ruler as parent, developed in England in the 17th and 18th centuries and then traveled to the young colonies in America. This doctrine gave the state the authority to take legal action on behalf of, or against, juveniles for their good or the good of the state. This doctrine is still present in the American justice system and still is the underlying authority for the juvenile justice system as well as the child protection system.

Before the development of the doctrine in America, the courts system treated juveniles as adults. The state would try juveniles in the adult courts and subject them to the same penalties as adults. Juveniles would serve their time, if convicted, in adult prisons alongside adult criminals. Juveniles could be subjected to the death penalty. In the big eastern cities in the mid-nineteenth century, "child savers" formed groups designed to rescue delinquent, abandoned, abused, and orphaned children. This was the genesis of the shift in the juvenile justice mission from a punitive one to a rehabilitative one.

JUVENILE STATUS OFFENDERS

Juvenile status offenders are before the court because their behavior endangers their welfare. They include runaways; at-risk youths; truants; children deemed unruly, unmanageable, or incorrigible; and children in need of mental health and substance abuse treatment.

Status offenses are actions that adults can do legally, but minors cannot. The behavior is not inherently criminal; it is only criminal when a minor engages in it. Consumption of alcoholic beverages is legal for an adult, but would constitute a status offense if a child did it. Other examples of status offenses are truancy, curfew violations, and running away from home.

State statutes vary in their terminology, but most contain references to children who are unruly, unmanageable, incorrigible, truant, or runaway. States refer to these children variously as *persons in need of supervision (PINS), children in need of supervision (CHINS), minors in need of supervision (MINS),* or *at-risk youth (ARY).* Some states include status offenses within their delinquency statutes, while others have separate unruly child statutes, and still others include unruly children in their abuse-neglect-dependency statutes.

Status Offenses Compared to Delinquency

Status hearings begin with a complaint stating that certain facts, if true, confer offender status upon the juvenile. The hearing proceeds as any other juvenile hearing; it is tried before a judge, the prosecution and the defense each present witnesses and documentary evidence, and the court determines whether the evidence supports the facts.

If the court finds the facts support the charges, it will adjudge the child a status offender or an unruly, unmanageable, truant, or incorrigible child, claim jurisdiction over the child, and proceed to disposition.

Status actions, like delinquency actions, can result in the loss of liberty. The court can take physical custody of minors who are unruly, unmanageable, incorrigible, truant, runaway, or determined to be PINS, CHINS, or MINS and place them in secure detention facilities or other residential facilities.

Vagueness

Status offenses are not criminal in nature; therefore the civil liberties and constitutional protections that accompany criminal actions do not accompany status actions. Some legal commentators and practitioners have attacked status statutes on the ground that they are unconstitutionally vague.

The courts have never accepted this argument. They have held that because of their mission to rehabilitate, reform, and protect children, they have the necessary leeway to fulfill this mission, and that leeway includes the prosecution of juvenile offenses in a manner that differs from the prosecution of criminal offenses. The juvenile courts' mission is to act always in the best interests of children. This broad and undefined mandate allows them tremendous freedom in their actions.

The test of whether a statute is constitutional is whether a person of reasonable intelligence can be expected to understand what is mandated or prohibited by that statute. The courts have held that any child can be reasonably expected to understand what it means to submit to the authority of her parents, attend school, or not run away from home.

Emancipation

Minors who are legally emancipated are not subject to status offense laws. Emancipation grants to minors the legal status of adulthood before they have attained the chronological age of majority. Thus, offenses based upon their status as minors will not stand. (*See* Chapter 13, Emancipation.)

DUE PROCESS IN THE JUVENILE COURT

due process
The correct and proper way of carrying on a legal action, prescribed by the Fifth and Fourteenth Amendments to the Constitution

Due process is the set of procedures that must be in place for a legal proceeding to be valid under the Constitution. Due process dictates that juvenile defendants must receive certain rights and have the opportunity to participate in certain procedures during their cases. There are two aspects of due process: **procedural due process,** which deals with the mechanical aspects of a proceeding, such as notice, and **substantive due process,** which deals with the content of the legal rights afforded a criminal or juvenile defendant.

procedural due process
The part of due process that deals specifically with the manner in which things proceed, for example, when, how, and to whom the state must give notice of a delinquency proceeding

Procedural Due Process

The juvenile court has traditionally been a less formal forum than its adult counterpart. By the terms of the Illinois Juvenile Court Act of 1899 (IJCA) and its progeny, the juvenile court is directed to "hear and dispose of the case in a summary manner."[ii]

substantive due process
The part of due process that deals specifically with the content of the legal rights afforded a criminal or juvenile defendant

Juvenile court judges have wider latitude than adult court judges do in the dispositions they can dispense, in the evidence they will consider, and in the way that they take testimony. They are not, however, excused from adherence to the dictates of the United States Constitution.

From 1966 to 1970 the Supreme Court carved out the due process requirements applicable to juvenile court with three important cases—Kent v. United States, 383 U.S. 541 (1966); In Application of Gault, 387 U.S. 1 (1967); and In re Winship, 397 U.S. 358 (1970).

Kent involved a juvenile who was charged in juvenile court with housebreaking, robbery, and rape. After the juvenile court social services director indicated the court's intention to waive jurisdiction over Kent and transfer him to the adult court for trial, Kent's attorney filed a motion requesting a hearing on the waiver and requesting permission to view Kent's social services file.

The juvenile court judge denied both these motions. He wrote that he had made these rulings "after full investigation" although there was no indication that he had conducted any investigation. Kent stood trial in adult court, where a jury convicted him. The appellate court upheld the conviction. Kent then appealed to the United States Supreme Court.

The Supreme Court observed that while juvenile courts had a good amount of latitude and discretion, that latitude and discretion were not absolute:

> We agree with the Court of Appeals that the [Juvenile Court Act statute] contemplates that the Juvenile Court should have considerable latitude within which to determine whether it should retain jurisdiction over a child or—subject to the statutory delimitation—should waive jurisdiction. But this latitude is not complete. At the outset, it assumes procedural regularity sufficient in the particular circumstances to satisfy the basic requirements of due process and fairness, as well as compliance with the statutory requirement of a "full investigation." The statute . . . does not confer upon the Juvenile Court a license for arbitrary procedure. . . . We do not mean by this to indicate that the hearing to be held must conform with all of the requirements of a criminal trial or even of the usual administrative hearing; but we do hold that the hearing must measure up to the essentials of due process and fair treatment.

In Gault the police took a juvenile into custody for allegedly making an obscene telephone call to his neighbor. Gault remained in custody for several days with no hearing, no access to an attorney, and no notice of the charges against him. The Court held that this was impermissible and that juveniles had the right to notice of the charges against them, the right to have counsel present during proceedings, the right to confrontation and cross-examination, and the privilege against self-incrimination.

The Gault court did not go so far as to hold that a juvenile hearing had all of the due process guarantees of a criminal hearing, but held that the Due Process Clause guarantees juveniles the right to an attorney and the privilege against self-incrimination. Gault, Kent, and Winship together formed the doctrine that principles of fundamental fairness must attend all juvenile proceedings.

Winship held that the requirement that the state must prove guilt beyond a reasonable doubt applied to delinquency proceedings as well as criminal trials.

Juveniles, therefore, have the right to notice of the charges against them, the right to have counsel present during proceedings, the right to confrontation and cross-examination, and the privilege against self-incrimination.

The right to notice of the charges against them means that they have the right to petition the prosecution for a full accounting of the charges the state will be filing or has filed against them. The state cannot change the charges nce the state makes such accounting without giving juveniles adequate notice of the change and affording them adequate time to prepare against them.

The right to have counsel present during the proceedings means that juveniles are allowed to have an attorney present at all phases of the proceedings, including during any formal interrogation or informal questioning. The right to counsel also contemplates that the counsel who represent the juveniles must be competent and have full access to any information they need in order to properly represent their clients. Further, the attorneys must enjoy access to the juveniles, and that access must be granted in an atmosphere of sufficient privacy that attorney and client can communicate effectively and prepare a defense.

The right to confrontation and cross-examination refer to the rights that juveniles enjoy during the actual court proceedings. Confrontation means that defendants are allowed to know the identity of, see, and confront the persons who are making the accusations against them. The right to cross-examination means that during the trial the juveniles' attorneys are allowed to cross-examine any witnesses against them.

SIDEBAR

CROSS-EXAMINATION

hostile or adverse witness
A person who is testifying against the interests of the person who is examining or questioning her in court, and who is thus subject to cross examination

Cross-examination is the examination on the witness stand of **hostile or adverse witness,** that is, witnesses who are testifying against the questioners' interest. A hostile or adverse witness from a juvenile defendant's perspective would be one who has testified against the defendant on behalf of the state.

The attorney conducting a cross-examination questions the witness through a series of yes-or-no questions designed to uncover inconsistencies, biases, or inaccuracies on the part of the witness. In the right hands, it is a powerful tool for uncovering the truth, and the court system depends heavily upon the art of cross-examination to guard against unfair or unfounded results at trial.

The privilege against self-incrimination means that neither the prosecution nor the court can compel juvenile defendants to take the witness stand and offer testimony against themselves. In other words, the defendant does not have to say anything at all during the proceedings unless he chooses to do so.

THE CONFLICT BETWEEN THE PUNITIVE APPROACH AND THE REHABILITATIVE APPROACH

Much debate has centered upon the question of whether the aim of the juvenile justice system should be punishment of delinquent juveniles or their rehabilitation.

A punishment-based juvenile justice system would try more juveniles as adults, would make the juvenile system more adult-like in its operations, and would punish juveniles in the same way as it punishes adults. It would subject juveniles to longer prison sentences in adult-style prisons for a greater array of offenses. The ultimate aim would be to punish juveniles for their wrongdoing and to protect society from delinquent juveniles.

Those who favor of punishment assert that juvenile crime has become more of a problem and that juveniles are committing crimes at ever-younger ages and of ever-increasing seriousness. They argue that society's right to be free from the threat of such crimes is more important than juveniles' right to receive preferential treatment.

A rehabilitation-based system would try fewer juveniles as adults, would tailor the juvenile hearing process to the needs of children by making it less intimidating, less formal, and more accommodating, and would offer juveniles therapeutic and educational programs in response to adjudications of delinquency rather than imprisonment or other deprivation of liberty. The ultimate aim would be to assess and address the needs of errant juveniles.

Those in favor of rehabilitation argue that society has an obligation to protect its youngest, most vulnerable members, even from themselves. They assert that most juvenile offenders have become offenders as a result of some failing or deficiency in their upbringing or their treatment at society's hands. Because the root cause of their delinquency is society's failures, society owes it to these children to help them, reform them, and rehabilitate them. They also argue that society will benefit in the long run by having adult citizens who received rehabilitative treatment rather than punishment as juveniles.

CASE PROBLEM

D.W., a 16-year-old tenth-grade student, was involved in an altercation with a teacher. The state presented a petition to the Juvenile Court charging D.W. with simple battery, a misdemeanor, after he allegedly used his fist to hit the teacher in the face and gave the teacher a black eye.

Following its case-in-chief and the testimony of two defense witnesses, the state made an oral motion to amend the petition to charge D.W. with a violation of battery against a school official, a felony. Defense counsel strenuously objected to the amendment, asserting that he was prepared to defend only against a charge of simple battery.

The trial court overruled the objection and the hearing continued under the amended petition. The trial court found that D.W. had committed the act of battery against a school official and was therefore delinquent. D.W. was committed to state custody for five years. D.W. appeals on the grounds that it was a violation of D.W.'s right to due process for the juvenile court to allow the state to amend the petition in the middle of the hearing without granting D.W. a continuance in order to prepare for the new charges.

Does the appellate court affirm or reverse the conviction?

ROLE-PLAY PROBLEM

Seventeen-year-old Lee Boyd Malvo, along with his 42-year-old accomplice, was charged in 2002 with a deadly series of sniper style shootings in the Washington, D.C., metro area. Together, Malvo and his accomplice are known as the Beltway Snipers.

Lee Malvo and his mother left their small Caribbean-island home in August 1990 after his father abandoned them. They moved around the Caribbean for a while looking for work, never having a permanent place to stay. Lee's mother often left him for months at a time with relatives, neighbors, or acquaintances. Many times she would not tell her son in advance that she was leaving or how long she would be gone. Despite this, Lee was a decent student and a generally likeable child, according to most accounts.

Lee and his mother ended up in Bellingham, Washington, in 2002. They met the handsome, charismatic, dominant John Alan Muhammad while living in a homeless shelter.

Lee Boyd Malvo became John Lee Malvo at some point, and he and Muhammad began to introduce themselves as father and son. It became apparent that the boy was under the older man's power. Muhammad regulated every bite of food that Lee ate (a strict diet of honey, crackers, and water), enforced a rigorous workout regimen for the boy, and prevented Malvo from attending school. No one knows what means Muhammad used to control Malvo.

The pair drifted about the southern United States in the summer of 2002. They appeared in Baton Rouge, Louisiana, and Montgomery, Alabama, before settling in the Washington, D.C., area in late summer or early fall of that year. In October of the same year, the two embarked on a deadly shooting spree. They terrorized the Washington region with a series of random, unprovoked, deadly attacks against people on the streets, in gas stations, in parking lots, and on a bus. The victims died from single gunshots. One of the victims was a high school student whom Malvo and Muhammad shot outside of his school.

Police found notes at some of the sites in which Muhammad and Malvo taunted and berated the police, threatened to shoot more people, specifically stated they would target children, and demanded a ransom of $10 million to stop the killing.

Your supervising attorney has asked you to work on this case.

One group of students should answer these questions as though they are working for the County District Attorney who is prosecuting the Beltway Sniper. Another group should answer them as though they are working for a law firm that is defending him.

1. What facts do you find the most significant in this case? Why are they significant? How will you use them?

2. What defense will you use on Malvo's behalf?

3. What more do you want to know? How will you acquire this information?

4. How will you research the issues underlying your arguments?

HYPOTHETICAL PROBLEM

Police took custody of 15-year-old Jorfey on suspicion of killing his mother's boyfriend, Ron. Jorfey's mother, Madeleine, never married. She conceived Jorfey while working as a prostitute. She has no idea who Jorfey's father is. She had Jorfey at home with the help of a friend, another prostitute, and did not report his birth for several days. Consequently, she does not know his birthday. Jorfey received his unusual name because his mother thought she was naming him "Jeffrey," but she misspelled it on the birth certificate and never bothered to fix it.

Jorfey spent his time moving from homeless shelter to homeless shelter. He and Madeleine often lived in her car. When she did not have a car or was too high to go to a shelter, they lived on the streets. At other times, they stayed with whatever man Madeleine happened to be seeing at the moment. These men beat Madeleine and Jorfey, and many of them sexually abused the boy. One man was particularly brutal with Jorfey, but when Jorfey complained about the man, his mother slapped him and told him to shut up, before he got them kicked out of the man's abode.

Jorfey did not attend school until he was seven years old. Nobody asked about him or missed him before then. When he finally started, he was two years older than the other children, but far behind them in every developmental realm: emotionally, physically, intellectually, and socially. Several teachers remarked upon Jorfey's delayed development, but despite this and his very poor grades, no one referred him to a special program.

Jorfey arrived at school on several occasions bearing bruises, cuts, and burn marks. His teachers noted them, but never called the authorities. His mother failed to pick him up from school several times. Once, a teacher had to take Jorfey home with him because his mother never showed up and the school administrators could not locate anyone to take him.

By the time Jorfey reached his teens, his mother had settled down somewhat. She was living with Ron, who supported her and Jorfey, but regularly beat them. He sexually abused Jorfey for years, always with his mother's knowledge. Jorfey tried to leave home, but felt he had nowhere to go. His classmates did not like him and teased him about his body odor, his dirty clothes, and his rotten teeth. He had no known relatives. He knew from experience that living on the streets was cold and dangerous. So, he stayed at home.

One night Ron was extra drunk and particularly volatile. He taunted Jorfey and hit him repeatedly. That night, while Ron slept, Jorfey got Ron's gun and shot him dead.

1. Should the state file a petition alleging Jorfey is a delinquent child for killing Ron?

2. If the state files such a petition, and the court adjudges him delinquent, what would be the most appropriate punishment for Jorfey?

3. Has anyone failed Jorfey? Should that matter in a delinquency hearing?

ETHICAL CONCERNS

Juvenile defense attorneys frequently encounter the problem of serving two masters. Often, the juveniles whom the attorneys are representing desire one outcome. The juveniles' parents, who are paying the attorneys, may desire another outcome. The attorneys may believe that a third outcome is most desirable for the children.

What are legal practitioners to do when they find themselves representing juvenile offenders who want the attorneys to use all their skill and art to beat the charges, while the parents who are paying the fees want the children to suffer the consequences of their actions, and the attorneys believe that the best possible situation for this juvenile would be his removal from their parents' custody entirely?

State law varies, but most professional codes require attorneys to advocate zealously for their clients, notwithstanding who is paying the fee, and notwithstanding what their personal preferences are.

DISCUSSION QUESTIONS

1. Do you favor the punitive approach or the rehabilitative approach to juvenile justice?

2. What do you view as the most significant factors in deciding whether to take a punitive or rehabilitative approach?

3. If you favor the punitive approach, do you believe that the punishment courts mete out to juveniles should be the same as those of adults, or should they be tailored in some way to juvenile needs?

4. If you favor the rehabilitative approach, what types of rehabilitation would you make available to juveniles?

5. Should the victims of the juvenile's acts have a voice in the determination of the treatment program or punishment?

   Some legal commentators, including Justice Stewart of the United States Supreme Court, believe that affording constitutional protections to juveniles is a backdoor way of treating juveniles more like adults, thus making them subject to more adult punishment. They assert that the juvenile court should be separate and distinct from criminal court in all aspects, that it should be tailored solely to fit the needs of juveniles, which are quite different from those of adults.

   In his dissent in In re Gault, Justice Stewart wrote: "The inflexible restrictions that the Constitution so wisely made applicable to adversary criminal trials have no inevitable place in the proceedings of those public social agencies known as juvenile or family courts. . . . In [the nineteenth century] there were no juvenile proceedings, and a child was tried in a conventional criminal court with all the trappings of a conventional criminal trial. So it was that a 12-year-old boy named James Guild was tried in New Jersey for killing Catharine Beakes. A jury found him guilty of murder, and he was sentenced to death by hanging. The sentence was executed. It was all very constitutional."

6. Do you agree with Justice Stewart that applying adult-style constitutional protections to juvenile proceedings will result in more severe punishments for juveniles?

7. Have Justice Stewart's fears proved well founded?

   A. Do you agree with Justice Stewart that applying adult-style constitutional protections to juvenile proceedings will result in more severe punishments for juveniles?

   B. Have Justice Stewart's fears proved well founded?

 TERMS

due process   procedural due process
hostile or adverse witness   substantive due process
parens patriae

END NOTES

[i] Code of Ala. Section 12-15-1(2002)
[ii] IJCA section 5.

Chapter 3

TAKING CUSTODY OF JUVENILES

OBJECTIVES

By the conclusion of this chapter, the student should know:

- The Search Incident to Arrest doctrine
- How the Fourth and Fourteenth Amendments to the United States Constitution work together to describe the parameters of legal searches and seizures
- The definition of probable cause
- The definition of a motion to suppress and the circumstances that warrant filing such a motion
- The Fruit of the Poisonous Tree doctrine and the Exclusionary Rule
- How the prohibition against unreasonable searches and seizures apply to the actions of various state agents
- The circumstances under which police officers may take custody of juveniles without a warrant
- The parameters of a Terry stop

INTRODUCTION

Taking custody of juveniles is the equivalent of arresting adults. It invokes the juvenile court's jurisdiction when the police take custody of a juvenile pursuant to a possible delinquent act. Once police take physical custody of a juvenile, they can bring the juvenile to the police station, a police juvenile center, or a youth detention facility. (See Chapter 5, Pretrial Detention.)

Police can choose at the outset not to take the juvenile into custody. Instead, they can issue a **citation in lieu of arrest,** in which case the police simply issue an order commanding the juvenile to appear in court on a certain date and then release the juvenile.

SEARCHES AND SEIZURES

When the police take custody of juveniles they may search them incident to taking custody of them under the search incident to arrest doctrine. This doctrine allows the police to search the juveniles' persons as well as their wingspans at the time and place of taking custody. Wingspan refers to the area that people can reach with their arms. It circles the body and travels with the person. As detained juveniles move about the room, so does the area the police can legally search. The rationale for this is that within their wingspans, people can hide evidence, destroy evidence, or reach weapons.

If the juvenile is in a car when the police take custody, the police can search the entire car thoroughly. This includes the trunk and any packages in the car or the trunk. The rationale for this is that a car is inherently mobile and therefore there is a high risk of losing any evidence that may be inside the car.

Constitutional Provisions Regarding Searches and Seizures

The Fourth Amendment and Fourteenth Amendments to the United States Constitution prohibit the state from subjecting any person to an unreasonable **search and seizure.** Search and seizure refers to situations where state agents— usually police officers—stop and temporarily detain a person, search the person's body, clothing, home, car, or bags, and then take items that they have found in the search without the person's consent.

The Fourth Amendment contains the language that expressly guarantees that people are to be safe from unreasonable, warrantless searches. It also requires that where a warrant does issue, the warrant must be specific, and those state authorities seeking the warrant must support it with **probable cause.**

AMENDMENT IV

The right of the people to be secure in their persons, houses, papers, and effects, against unreasonable searches and seizures, shall not be violated, and no warrants shall issue, but upon probable cause, supported by oath or affirmation, and particularly describing the place to be searched, and the persons or things to be seized.

The Fourteenth Amendment makes all the other Constitutional provisions applicable to the states as well as to the federal government, and expressly prohibits any state from making a law that will abridge the privileges and immunities of citizens of the United States.

citation in lieu of arrest
An order, issued by the police, to appear in court before a magistrate or judge at a later date

search and seizure
To actively seek out and then take possession of the property or person of another

probable cause
A level of certainty that is more than a "hunch" but less than total or even near total certainty. A reasonable ground for belief in the existence of facts warranting an action

AMENDMENT XIV

Section 1. All persons born or naturalized in the United States, and subject to the jurisdiction thereof, are citizens of the United States and of the State wherein they reside. No State shall make or enforce any law which shall abridge the privileges or immunities of citizens of the United States; nor shall any State deprive any person of life, liberty, or property, without due process of law; nor deny to any person within its jurisdiction the equal protection of the laws.

The prohibition against unreasonable search and seizure means that police and other state agents may not stop people arbitrarily and search their possessions. State agents must have probable cause to believe that someone has committed or is committing a crime before they can legally to stop, detain, and search them.

Probable cause means that the person seeking the warrant have reasonably clear, articulable facts to support a belief that certain items will be at a certain location. The test for probable cause is whether facts and circumstances within the police officer's knowledge are sufficient to cause a prudent person to believe someone has committed, is committing, or is about to commit a crime.

SIDEBAR

CHALLENGES TO SEARCHES AND SEIZURES

If you are working for the defense and the case involves a search and seizure, you must thoroughly acquaint yourself with the facts and circumstances surrounding the search and seizure.

Every fact will have an impact upon the ultimate determination whether probable cause existed. The court will look at such facts as where the juvenile was standing when the police became aware of him, where the police officer was standing at the time, what time of day it was, and what the juvenile did with his hands.

Once you ascertain all of the facts, you must do the research to determine whether that set of facts constitutes probable cause. In almost every case you should file a **motion to suppress** any evidence that the state has obtained as a result of a search and seizure. A motion to suppress is an application to the court for an order prohibiting the introduction of certain evidence that the defense. (See Appendix for a sample Motion to Suppress.)

The defense will assert in its motion to suppress that the police gained possession of the evidence through the use of an illegal search. If the root

motion to suppress

An application to the court for an order prohibiting the introduction of certain evidence that the defense

(continues)

search was illegal, any evidence harvested from it will also be illegal. This is the **Fruit of the Poisonous Tree doctrine.** A corollary to this doctrine is the **Exclusionary Rule,** which states that courts must not admit evidence that the state has obtained illegally.

If you are working for the prosecution, you should be no less familiar with the facts and details than you would be as a defense attorney. Rather than filing a motion to suppress as a prosecutor, you will be responding to one, and you need to be prepared to defend the state's actions.

The law in this area is subtle, complex, and continually evolving due to the vast number of challenges to searches and seizures. You will need to re-search each case anew.

Fruit of the Poisonous Tree doctrine

If the root search was illegal, any evidence harvested from it also will be illegal

Exclusionary Rule

This rule states that the court must not admit evidence that the state has obtained illegally

---

Fourth Amendment considerations apply to juveniles just as they do to adults. The juvenile court will exclude evidence that the state has obtained in violation of the Fourth Amendment.

Applications of the Prohibition Against Unreasonable Searches and Seizures

The Fourth Amendment does not only apply to searches and seizures that police officers conduct. The Fourth Amendment guards against unreasonable action on the part of any state official or actor including public school personnel, as the following case, New Jersey v. T.L.O., illustrates.

This case also presents a succinct description of the law of search and seizure, and presents issues of importance and significance to practitioners of juvenile law, who will find themselves frequently exploring issues concerning the rights of students and school-based behavior.

New Jersey v. T.L.O.
469 U.S. 325 (1985)
JUSTICE WHITE delivered the opinion of the Court.

A teacher at Piscataway High School discovered two girls smoking in a lavatory. One of the two girls was T.L.O. The teacher took the two girls to [meet] Assistant Vice Principal Choplick. In response to questioning by Mr. Choplick, T.L.O. denied that she had been smoking in the lavatory and claimed that she did not smoke at all.

Mr. Choplick demanded to see [T.L.O.'s] purse. Opening the purse, he found a pack of cigarettes. As he reached into the purse for the cigarettes, Mr. Choplick also noticed a package of cigarette rolling papers. In his experience, possession of rolling papers by high school students was closely associated with the use of marihuana. Suspecting that a closer examination of the

(continues)

New Jersey v. T.L.O. (Continued)

purse might yield further evidence of drug use, Mr. Choplick proceeded to search the purse thoroughly. The search revealed a small amount of marihuana, a pipe, a number of empty plastic bags, a substantial quantity of money in one-dollar bills, an index card that appeared to be a list of students who owed T.L.O. money, and two letters that implicated T.L.O. in marihuana dealing.

[T]he State brought delinquency charges against T.L.O. Contending that Mr. Choplick's search of her purse violated the Fourth Amendment, T.L.O. moved to suppress the evidence found in her purse as well as her confession, which, she argued, was tainted by the allegedly unlawful search. The Juvenile Court denied the motion to suppress.

[T]he court concluded that the search conducted by Mr. Choplick was a reasonable one. The initial decision to open the purse was justified by Mr. Choplick's well-founded suspicion that T.L.O. had violated the rule forbidding smoking in the lavatory. Once the purse was open, evidence of marihuana violations was in plain view, and Mr. Choplick was entitled to conduct a thorough search to determine the nature and extent of T.L.O.'s drug-related activities. The court found T.L.O. to be a delinquent and sentenced her to a year's probation.

On appeal [the] Appellate Division affirmed the trial court's finding that there had been no Fourth Amendment violation. T.L.O. appealed the Fourth Amendment ruling, and the Supreme Court of New Jersey reversed the judgment of the Appellate Division and ordered the suppression of the evidence found in T.L.O.'s purse.

The New Jersey Supreme Court agreed with the lower courts that the Fourth Amendment applies to searches conducted by school officials.

In determining whether the search at issue in this case violated the Fourth Amendment, we are faced initially with the question whether that Amendment's prohibition on unreasonable searches and seizures applies to searches conducted by public school officials. We hold that it does.

It is now beyond dispute that "the Federal Constitution, by virtue of the Fourteenth Amendment, prohibits unreasonable searches and seizures by state officers." Equally indisputable is the proposition that the Fourteenth Amendment protects the rights of students against encroachment by public school officials.

The State of New Jersey has argued that the history of the Fourth Amendment indicates that the Amendment was intended to regulate only searches and seizures carried out by law enforcement officers; accordingly, although public school officials are concededly state agents for purposes of the Fourteenth Amendment, the Fourth Amendment creates no rights enforceable against them.

This Court has never limited the Amendment's prohibition on unreasonable searches and seizures to operations conducted by the police. Rather, the Court has long spoken of the Fourth Amendment's strictures as restraints imposed upon "governmental action"—that is, "upon the activities of sovereign authority."

Against the child's interest in privacy must be set the substantial interest of teachers and administrators in maintaining discipline in the classroom and on school grounds. Maintaining order in the classroom has never been easy, but in recent years, school disorder has often taken particularly ugly forms: drug use and violent crime in the schools have become major social problems.

(continues)

New Jersey v. T.L.O. (Continued)

We join the majority of courts that have examined this issue in concluding that the legality of a search of a student should depend simply on the reasonableness, under all the circumstances, of the search. Determining the reasonableness of any search involves a twofold inquiry: first, one must consider "whether the action was justified at its inception," second, one must determine whether the search as actually conducted "was reasonably related in scope to the circumstances which justified the interference in the first place."

Under ordinary circumstances, a search of a student by a teacher or other school official will be "justified at its inception" when there are reasonable grounds for suspecting that the search will turn up evidence that the student has violated or is violating either the law or the rules of the school. Such a search will be permissible in its scope when the measures adopted are reasonably related to the objectives of the search and not excessively intrusive in light of the age and sex of the student and the nature of the infraction.

This standard will, we trust, neither unduly burden the efforts of school authorities to maintain order in their schools nor authorize unrestrained intrusions upon the privacy of schoolchildren. By focusing attention on the question of reasonableness, the standard will spare teachers and school administrators the necessity of schooling themselves in the niceties of probable cause and permit them to regulate their conduct according to the dictates of reason and common sense. At the same time, the reasonableness standard should ensure that the interests of students will be invaded no more than is necessary to achieve the legitimate end of preserving order in the schools.

Because the search resulting in the discovery of the evidence of marihuana dealing by T.L.O. was reasonable, the New Jersey Supreme Court's decision to exclude that evidence from T.L.O.'s juvenile delinquency proceedings on Fourth Amendment grounds was erroneous. Accordingly, the judgment of the Supreme Court of New Jersey is Reversed.

TAKING CUSTODY OF JUVENILES WITHOUT A WARRANT

Police officers can take juveniles into custody without arrest warrants if they have probable cause to believe that the juveniles have committed acts that would be crimes if adults had committed them.

Police may conduct **Terry stops,** in which they briefly detain people for investigative purposes. They can do this under an exception to the probable cause requirement if they have reasonable suspicion supported by articulable facts that someone may be engaged in criminal activity. Officers are only permitted to pat down suspects for weapons. The court will allow the admission of any material they find as a result of the **stop and frisk.** *Stop and frisk* refers to the very short detention and pat down of a suspect's outerwear for the purpose of finding weapons.

Terry stop

A brief stop predicated upon a reasonable suspicion by the police that criminal activity might be afoot

stop and frisk

Where a police officer briefly detains a person and pats down the person looking for weapons

SIDEBAR

TERRY V. OHIO

The Terry stop grew out of Terry v. Ohio, 88 S.Ct. 1868 (1968). In that case, a police officer observed two men walking back and forth past a jewelry store. One would stand on the corner and look around while the other peered in the store window. This behavior is not illegal. But it did cause the veteran officer observing it to suspect that the men were casing the store for a future burglary. The officer stopped the men and without first informing them of their Miranda rights patted them down for weapons. In so doing he discovered a weapon in the pocket of one of the men. The Supreme Court upheld Terry's conviction for carrying a concealed weapon in the face of a Fourth Amendment challenge.

The Court noted that "[W]e deal here with an entire rubric of police conduct—necessarily swift action predicated upon the on-the-spot observations of the officer on the beat—which historically has not been, and as a practical matter could not be, subjected to the warrant procedure." Police officers must be able to point to specific and articulable facts which, taken together with rational inferences from those facts, reasonably warrant an intrusion.

FINGERPRINTS AND MUG SHOTS

Police may fingerprint juveniles and take mug shots of them pursuant to taking custody of them. At one time laws prohibited the practice due to the rehabilitative and non-punitive mission of the juvenile courts. Police were allowed to fingerprint and photograph juveniles only when it was necessary for the investigation or when a court specifically approved it.

Now, as a general rule, most states allow police to take fingerprints and mug shots, especially with older offenders and more serious criminal acts. Some states mandate it.

Among those states that allow or mandate police to take fingerprints and mug shots of juveniles, several mandate that the police department must destroy the mug shots and fingerprints if the court ultimately dismisses the case. Other states allow this information to become part of the record subject to the rules, policies, and procedures attendant to juvenile records in general.

CASE PROBLEM

Park security officers saw four people in an area known as a hot spot for drug activity. The officers observed Maxwell, a teenage boy, smoking what was readily observable as a marijuana pipe. As the officers approached the group, the officers detected the distinct odor of burning marijuana. The officers were wearing bulletproof vests under T-shirts bearing gold badges with the words "Security Officer" on them. Although they did not carry firearms, each officer also wore a duty belt containing pepper spray, a collapsible baton, handcuffs, a radio, and a flashlight holder.

The officers told Maxwell that they had seen what he had been doing. They also told the group that they were not police officers and that no one was going to be arrested by either officer. They repeatedly told everyone in the group that they were not under arrest and were not being detained. The officers asked the group if they would please answer some questions. At no time during the incident was there any display of handcuffs or pepper spray, nor were there any sort of forceful actions against the members of the group designed to detain any of them.

In the course of the contact, the officers asked Maxwell, "Is that your marijuana pipe?" When Maxwell denied that it was his pipe, the officers asked the entire group, "Whose marijuana pipe is it?"

Tiffany, who was also present, said, "It's my pipe." One of the security officers used a cell phone to call the Spokane police. The police arrived within five minutes and arrested Tiffany. The state charged her with possession of drug paraphernalia.

Tiffany moved to suppress the pipe and her statement, arguing that the security officers were state actors and the questioning and detention were unlawful. The court denied the motion because the officers were not agents of the state but rather "had the status of private citizens." The juvenile court denied her motion to suppress and adjudicated Tiffany delinquent. She appeals.

Does the appellate court affirm or reverse?

ROLE-PLAY PROBLEM

Eddy, 17 years old, was standing on the corner of 13th Street and Tremont Avenue, on the main drag of a high-crime neighborhood that local police know to be a hotbed of drug dealing and gang activity. It was about 6:15 on an evening in mid-October. The sun had just set, and the streetlights were just coming on. It was a cold evening, and Eddy was wearing a down jacket.

A police officer sat in his car at the entrance to an alley a block-and-a-half away from the corner where Eddy was standing. He says that he saw a male approach Eddy. The male turned out to be Jake, 15 years old. As Jake approached, he and Eddy put out their hands. The police officer says that he saw a small plastic bag in Eddy's hand and money in Jake's hand. This led the officer to believe that a drug transaction had just taken place.

Further, the officer knew both Eddy and Jake, and knew them to be members of a local gang that was heavily involved in drug dealing. This particular corner was the favored corner for this gang to conduct their drug transactions. It was called the "Market at 13th and Tre."

The officer pulled out of the alley and pulled up next to the Eddy and Jake. He asked them what they had just done. Jake replied that he was saying hello to his friend Eddy. The officer asked Eddy if he had just sold Jake drugs. Eddy replied that he had not. The officer told the two that he had just witnessed them exchanging drugs and money. "No," returned Eddy, "we were just shaking hands."

The officer got out of the car and ordered to two to put their hands up against the car. He patted the two down and found nothing. The he reached into Eddy's pocket and found four twenty-dollar bills folded together into a small square. He found in Jake's pocket a 2-inch-square plastic baggy containing rocks of crack. He took the two into custody. The state filed a petition in juvenile court asserting that Eddy was delinquent because he engaged in drug trafficking, a felony. It filed a petition against Jake charging that he was delinquent because he had engaged in drug abuse, a misdemeanor.

You are working for the defense.

1. What motion will you file?
2. What arguments will you make in your motion?
3. What facts will you use to buttress your arguments?

You are working for the prosecution.

4. How will you respond to the defense's motion?
5. What legal arguments will you make?
6. What facts will you use to buttress your argument?

HYPOTHETICAL PROBLEM

Fourteen-year-old Sloan was standing outside of a convenience store in a high-crime neighborhood. She was waiting for her friend, Rebecca, who was inside buying candy and soft drinks. Officers Klein and Zepp pulled into the parking lot and sat in their patrol car, watching Sloan. Rebecca came out, and the two girls stood on the walk in front of the store, drinking their drinks and sharing their candy. Soon, Tyler, Justin, Kyle, and Jonathan joined the girls.

All of the teenagers were wearing matching jean jackets with red symbols and letters on the backs. The letters and symbols did not represent any youth gang that the officers knew, but they resembled gang writing. The officers continued to watch the teenagers, who continued to eat, drink, and engage in horseplay.

The officers approached the teens and asked them their names. The teens refused to say. Officer Zepp ordered them to stand against the wall while she patted them down for weapons. She discovered a cigarette pack in Kyle's pocket and a makeup bag in Sloan's pocket. She opened each of them and found drugs inside. The state filed delinquency petitions against Sloan and Kyle.

Defense attorneys filed motions to suppress the drugs as evidence based upon the Fruit of the Poisonous Tree doctrine. What are the defendants' specific arguments?

The state cites *Terry v. Ohio* in its response. What are the state's specific arguments?

How will the court rule? Why?

ETHICAL CONCERNS

The classic dilemma that all practitioners face is protecting a juvenile offender's constitutional rights even in the face of known wrongdoing. Every lawyer and paralegal who works in the area of adult or juvenile criminal defense has heard the question, "How can you defend someone whom you *know* to be guilty?"

Prosecutors and police officers face the dilemma of knowing that criminal action is taking place, but feeling powerless to stop it because they cannot back up their gut feeling—certain though it may be—with articulable facts and circumstances sufficient to support a finding of probable cause.

Defenders usually respond that in protecting the constitutional rights of the admittedly guilty person in *this* case, they are protecting *every* citizen's constitutional rights, including the rights of innocent people.

Prosecutors and police officers must take solace in the knowledge that while the Constitution may prevent them from acting on their gut feelings, it also allows them to act decisively when they can articulate those feelings properly.

DISCUSSION QUESTIONS

Consider the case of *New Jersey v. T.L.O.*:

1. Do you believe that the exigencies present in a school environment justify compromising students' right to privacy?

2. Note the court's explanation that requiring schools to adhere to a standard of reasonableness will "spare teachers and school administrators the necessity of schooling themselves in the niceties of probable cause and permit them to regulate their conduct according to the dictates of reason and common sense." Do you agree that this is a desirable outcome?

3. Will loosening the standard allow schools to act more arbitrarily?

4. Do schools require the kind of flexibility that the court is allowing them just to maintain a safe and orderly environment?

5. What factors would you consider to be significant in such an inquiry?

6. Under what circumstances should a student be able to expect privacy?

7. Do you agree that Mr. Choplick's actions were reasonable?

8. Would you still think Mr. Choplick's actions were reasonable if T.L.O. had admitted outright that she was smoking but Mr. Choplick searched her purse anyway?

9. Would you change your mind if Mr. Choplick found a loaded gun in T.L.O.'s purse?

10. Does the prohibition against unreasonable searches and seizures unfairly restrict police action or guard against police abuse?

11. Should police and other state agents have more latitude when dealing with juveniles because of juveniles' inherent vulnerability?

KEY TERMS

citation in lieu of arrest	probable cause
Exclusionary Rule	search and seizure
Fruit of the Poisonous Tree doctrine	stop and frisk
motion to suppress	Terry stop

INTERROGATION

OBJECTIVES

By the end of this chapter, the student should know:

- The outlines of the landmark case *Miranda v. Arizona*
- *Miranda's* place in the development of the interrogation law
- How *Miranda* applies to juvenile interrogations
- The contents of the Miranda warnings
- Why *Miranda* and other interrogation issues are particularly important in juvenile justice
- The results of professor Thomas Grisso's study of juveniles' understanding of the Miranda warnings
- The bases for constitutional challenges to juveniles' statements
- How to determine if a juvenile was in custody during questioning
- How to attack or defend juveniles' statements in court
- The requirements for juveniles to invoke or waive their Miranda rights
- How courts apply the totality of the circumstances doctrine to interrogation challenges

INTRODUCTION

Interrogation is the formal questioning of a suspected offender by the police while the offender is in custody. Historically, confessions that the police obtain from offenders while in custody have been suspect. Police routinely used forceful and sometimes deceptive practices to obtain confessions at one time. These practices offended the American sensibility, which is founded upon the basic and inviolate freedoms and privileges we possess by virtue of the Constitution.

A large body of law exists regarding interrogation. There are strict precepts as to when, where, and how the state may interrogate a criminal defendant, who may

interrogation

The formal questioning of a suspected offender by the police while the offender is in custody

Miranda warnings

The set of cautions and instructions that police must provide to a criminal suspect when that suspect is in custody before the police may ask any questions of the suspect

and who must be present during interrogation, and how the state can use results of interrogation.

THE IMPORTANCE OF *MIRANDA V. ARIZONA*

The most important case on interrogation is *Miranda v. Arizona,* the landmark case that gave us the **Miranda warnings,** which are still the law. The following excerpt details the court's reasoning as it lays out the structure of the familiar Miranda warning. The full case is quite lengthy, but deserving of close perusal for its beautifully written and elegantly argued positions and historical perspectives.

Miranda v. Arizona
384 U.S. 436 (1966)
MR. CHIEF JUSTICE WARREN delivered the opinion of the Court.

The cases before us raise questions which go to the roots of our concepts of American criminal jurisprudence: the restraints society must observe consistent with the Federal Constitution in prosecuting individuals for crime. More specifically, we deal with the admissibility of statements obtained from an individual who is subjected to custodial police interrogation and the necessity for procedures which assure that the individual is accorded his privilege under the Fifth Amendment to the Constitution not to be compelled to incriminate himself.

In the cases before us today, given this background, we concern ourselves primarily with this interrogation atmosphere and the evils it can bring. In No. 759, Miranda v. Arizona, the police arrested the defendant and took him to a special interrogation room, where they secured a confession.

The question in these cases is whether the privilege [against self-incrimination] is fully applicable during a period of custodial interrogation. In this Court, the privilege has consistently been accorded a liberal construction. We are satisfied that all the principles embodied in the privilege apply to informal compulsion exerted by law enforcement officers during in-custody questioning. An individual swept from familiar surroundings into police custody, surrounded by antagonistic forces, and subjected to the techniques of persuasion described above cannot be otherwise than under compulsion to speak. As a practical matter, the compulsion to speak in the isolated setting of the police station may well be greater than in courts or other official investigations, where there are often impartial observers to guard against intimidation or trickery.

Today, then, there can be no doubt that the Fifth Amendment privilege is available outside of criminal court proceedings, and serves to protect persons in all settings in which their freedom of action is curtailed in any significant way from being compelled to incriminate themselves. We have concluded that, without proper safeguards, the process of in-custody interrogation of persons suspected or accused of crime contains inherently compelling pressures which work to undermine the individual's will to resist and to compel him to speak where he would not otherwise do so freely. In order to combat these pressures and to

(continues)

Miranda v. Arizona (Continued)

permit a full opportunity to exercise the privilege against self-incrimination, the accused must be adequately and effectively apprised of his rights, and the exercise of those rights must be fully honored.

At the outset, if a person in custody is to be subjected to interrogation, he must first be informed in clear and unequivocal terms that he has the right to remain silent. For those unaware of the privilege, the warning is needed simply to make them aware of it—the threshold requirement for an intelligent decision as to its exercise. More important, such a warning is an absolute prerequisite in overcoming the inherent pressures of the interrogation atmosphere. It is not just the subnormal or woefully ignorant who succumb to an interrogator's imprecations, whether implied or expressly stated, that the interrogation will continue until a confession is obtained or that silence in the face of accusation is itself damning, and will bode ill when presented to a jury. Further, the warning will show the individual that his interrogators are prepared to recognize his privilege should he choose to exercise it.

The warning of the right to remain silent must be accompanied by the explanation that anything said can and will be used against the individual in court. This warning is needed in order to make him aware not only of the privilege, but also of the consequences of forgoing it. It is only through an awareness of these consequences that there can be any assurance of real understanding and intelligent exercise of the privilege. Moreover, this warning may serve to make the individual more acutely aware that he is faced with a phase of the adversary system—that he is not in the presence of persons acting solely in his interest.

The circumstances surrounding in-custody interrogation can operate very quickly to overbear the will of one merely made aware of his privilege by his interrogators. Therefore, the right to have counsel present at the interrogation is indispensable to the protection of the Fifth Amendment privilege under the system we delineate today. Our aim is to assure that the individual's right to choose between silence and speech remains unfettered throughout the interrogation process. A once-stated warning, delivered by those who will conduct the interrogation, cannot itself suffice to that end among those who most require knowledge of their rights. A mere warning given by the interrogators is not alone sufficient to accomplish that end. Prosecutors themselves claim that the admonishment of the right to remain silent, without more, "will benefit only the recidivist and the professional." Even preliminary advice given to the accused by his own attorney can be swiftly overcome by the secret interrogation process. Thus, the need for counsel to protect the Fifth Amendment privilege comprehends not merely a right to consult with counsel prior to questioning, but also to have counsel present during any questioning if the defendant so desires.

An individual need not make a pre-interrogation request for a lawyer. While such request affirmatively secures his right to have one, his failure to ask for a lawyer does not constitute a waiver. No effective waiver of the right to counsel during interrogation can be recognized unless specifically made after the warnings we here delineate have been given. The accused who does not know his rights and therefore does not make a request may be the person who most needs counsel.

If an individual indicates that he wishes the assistance of counsel before any interrogation occurs, the authorities cannot rationally ignore or deny his request on the basis that the individual does not have or cannot afford a retained attorney. The financial ability of the individual has no relationship to the scope of the rights involved here. The privilege

(continues)

Miranda v. Arizona (Continued)

against self-incrimination secured by the Constitution applies to all individuals. The need for counsel in order to protect the privilege exists for the indigent as well as the affluent. In fact, were we to limit these constitutional rights to those who can retain an attorney, our decisions today would be of little significance. The cases before us, as well as the vast majority of confession cases with which we have dealt in the past, involve those unable to retain counsel. While authorities are not required to relieve the accused of his poverty, they have the obligation not to take advantage of indigence in the administration of justice. Denial of counsel to the indigent at the time of interrogation while allowing an attorney to those who can afford one would be no more supportable by reason or logic than the similar situation at trial and on appeal struck down in *Gideon v. Wainwright,* 372 U.S. 335 (1963), and *Douglas v. California,* 372 U.S. 353 (1963).

In order fully to apprise a person interrogated of the extent of his rights under this system, then, it is necessary to warn him not only that he has the right to consult with an attorney, but also that, if he is indigent, a lawyer will be appointed to represent him. Without this additional warning, the admonition of the right to consult with counsel would often be understood as meaning only that he can consult with a lawyer if he has one or has the funds to obtain one. The warning of a right to counsel would be hollow if not couched in terms that would convey to the indigent—the person most often subjected to interrogation—the knowledge that he too has a right to have counsel present. As with the warnings of the right to remain silent and of the general right to counsel, only by effective and express explanation to the indigent of this right can there be assurance that he was truly in a position to exercise it.

Once warnings have been given, the subsequent procedure is clear. If the individual indicates in any manner, at any time prior to or during questioning, that he wishes to remain silent, the interrogation must cease.

If the interrogation continues without the presence of an attorney and a statement is taken, a heavy burden rests on the government to demonstrate that the defendant knowingly and intelligently waived his privilege against self-incrimination and his right to retained or appointed counsel.

Our decision is not intended to hamper the traditional function of police officers in investigating crime. When an individual is in custody on probable cause, the police may, of course, seek out evidence in the field to be used at trial against him. Such investigation may include inquiry of persons not under restraint. General on-the-scene questioning as to facts surrounding a crime or other general questioning of citizens in the fact-finding process is not affected by our holding. It is an act of responsible citizenship for individuals to give whatever information they may have to aid in law enforcement. In such situations, the compelling atmosphere inherent in the process of in-custody interrogation is not necessarily present.

In dealing with statements obtained through interrogation, we do not purport to find all confessions inadmissible. Confessions remain a proper element in law enforcement. Any statement given freely and voluntarily without any compelling influences is, of course, admissible in evidence. The fundamental import of the privilege while an individual is in custody is not whether he is allowed to talk to the police without the benefit of warnings and counsel, but whether he can be interrogated. There is no requirement that police stop a person who enters a police station and states that he wishes to confess to a crime, or a person who calls the police to offer a confession or any other statement he desires to make. Volunteered statements of any kind are not barred by the Fifth Amendment, and their admissibility is not affected by our holding today.

SIDEBAR

MR. CHIEF JUSTICE WARREN'S DESCRIPTION
OF INTERROGATION TECHNIQUES

[Police] officers [who are trained in interrogation] are told by the manuals that the "principal psychological factor contributing to a successful interrogation is privacy—being alone with the person under interrogation." The efficacy of this tactic has been explained as follows,

> "If at all practicable, the interrogation should take place in the investigator's office or at least in a room of his own choice. The subject should be deprived of every psychological advantage. In his own home he may be confident, indignant, or recalcitrant. He is more keenly aware of his rights and more reluctant to tell of his indiscretions or criminal behavior within the walls of his home. Moreover his family and other friends are nearby, their presence lending moral support. In his own office, the investigator possesses all the advantages. The atmosphere suggests the invincibility of the forces of the law."

To highlight the isolation and unfamiliar surroundings, the manuals instruct the police to display an air of confidence in the suspect's guilt and from outward appearance to maintain only an interest in confirming certain details. The guilt of the subject is to be posited as a fact. The interrogator should direct his comments toward the reasons why the subject committed the act, rather than court failure by asking the subject whether he did it. Like other men, perhaps the subject has had a bad family life, had an unhappy childhood, had too much to drink, had an unrequited desire for women. The officers are instructed to minimize the moral seriousness of the offense, to cast blame on the victim or on society. These tactics are designed to put the subject in a psychological state where his story is but an elaboration of what the police purport to know already—that he is guilty. Explanations to the contrary are dismissed and discouraged.

The texts thus stress that the major qualities an interrogator should possess are patience and perseverance. One writer describes the efficacy of these characteristics in this manner:

> "In the preceding paragraphs emphasis has been placed on kindness and stratagems. The investigator will, however, encounter many situations where the sheer weight of his personality will be the deciding factor. Where emotional appeals and tricks are employed to no avail, he must rely on an oppressive atmosphere of dogged persistence. He must interrogate steadily and without relent, leaving the subject no prospect of surcease. He must dominate his subject and overwhelm him with his inexorable will to obtain the truth. He should interrogate for a spell of

(continues)

several hours pausing only for the subject's necessities in acknowledgment of the need to avoid a charge of duress that can be technically substantiated. In a serious case, the interrogation may continue for days, with the required intervals for food and sleep, but with no respite from the atmosphere of domination. It is possible in this way to induce the subject to talk without resorting to duress or coercion. The method should be used only when the guilt of the subject appears highly probable."

The manuals suggest that the suspect be offered legal excuses for his actions in order to obtain an initial admission of guilt. Where there is a suspected revenge-killing, for example, the interrogator may say:

"Joe, you probably didn't go out looking for this fellow with the purpose of shooting him. My guess is, however, that you expected something from him and that's why you carried a gun—for your own protection. You knew him for what he was, no good. Then when you met him he probably started using foul, abusive language and he gave some indication that he was about to pull a gun on you, and that's when you had to act to save your own life. That's about it, isn't it, Joe?"

Having then obtained the admission of shooting, the interrogator is advised to refer to circumstantial evidence which negates the self-defense explanation. This should enable him to secure the entire story. One text notes that "Even if he fails to do so, the inconsistency between the subject's original denial of the shooting and his present admission of at least doing the shooting will serve to deprive him of a self-defense 'out' at the time of trial."

When the techniques described above prove unavailing, the texts recommend they be alternated with a show of some hostility. One ploy often used has been termed the "friendly-unfriendly" or the "Mutt and Jeff" act:

"In this technique, two agents are employed. Mutt, the relentless investigator, who knows the subject is guilty and is not going to waste any time. He's sent a dozen men away for this crime and he's going to send the subject away for the full term. Jeff, on the other hand, is obviously a kindhearted man. He has a family himself. He has a brother who was involved in a little scrape like this. He disapproves of Mutt and his tactics and will arrange to get him off the case if the subject will cooperate. He can't hold Mutt off for very long. The subject would be wise to make a quick decision. The technique is applied by having both investigators present while Mutt acts out his role. Jeff may stand by quietly and demur at some of Mutt's tactics. When Jeff makes his plea for cooperation, Mutt is not present in the room."

The interrogators sometimes are instructed to induce a confession out of trickery. The technique here is quite effective in crimes which require identification or which run in series. In the identification situation, the interrogator

(continues)

may take a break in his questioning to place the subject among a group of men in a line-up. "The witness or complainant (previously coached, if necessary) studies the line-up and confidently points out the subject as the guilty party." Then the questioning resumes "as though there were now no doubt about the guilt of the subject." A variation on this technique is called the "reverse line-up":

"The accused is placed in a line-up, but this time he is identified by several fictitious witnesses or victims who associated him with different offenses. It is expected that the subject will become desperate and confess to the offense under investigation in order to escape from the false accusations."

The manuals also contain instructions for police on how to handle the individual who refuses to discuss the matter entirely, or who asks for an attorney or relatives. The examiner is to concede him the right to remain silent. "This usually has a very undermining effect. First of all, he is disappointed in his expectation of an unfavorable reaction on the part of the interrogator. Secondly, a concession of this right to remain silent impresses the subject with the apparent fairness of his interrogator." After this psychological conditioning, however, the officer is told to point out the incriminating significance of the suspect's refusal to talk:

"Joe, you have a right to remain silent. That's your privilege and I'm the last person in the world who'll try to take it away from you. If that's the way you want to leave this, O. K. But let me ask you this. Suppose you were in my shoes and I were in yours and you called me in to ask me about this and I told you, 'I don't want to answer any of your questions.' You'd think I had something to hide, and you'd probably be right in thinking that. That's exactly what I'll have to think about you, and so will everybody else. So let's sit here and talk this whole thing over."

Few will persist in their initial refusal to talk, it is said, if this monologue is employed correctly.

In the event that the subject wishes to speak to a relative or an attorney, the following advice is tendered:

"The interrogator should respond by suggesting that the subject first tell the truth to the interrogator himself rather than get anyone else involved in the matter. If the request is for an attorney, the interrogator may suggest that the subject save himself or his family the expense of any such professional service, particularly if he is innocent of the offense under investigation. The interrogator may also add, 'Joe, I'm only looking for the truth, and if you're telling the truth, that's it. You can handle this by yourself.'"

How *Miranda* Applies to Juveniles

When the Supreme Court decided *Miranda* in 1966 it applied only to adult criminal defendants. *Miranda* yielded the now-famous "Miranda warnings" that every person who has ever watched a police show on television knows by heart: "You have the right to remain silent. Anything you say can and will be used against you in a court of law. You have the right to an attorney. If you cannot afford an attorney, one will be appointed for you at the state's expense."

The Supreme Court ruled in *Miranda* the police must make certain rights known to any person who is in custody prior to any interrogation of that person. As initially decided, it applied only to adult criminal defendants.

The Supreme Court expanded its application of Miranda to juveniles the following year, in *Application of Gault*, 87 S.Ct. 1428 (1967). Observing that "it would indeed be surprising if the privilege against self-incrimination were available to hardened criminals but not to juveniles," the Court held that *Miranda* applied to juveniles who were in a "proceeding to determine whether a minor is 'delinquent' and which may result in commitment to a state institution."

As far back as 1948 in the case of *Haley v. Ohio*, 332 U.S. 596, the Supreme Court recognized that juveniles were especially vulnerable to the strength, power, and authority of adult law enforcement figures. The court wrote:

> What transpired would make us pause for careful inquiry if a mature man were involved. And when, as here, a mere juvenile—an easy victim of the law—is before us, special care in scrutinizing the record must be used. Age 15 is a tender and difficult age for a boy of any race. He cannot be judged by the more exacting standards of maturity. That which would leave a man could and unimpressed can overawe and overwhelm a lad in his early teens. This is the period of great instability which the crisis of adolescence produces. A 15-year-old lad, questioned through the dead of night by relays of police, is a ready victim of the inquisition. Mature men possibly might stand the ordeal from midnight to 5 a.m. But we cannot believe that a lad of tender years is a match for the police in such a contest.

That solicitous attitude has not survived entirely intact. While juveniles are now afforded the same rights as adults, they are afforded no special or extra rights.

The prosecution in a juvenile case can use any incriminatory statements juveniles make while in police custody against them in a subsequent delinquency if the statement is constitutionally valid. If the juvenile gave the statement either under the advisement of an attorney, or gave the statement after having knowingly, intelligently, and voluntarily waived his right to have an attorney present, it is constitutionally valid.

The only difference between the treatment of juveniles and adults in the interrogation process is that some states allow or require an interested, concerned, independent adult—sometimes a parent, though not necessarily—to be present during the interrogation of a juvenile if an attorney is not present.

SIGNIFICANCE OF THE INTERROGATION ISSUE

The issues of interrogation techniques, **waiver**—or the voluntary giving up of one's rights—and the right against self-incrimination are particularly important in juvenile law because many delinquency cases involve confessions and inculpatory statements.

waiver
The voluntary giving up of a right or privilege

Professor Thomas Grisso has done extensive work in the area of juveniles and confessions. He has found that juveniles are especially prone to confess and give statements to police and other authorities. Even when interrogators read Miranda warnings to a juveniles who are in custody, there is no assurance that they understand or appreciate the significance of the warnings.

Professor Grisso determined that 67 percent of juveniles do not understand the basic words used in the Miranda warnings—words such as "attorney," "right," and "statement." The majority of juveniles who heard the phrase "anything you say can and will be used against you in a court of law" interpreted that to mean that the judge would punish them if they refused to answer the interrogators' questions.

SIDEBAR

PROFESSOR THOMAS GRISSO'S STUDY

In 1980, Dr. Thomas Grisso, an Associate Professor of Psychology at St. Louis University, conducted a series of tests to determine how well juveniles and adults understood the Miranda warnings.

One of his most significant findings was that the less people understood their rights, the more likely they were to waive those rights. Grisso found that juveniles' understanding of the Miranda warnings was much less than that of similarly situated adults and that neither group exhibited the complete understanding the law requires. Professor Grisso used the following statement:

You do not have to make a statement and have the right to remain silent. Anything you say can and will be used against you in a court of law. You have the right to consult an attorney before interrogation and to have an attorney present at the time of interrogation. If you cannot afford an attorney, one will be appointed for you.

(continues)

The professor conducted two studies. Study I comprised three tests and was designed to measure the subjects' comprehension of the actual words used in the Miranda warning.

The Comprehension of Miranda Rights (CMR) portion of Study I asked subjects to explain in their own words what the statements in the Miranda warning mean.

The Comprehension of Miranda Vocabulary (CMV) segment gave subjects a list of key words used in the Miranda warning (*consult, attorney, interrogation, appoint, entitled,* and *right*) and asked the subject to define them.

The Comprehension of Miranda Rights, True/False (CMR-T/F) part consisted of a list of statements concerning the Miranda warning and asked subjects to state whether those statements were true or false. The CMR-T/F was meant to compensate for those subjects with limited language skills.

Study II was the Function of Rights in Interrogation (Function) test. Examiners showed subjects three pictures and asked open-ended questions about the pictures. The pictures were an artist's renderings of an interrogation scene, an attorney/client consultation, and a courtroom scene. They were labeled as to the characters and the setting. The artist used neutral facial expressions and body gestures.

The panel of attorneys, nationally recognized experts, scholars, and psychologists who devised the tests determined that three crucial areas of perception must be present for the subject to demonstrate meaningful comprehension of Miranda rights.

First, the subject must understand the nature of an interrogation. That is, he must understand that the police are adversaries and are trying to convict him in a court of law. Second, he must understand the right to counsel includes the requirement that the attorney maintain confidentiality about any criminal admission the defendant makes. Finally, he must understand the right to remain silent as an absolute protection from self-incrimination at all stages of the proceeding from interrogation through trial.

The study team formulated a series of responses that they deemed adequate and another series that they deemed questionable. Any response that didn't fall into one of those categories would be deemed inadequate.

Examples of adequate and inadequate CMR responses follow:

"You have the right to remain silent."

Adequate: Encompasses the idea that the defendant does not have to say anything to the police, answer any question, and/or make any formal or informal statement. Also, that the defendant has a choice whether to talk, and if he chooses not to talk, it cannot be held against him.

"You don't have to say a word to
the police or anyone."

(continues)

*"You don't have to say anything to anyone
but if you want to you can."*

*"You don't have to say anything, and if you don't, it will not be
held against you in court."*

Questionable: Choice or implied choice is present, but rationale is incorrect or illogical.

*"You don't have to talk if you don't want to, because
you might not have done it."*

*"You don't have to talk if you don't want to, because the police
might not want you to."*

"It means don't talk to the police."

Examples of adequate and questionable responses to the CMV follow:

Consult

Criterion: The idea that information or advice is provided or sought pursuant to a decision.

Examples: "To ask for (give) advice about something."
"To make plans with someone."
"To talk over problems."

Examples of Function test questions:

Examiners show juvenile subjects a picture of a juvenile and two policemen seated at a table. Examiners showed adults a picture of an adult and two policemen seated at a table. The examiners told the subjects that this was a picture of a person whom the police had arrested and wished to question. Subjects answered the following questions:

1. "What is it that the policemen will want Joe to do?"

2. "Finish this sentence: 'The police think that Joe . . .'"

3. "What is the most important thing the police might want Joe to tell them?"

4. "How are the policemen probably feeling?"

5. "How is Joe probably feeling?"

After scoring the responses the team analyzed the data in relation to age, IQ, race, sex, socioeconomic status, and prior criminal record. The results revealed a sharp difference in the level of juvenile understanding and the level of adult understanding.

In the CMR test, 20.9 percent of juveniles and 42.3 percent of adults received a perfect score indicating complete and legally adequate understanding of all four warnings. 55.3 percent of juvenile and 23.1 percent of

(continues)

adults demonstrated a total lack of understanding of at least one of the four warnings.

Subjects fared slightly better in the CMV, where 33.2 percent of juveniles and 60.1 percent of adults demonstrated adequate understand of all six crucial terms in the Miranda warning. 63.3 percent or juveniles and 37.3 percent of adults completely misunderstood at least one word.

In the CMV-T/F, 27.6 percent or juvenile and 62.7 percent of adults received adequate scores on all parts.

In Study II, the great majority of juveniles and adults (90–99 percent) understood the adversarial nature of a police interrogation. However, 28.6 percent of juveniles, as opposed to only 12 percent of adults, described the police in the interrogation picture as "friendly" or "apologetic."

The great majority of juveniles and adults (80 percent and 89 percent, respectively) understood the attorney/client relationship and understood that the attorney was supposed to defend the defendant. However, 28 percent of juveniles did not understand that an attorney must maintain client confidences, incorrectly believing that the attorney's advocacy would be compromised if she were aware of her client's guilt. Only 6 percent of adults made this mistake.

Finally, 61.8 percent of juveniles and 21.7 percent of adults incorrectly believed that a judge could penalize a defendant for invoking or having invoked his right to remain silent. The majority of juveniles (55.3 percent) and a large number of adults (42.9 percent) stated that they would have to answer the judge's questions about their criminal activity.

Many police departments have incorporated new methods and techniques of interrogation of juveniles based upon Dr. Grisso's work. There are written tests and evaluations that are available for purchase that police departments can use to assess juveniles' understanding of important concepts and terms.

Grisso, T. (1980). Juveniles' capacities to waive Miranda rights: An empirical analysis. *California Law Review, 68,* 1134–1166.

CONSTITUTIONAL CHALLENGES TO JUVENILE CONFESSIONS

Attorneys and paralegals for the defense and the prosecution should be aware of the existence of any statements the juvenile has made in any delinquency action so they can assess whether the juvenile made the statements are vulnerable to a constitutional challenge.

It is reasonable to assume that defense attorneys will challenge many statements and confessions on the basis of state coercion or the juveniles' lack of understanding.

The prosecution should prepare to defend the interrogation process and the resultant statement or confession. The main areas to examine are whether the juvenile was in fact in custody at the time of the statements; whether a responsible adult—a parent or guardian—was present during the questioning, and if not, why not; whether the juvenile received Miranda warnings, and if so, the adequacy of the warnings; whether the juvenile invoked his Miranda rights; and whether the police did anything to elicit a statement from the juvenile after he invoked his rights.

In Custody

The first consideration is whether the juvenile was indeed in custody when he made the statements. Constitutional protections do not apply to pre-custodial interrogations or investigations. They begin to apply only once the juvenile is in custody.

Juveniles are in custody when they are not free to leave or when they believe they are not free to leave. In making this determination the court will assess "whether, based on the objective circumstances, a reasonable juvenile of the same age would believe is freedom of movement was significantly restricted."

The Supreme Court ruled in the 2004 case *Yarborough v. Alvarado* that the police do not need to take into account a juvenile's age when determining whether a juvenile is in custody for the purpose of issuing Miranda warnings.

Remember that a juvenile is not "under arrest" or "arrested" but rather "in custody" or "taken into custody." The state of being in custody will not always be readily apparent to the juvenile at the time, or to the attorney or paralegal reviewing the situation after the fact. Ideally, there will be a point where all can agree that at that point the juvenile was no longer free to leave.

There may or may not be a formal statement wherein a police officer explicitly says to a juvenile, "You are now in custody," or similar words. Such an explicit statement would make the legal teams' jobs easier, but rarely does one encounter such clarity.

There may be chaos, confusion, and perhaps violence when the police take juveniles into custody. There may not be a clear moment when the juvenile is in custody. If the police observe juveniles committing illegal acts, then the juveniles will be in custody at the moment the police get physical control of them.

When the police visit to a juveniles' homes or schools to speak to them, and then take them into custody during the visit, it will be difficult to determine exactly when the juveniles lost their freedom of movement.

Parental or Other Adult Presence

The next consideration in evaluating a confession or statement is whether a responsible adult was present during the interrogation. Some, but not all, states have a rule requiring the presence of parentsor other adults during any interrogation of people under a certain age, usually 14, unless the juveniles knowingly, intelligently, and voluntarily waive that right. A valid waiver occurs after the juveniles have consulted with the adults and the adults have explained the juveniles' rights to them.

The states that require an adult presence do so to prevent "the [Miranda] warning from becoming merely a ritualistic recitation wherein the effect of actual comprehension is ignored."[1] As the Grisso study shows, this is a valid concern.

Some states, such as Louisiana and Pennsylvania, had such rules, but have repealed them, so that an adult or parental presence is no longer required.

Those states that have such rules generally require that juveniles have an opportunity to consult with adults. Courts have interpreted this to require that the consultation be in private. The rules also usually require that the same adults be present during the interrogation, if they choose to be, and if the juveniles desire it.

The adults must be sufficiently interested in the juveniles' welfare and completely independent of the prosecuting authority to afford the juvenile real protection.

Finally, the adults must understand the juveniles' rights, be able to explain those rights to them, and assert those rights on their behalf.

Professor Grisso's studies show that there is a significant percentage of adults who suffer from the same lack of understanding as many juveniles. Even intelligent, educated adults and juveniles can lack a full appreciation of the constitutional principles elucidated in *Miranda*. It is, therefore, important to focus on both the juveniles' and the adults' understanding.

Juveniles can waive their rights to have parents or other interested adults present at interrogation only after consultation with those parents or adults. The adults must be informed of, and understand, the juveniles' constitutional rights for it to be a genuine consultation.

Juveniles can waive their rights to have parents or other adults present at interrogation without prior consultation if they exhibit a high degree of intelligence, experience, knowledge, or sophistication.

Issuing Miranda Warnings

Police must inform juveniles that

- They have the right to remain silent.
- The state can, and will, use any statements they make against them in court.

Chapter 4 Interrogation 55

- They have the right to have an attorney present.
- If they cannot afford an attorney, the state will appoint them one at the state's expense.

Many police departments have Miranda warnings printed onto sheets that detainees must read and sign. They indicate by their signature that they have read the document and understand all of the rights they possess under *Miranda.*

Invoking *Miranda*

Another consideration in assessing juveniles' statements is whether they invoked, or attempted to invoke, their Miranda rights. If the juveniles ask for attorneys, the police must immediately halt all questioning until the attorney arrives. They may not attempt to elicit a response or statement from the juveniles in any fashion, even if that invocation takes a form other than overt questioning.

The following case, *Fare v. Michael C.,* demonstrates the test that courts apply in determining whether a juvenile has invoked his Miranda rights, and the factors the courts take into account in assessing a juvenile's understanding of the interrogation process. The court also addresses the issue of whether a juvenile's request to speak to his probation officer is equivalent to asking to see an attorney, and concludes that it is not.

Fare v. Michael C.
99 S.Ct. 2560 (1979)
MR. JUSTICE BLACKMUN delivered the opinion of the Court.

Respondent Michael C. was implicated in the murder of Robert Yeager. A small truck registered in the name of respondent's mother was identified as having been near the Yeager home at the time of the killing, and a young man answering respondent's description was seen by witnesses near the truck and near the home shortly before Yeager was murdered.

On the basis of this information, Van Nuys, Cal., police took respondent into custody. Respondent then was 16½ years old and on probation to the Juvenile Court. He had been on probation since the age of 12. Approximately one year earlier he had served a term in a youth corrections camp under the supervision of the Juvenile Court. He had a record of several previous offenses, including burglary of guns and purse snatching, stretching back over several years.

Upon respondent's arrival at the Van Nuys station house two police officers began to interrogate him. The officers and respondent were the only persons in the room during the interrogation. The conversation was tape-recorded. One of the officers initiated the interview by informing respondent that he had been brought in for questioning in relation to a murder. The officer fully advised respondent of his *Miranda* rights. The following exchange then occurred, as set out in the opinion of the California Supreme Court,

"**Q.** . . . Do you understand all of these rights as I have explained them to you?

A. Yeah.

Q. Okay, do you wish to give up your right to remain silent and talk to us about this murder?

A. What murder? I don't know about no murder.

(continues)

Fare v. Michael C. (Continued)

Q. I'll explain to you which one it is if you want to talk to us about it.

A. Yeah, I might talk to you.

Q. Do you want to give up your right to have an attorney present here while we talk about it?

A. Can I have my probation officer here?

Q. Well I can't get a hold of your probation officer right now. You have the right to an attorney.

A. How I know you guys won't pull no police officer in and tell me he's an attorney?

Q. Huh?

A. [How I know you guys won't pull no police officer in and tell me he's an attorney?]

Q. Your probation officer is Mr. Christiansen.

A. Yeah.

Q. Well I'm not going to call Mr. Christiansen tonight. There's a good chance we can talk to him later, but I'm not going to call him right now. If you want to talk to us without an attorney present, you can. If you don't want to, you don't have to. But if you want to say something, you can, and if you don't want to say something you don't have to. That's your right. You understand that right?

A. Yeah.

Q. Okay, will you talk to us without an attorney present?

A. Yeah I want to talk to you."

Respondent thereupon proceeded to answer questions put to him by the officers. He made statements and drew sketches that incriminated him in the Yeager murder.

Largely on the basis of respondent's incriminating statements, probation authorities filed a petition in Juvenile Court alleging that respondent had murdered Robert Yeager.

Respondent thereupon moved to suppress the statements and sketches he gave the police during the interrogation. He alleged that the statements had been obtained in violation of *Miranda* in that his request to see his probation officer at the outset of the questioning constituted an invocation of his Fifth Amendment right to remain silent, just as if he had requested the assistance of an attorney. Accordingly, respondent argued that since the interrogation did not cease until he had a chance to confer with his probation officer, the statements and sketches could not be admitted against him in the Juvenile Court proceedings.

In a ruling from the bench, the court denied the motion to suppress. It held that the question whether respondent had waived his right to remain silent was one of fact to be determined on a case-by-case basis, and that the facts of this case showed a "clear waiver" by respondent of that right. The court observed that the transcript of the interrogation revealed that respondent specifically had told the officers that he would talk with them, and that this waiver had come at the outset of the interrogation and not after prolonged questioning. The court noted that respondent was a "16 and a half year old minor who has been through the court system before, has been to [probation] camp, has a probation officer, [and is not] a young, naive minor with no experience with the courts." Accordingly, it found that on the facts of the case respondent had waived his Fifth Amendment rights, notwithstanding the request to see his probation officer.

On appeal, the Supreme Court of California reversed. The court held that respondent's "request to see his probation officer at the commencement of interrogation negated any possible willingness on his part to discuss his case with the police [and] thereby invoked his Fifth Amendment privilege." The court based this conclusion on its view that, because of the juvenile court system's emphasis on the relationship between a

(continues)

Fare v. Michael C. (Continued)

probation officer and the probationer, the officer was "a trusted guardian figure who exercises the authority of the state as *parens patriae* and whose duty it is to implement the protective and rehabilitative powers of the juvenile court." As a consequence, the court found that a minor's request for his probation officer was the same as a request to see his parents during interrogation, and thus under the rule of *Burton* constituted an invocation of the minor's Fifth Amendment rights.

The fact that the probation officer also served as a peace officer did not alter, in the court's view, the fact that the officer in the eyes of the juvenile was a trusted guardian figure to whom the minor normally would turn for help when in trouble with the police. The court ruled that it would unduly restrict *Miranda* to limit its reach in a case involving a minor to a request by the minor for an attorney, since it would be "fatuous to assume that a minor in custody will be in a position to call an attorney for assistance and it is unrealistic to attribute no significance to his call for help from the only person to whom he normally looks—a parent or guardian."

The State of California petitioned this Court for a writ of certiorari [and] we thereafter issued the writ.

II

The rule the Court established in *Miranda* is clear. In order to be able to use statements obtained during custodial interrogation of the accused, the State must warn the accused prior to such questioning of his right to remain silent and of his right to have counsel, retained or appointed, present during interrogation.

The California court in this case, however, significantly has extended this rule by providing that a request by a juvenile for his probation officer has the same effect as a request for an attorney.

The rule in *Miranda,* however, was based on this Court's perception that the lawyer occupies a critical position in our legal system because of his unique ability to protect the Fifth Amendment rights of a client undergoing custodial interrogation. The lawyer's presence helps guard against overreaching by the police and ensures that any statements actually obtained are accurately transcribed for presentation into evidence.

A probation officer is not in the same posture with regard to either the accused or the system of justice as a whole. Moreover, the probation officer is the employee of the State which seeks to prosecute the alleged offender. He is a peace officer, and as such is allied, to a greater or lesser extent, with his fellow peace officers.

In these circumstances, it cannot be said that the probation officer is able to offer the type of independent advice that an accused would expect from a lawyer retained or assigned to assist him during questioning.

We thus believe it clear that the probation officer is not in a position to offer the type of legal assistance necessary to protect the Fifth Amendment rights of an accused undergoing custodial interrogation that a lawyer can offer.

If it were otherwise, a juvenile's request for almost anyone he considered trustworthy enough to give him reliable advice would trigger the rigid rule of *Miranda*.

Nor do we believe that a request by a juvenile to speak with his probation officer constitutes a *per se* request to remain silent. In the absence of further evidence that the minor intended in the circumstances to invoke his Fifth Amendment rights by such a request, we decline to attach such overwhelming significance to this request.

We hold, therefore, that it was error to find that the request by respondent to speak with his probation officer *per se* constituted an invocation of respondent's Fifth Amendment right to be free from compelled

(continues)

Fare v. Michael C. (Continued)

self-incrimination. It therefore was also error to hold that because the police did not then cease interrogating respondent the statements he made during interrogation should have been suppressed.

We feel that the conclusion of the Juvenile Court was correct. The transcript of the interrogation reveals that the police officers conducting the interrogation took care to ensure that respondent understood his rights. They fully explained to respondent that he was being questioned in connection with a murder. They then informed him of all the rights delineated in *Miranda,* and ascertained that respondent understood those rights. There is no indication in the record that respondent failed to understand what the officers told him. Moreover, after his request to see his probation officer had been denied, and after the police officer once more had explained his rights to him, respondent clearly expressed his willingness to waive his rights and continue the interrogation.

Further, no special factors indicate that respondent was unable to understand the nature of his actions. He was a 16½-year-old juvenile with considerable experience with the police. He had a record of several arrests. He had served time in a youth camp, and he had been on probation for several years. He was under the full-time supervision of probation authorities. There is no indication that he was of insufficient intelligence to understand the rights he was waiving, or what the consequences of that waiver would be. He was not worn down by improper interrogation tactics or lengthy questioning or by trickery or deceit.

On these facts, we think it clear that respondent voluntarily and knowingly waived his Fifth Amendment rights.

The judgment of the Supreme Court of California is reversed, and the case is remanded for further proceedings not inconsistent with this opinion.

It is so ordered.

SIDEBAR

PREPARING TO ATTACK OR DEFEND A JUVENILE'S STATEMENT

When evaluating a case that involves interrogation and a confession or statement, assess and evaluate all of the facts and circumstances. Your assessment should focus on the juvenile's age, intelligence, education, and prior experience with the court system, as well as where the events took place and at what time of day the interrogation took place. If possible, you should also determine who else was present during the interrogation, and the words, actions, and demeanor of the police officers.

If you work for the prosecution, obtain or prepare your own *Miranda* comprehension assessment. Police officers can administer this assessment before interrogation to ensure that the juvenile understands the words and meanings of the Miranda warnings, thus staving off a constitutional challenge.

The Supreme Court treats juveniles the same as it treats adults when it rights to those facing criminal or quasi-criminal proceedings. Juveniles possess the right against self-incrimination, right to an attorney, and right to appointed counsel for indigents, just as adults. But juveniles do not get any extra protection or different treatment. In fact, the Supreme Court has on many occasions specifically declined to afford juveniles greater protections than adults.

The court requires juveniles to affirmatively invoke their Miranda rights in order to avail themselves of those rights. Juveniles facing police interrogation must clearly, unambiguously, and unequivocally ask for an attorney. Unless and until they do so, the police are under no obligation to stop or postpone the interrogation. Asking to see a probation officer, parent, or other adult is not sufficient to invoke *Miranda*.

WAIVER

Juveniles can waive their Miranda rights, just as adults can waive them. The courts require that any waiver be voluntary.

Voluntary has two senses in this context. First, it means the absence of coercion. The police cannot physically or mentally abuse, harm, or threaten to harm juveniles to procure their waivers. Alternatively, the police cannot make lavish promises in order to induce waivers. They cannot, for instance, promise juveniles that the judge will go easy on them if they confess.[2]

Voluntariness also means to reach the decision to waive constitutional rights knowingly, intelligently, and with comprehension. *Comprehension* is to understand the meaning of the words police use during interrogation: what an "attorney" is, what "court" means, what "against you" means. Courts do not require that juveniles understand or appreciate the implications and ramifications of a waiver. The decision to waive need not be intelligent, wise, or reasonable. It is enough to demonstrate that the juvenile understood the words. If a state statute does not specifically require the presence of an adult during waiver or interrogation, then the courts will not impose such a requirement.

Totality of the Circumstances Doctrine

Courts determine the validity of waiver or assertions of rights on a case-by-case basis by examining the totality of the circumstances. Courts will consider, among other factors related to the juvenile:

- Age
- Education
- Intelligence
- Knowledge of the court system, as evidenced by their previous experiences with the system

- A demonstration of knowledge of the charges against them
- A demonstration of knowledge of the rights afforded them

The courts will look at the following factors involving the police or state's actions:

- The time and place of interrogation
- The number of officers present
- Whether the police provided food, sleep, and toilet facilities
- Whether the juvenile was allowed to consult, or did consult, with a parent or interested adult
- The duration of the interrogation
- Whether the juvenile had refused to give a statement on prior occasions
- Whether the juvenile had reason to exhibit bravado[3]
- The attitude of the police

CASE PROBLEM

Police interviewed Michael, 17, without his parents at a police station about his involvement in a crime. Police neither took custody of nor Mirandized Michael. Michael confessed involvement during the interview. The court convicted Michael of second-degree murder and attempted robbery based, in part, on these statements. After failed appeals in the California courts, Michael unsuccessfully sought a writ of habeas corpus in federal district court in California.

The Ninth Circuit Court of Appeals reversed. Recognizing the "in custody" standard to be whether a reasonable person would feel free to end interrogation, the appeals court held that a juvenile is more likely than an adult to believe he is in custody. Because Michael was "in custody," the Fifth Amendment required that police read his rights under *Miranda v. Arizona* to him.

When deciding whether a suspect is "in custody" and therefore entitled to his Miranda warnings, must an officer consider the suspect's age and previous history with law enforcement?

ROLE-PLAY PROBLEM

Chuck is a 14-year-old boy who is in the seventh grade. He appears to be on the low end of the average range of intelligence.

Witnesses in Chuck's neighborhood who know him told police they saw Chuck hanging around outside of the home of Linda Black, a teenager who had been found dead of a blunt instrument blow to her head. There was a large, heavy candlestick next to her. Later forensic analysis revealed this to be the murder weapon. There were no traces of DNA other than Linda's on the candlestick.

Police also found Chuck's sweater inside her home. Chuck had seventy dollars and a man's watch in his pocket when police took custody of him.

Officers Adams and Flint went to Chuck's house on a Friday evening. Chuck's parents were not at home when the officers arrived. They asked Chuck if he would go with them to the police station. Smiling, Chuck said it sounded like fun and went eagerly along with them.

The officers took Chuck into a small, windowless room in the station, where they sat him down at a table. Officer Adams sat next to Chuck and patted him on the back as they spoke. Officer Flint stood over them, glaring and grimacing at everything Chuck said.

The first thing the officers asked Chuck was if he wanted to stay and just talk about a few things. Chuck said he did. They began by asking Chuck where he had been on the night of the murder and he told them he had gone to Linda Black's house for tutoring. They did their lesson, had a snack, and then he went home. Officer Adams told Chuck that somebody had murdered Linda later that very night. At this, Officer Flint glared at Chuck and mumbled something about the electric chair.

Chuck began to get frightened and the following exchange took place:

Chuck: Can I call my Mom?

Adams: Well, I'm sure you can if you want to Chuck? Is that what you want? You want your Mom to have to listen to all this?

Flint: He wants his Mommy. I bet Linda Black would have liked to have had her mother there to protect her, but she didn't get that. Did she, Chuck?

Adams: Flint, leave him alone. Chuck, do you want your mom here?

Chuck: I don't know. Should I call my mom or something? Maybe I should call someone else? Maybe my teacher?

Flint: What are you worried about, Chucky? You worried we're gonna find out you killed Linda Black? What are you trying to hide?

Adams: He's all right. Aren't you all right, Chuck? Listen, Chuck, you have the right to remain silent. Anything you say can, and will, be used against you in a court of law. You have the right to have an attorney present. If you can't afford an attorney, the county will appoint one for you at its expense. You got all that?

Chuck: Uh huh.

Adams: Good. Now do you want to just go ahead and answer some real simple questions? Or do you want to do that?

Chuck: Do what?

Adams: What I just said.

Chuck: I'll answer your questions.

Chuck went on to give a statement in which he took full responsibility for the murder. He got some of the details wrong, but he agreed to everything the officers put before him.

You are working for the defense.

1. What facts will you use to formulate an argument to suppress Chuck's statement?

2. What cases and legal concepts will you rely upon in formulating your argument?

3. As a paralegal, what kind of investigation will you conduct?

4. Whom will you interview and what documents will you review?

You are working for the prosecution.

5. What facts will you rely upon in formulating an argument against suppression of Chuck's statement?

6. What cases and legal concepts will you rely upon in formulating your argument?

7. As a paralegal, how will you conduct your investigation?

8. Whom will you interview and what documents will you collect?

HYPOTHETICAL PROBLEM

Several 14- and 15-year-old high school lacrosse players had just returned from an away game in which they suffered a devastating loss. They were waiting for their parents in the school parking lot. The boys had returned much earlier than anticipated and there was a miscommunication among the coaches, which resulted in the boys being left alone for over an hour.

The boys were arguing about the game, and Brett began to taunt George, who had made an error at a crucial moment. The arguing escalated to physical fighting and got so violent and loud that a neighbor called the police. When the police arrived most of the boys were bloody and had ripped clothes. It took the police several minutes to gain control of the boys.

When the police officers gained control of the boys, they saw that Brett had been stabbed. All of the boys seemed shocked and surprised by Brett's injury. None of the boys appeared to know who injured Brett.

There was a bloody knife lying on the ground on the edge of the parking lot. It was partially buried in the dirt and had been stepped on and scraped.

George began to run away, and one of the officers ran and caught him. George resisted, and it took the officer several minutes to subdue George. After the officer calmed George, he asked if George knew anything about Brett being stabbed. George began to cry. The officer said, "Son, your friend's hurt, and if we don't know exactly what happened to him, and when, and how, he could die. Do you know how he got hurt?" George answered, "I stabbed Brett." The state filed a delinquency petition against George and George has filed a motion to suppress his statement, "I stabbed Brett."

1. What will the defense argue?

2. How will the state respond?

3. How will the court rule?

ETHICAL CONCERNS

As in many areas of criminal law in general and juvenile justice in particular, the area of interrogations is fraught with ethical dilemmas. What should a court do when a juvenile defendant has given a statement confessing responsibility for a crime, but the circumstances under which the juvenile gave the statement are less than ideal? Should the court just throw away the evidence and allow the case to go unsolved? Or should the court admit the statement and compromise the constitutional rights of not just this defendant, but also of all defendants after him?

Often police officers do not have the luxury of sitting down and methodically administering a legally perfect version of the Miranda warnings and then conducting a legally perfect interrogation. Sometimes people blurt things out. Sometimes there is confusion in the station, and one officer is unaware of what another officer has said or done.

As always, the court must look at all of the circumstances and weigh society's interest in solving crime against society's interest in protecting the Constitution.

DISCUSSION QUESTIONS

1. The Supreme Court, in the 2004 case *Yarborough v. Alvarado,* specifically declined to extend special protections to juveniles in interrogation situations. Do you agree with that decision?

2. Should there be special provisions for juvenile defendants who are mentally retarded or mentally ill?

3. Should there be special provisions for juvenile defendants who are victims of abuse?

4. Do you believe that there should be a blanket requirement that a parent or other interested adult be present with the juvenile at any interrogation?

5. Should there be a blanket requirement that an attorney for the juvenile be present at any interrogation?

6. What is more important—that police solve crimes, or that juveniles are afforded all of their constitutional rights? What would be the result if either

option were taken to its logical conclusion, i.e., that police be allowed to use any tactic at all to solve crimes, as long as it gets results, or that police be required to follow every single rule and regulation possible in questioning juveniles so that none of their rights are compromised?

7. In Miranda v. Arizona, Chief Justice Warren quotes the 1933 Wickersham Commission Report, which in turn quotes the Lord Chancellor of England, Lord Sankey, "It is not admissible to do a great right by doing a little wrong. . . . It is not sufficient to do justice by obtaining a proper result by irregular or improper means." Do you agree with this?

8. If you were a Supreme Court justice, and you had the chance to rewrite the Miranda warnings, would you do so? If so, how would you change them?

KEY TERMS

interrogation   waiver
Miranda warning

END NOTES

[1] *Com. v. Alfonso A.,* 780 NE2d 1244 (Mass. 2003).

[2] In fact, research suggests that judges tend to sentence more severely defendants who admit their criminal involvement than those who deny it. Suback & Vardaman. (1997). "Decision making in delinquency cases. . . ." *Law and Human Behavior, 21,* 47.

[3] In *Alfonso A.* (ibid) the police went to a private home to question two boys, one of whom was 18 years old, and the other, a juvenile. The first, older boy boldly acquiesced to interrogation and waved off the notion of having his mother present in front of the juvenile. When it came time for the police to interrogate the juvenile, he waived his right to have his mother or another adult present during the interrogation. The appellate court held that this was not a valid waiver by the juvenile of his right to consult with an adult and cited, among other reasons, the bravado the juvenile witnessed his older compatriot display. Grisso, T. (1980). Juveniles' capacities to waive Miranda rights: An empirical analysis. *California Law Review, 68,* 1134–1166.

Chapter 5

PRETRIAL DETENTION

OBJECTIVES

By the end of this chapter, the student should know:

- The procedures that police follow in deciding whether to detain a juvenile after taking the juvenile into custody for delinquency
- The procedures for removing juveniles to detention facilities
- The outlines of a detention hearing
- The procedural safeguards that accompany pretrial detention proceedings
- That private attorneys can act as public defenders
- That states must always separate juveniles and adults in a detention facility, and the ramifications of the state's failure to do so
- The difference between procedural due process and substantive due process, and how procedural due process applies to juvenile proceedings
- How the Fifth Amendment applies to delinquency proceedings
- How juvenile detention rates changed throughout the 1990s

INTRODUCTION

When police take juveniles into custody, they must make a series of decisions that will have tremendous impact on the juveniles' immediate and distant futures.

The detaining officers must make an initial assessment whether to take the juveniles into custody or release them to the custody of parents or guardians. Officers are more likely to release the juveniles if the acts they committed were not serious or violent, if the officers believe there is little danger that the juveniles will re-offend if released, or if it is clear that the juveniles pose no threat to themselves or others.

warrant

A written order commanding the sheriff or the police to take custody of a certain person and bring that person before the court

Juveniles are obligated to attend all subsequent court proceedings. The court will issue a **warrant**—a written order commanding a sheriff or the police to take custody of a certain person and bring that person before the court—to the police, authorizing them to take the juvenile into custody if the juvenile fails to appear. Often, the police require the parent or guardian to sign an agreement to appear in court with the juvenile before the officer will release the juvenile to the parent or guardian.

Officers will not release juveniles at the point of initial detention if they cannot locate a parent, guardian, or other responsible adult to take custody of the juvenile. Officers may choose not to release the juveniles if they were involved in particularly serious or dangerous activities or if the officers have reason to believe the juveniles represent a danger to themselves or to others.

PROCEDURES

The states prescribe that police must follow certain procedures in detaining juveniles. First, the police must deliver Miranda warnings after they take the juvenile into custody and before they begin interrogation. The officer must inform the juvenile of his legal rights in language that he can understand. Most police officers carry written forms imprinted with Miranda warnings. They read the warnings to the juvenile, then they have the juvenile read the warnings and initial or check a box next to each paragraph stating, "I have read and understand this document." (See Chapter 4, Interrogation.)

Second, the police must attempt to contact the juvenile's parent, guardian, or other responsible adult. They must allow that adult to be present during the interrogation if the adult is available and willing to do so, and if the juvenile does not legally waive his right to have the adult present. The officer must inform the parent or guardian that they are taking the juvenile into custody and must describe the nature of the offense to the degree that it is practicable. The officer must also inform the state **attorney general,** or state prosecutor, of the detention.

attorney general

The head of the state's justice department; the state's chief law enforcement attorney

Third, if the police are able to contact the parent, and the parent asks to be present during questioning and makes himself available, all questioning must stop until the parent arrives. If the parent is not notified but the lack of notice does not have a discernibly adverse effect upon the outcome of the case, a reviewing court will not hold that to be a constitutional violation.

Last, the court must conduct a detention hearing within a legally prescribed time period. A detention hearing is an informal procedure wherein the juvenile court judge hears evidence pertaining to whether it is in the best interests of the juvenile and of society to detain the juvenile.

REMOVAL TO A DETENTION FACILITY

If the police choose to detain the juvenile, they will bring him to a detention facility, which is any secure facility for the temporary housing of juveniles who have committed or are suspected of having committed delinquent acts. Most big cities in the United States have juvenile detention facilities. Communities without their own detention facilities have arrangements with nearby cities to use their facilities as needed.

An **intake worker,** a detention facility employee who is available to receive juveniles, is on duty 24 hours a day in most detention facilities. These social workers or probation officers take temporary charge of the child and make initial assessments. They will attempt to contact the child's parent or guardian to provide notice of the child's custody and potential detention and to give the parent a chance to confer with and obtain counsel for the juvenile.

At this point, detention center personnel must decide whether to further detain or release the juvenile to a parent or guardian. If facility personnel release the juvenile, they will require the parent or guardian to sign an agreement to appear in court with the juvenile. If they cannot find the parent or guardian, or the parent or guardian refuses to come to the detention facility to receive the juvenile, the detention center personnel will detain the juvenile.

The prosecutor must decide whether to file a **petition,** or formal, written notice of the charges that the state is bringing against the juvenile, within 24 hours in most jurisdictions. If the prosecutor chooses not to file a petition, the detaining authorities will release the juvenile to a parent or guardian if one is available.

The authorities can choose to release the child even if the prosecutor files a petition. In this instance, the state must conduct a detention hearing. Most jurisdictions require detention hearings to occur within 72 hours of the juvenile's initial detention.

DETENTION HEARING

Delinquency proceedings are noncriminal, and detention is considered protective custody rather than punitive imprisonment. The detention hearing, therefore, is informal. The judge will generally permit police officers, detention facility personnel, and other authorities to testify without strict regard to the Rules of Evidence. The child's parent or guardian must receive notice of the hearing if possible.

intake worker
A social worker, probation officer or other state or county official who is the first contact between the public and a state- or county-run institution

petition
A formal, written document that begins a delinquency proceeding

probable cause

A level of certainty sufficient to sustain the initiation of a criminal or delinquency proceeding. Probable cause is a relatively low level burden of proof

At the detention hearing the judge must first determine whether **probable cause** exists to believe the juvenile committed a delinquent act. In order to sustain a finding of probable cause, the judge must find that there exists sufficient evidence to form a reasonable belief that the juvenile committed the act. Without such probable cause, the state cannot hold the child regardless of what other factors may be present.

The following case illustrates how courts assess the facts of a matter to determine whether officers had probable cause to detain juveniles. It also demonstrates how probable cause may be a product of external facts and circumstances, in this case, the fact that the events occurred immediately after the massacre at Columbine High School weighed heavily in the court's appraisal.

Williams ex rel. Allen v. Cambridge Bd. of Educ.
370 F.3d 630 C.A.6 (Ohio), 2004.

On April 20, 1999, fourteen students and one teacher were killed at Columbine High School in Littleton, Colorado. Two students at the school, we eventually learned, were responsible for the killing spree.

In April 1999, Rhys Williams and Zach Durbin were fourteen years old and were in the eighth grade at Cambridge Junior High School. Both students had previous criminal problems and were on juvenile probation in April 1999. Rhys also had been disciplined by the school for several incidents of threatening behavior.

On Wednesday, April 21, 1999, one day after the Columbine tragedy, Zach spoke with a classmate, Kayla Hollins, on the telephone. According to Zach, he merely told Kayla about [a] conversation [concerning Columbine] earlier in the day. According to Kayla, Zach told her that he was "getting sick of the way things were going" and was planning on bringing a gun to school or bombing the school. Kayla alleged that Zach also said he would kill the "preps" first— meaning that he would kill Sadie LePage and that Kayla would be "one of the first to go"—but that he would not hurt Katie Spittle because he liked her.

On Friday morning of that week, two days after her conversation with Zach, Kayla wrote a note to

Sadie LePage, saying that Zach "was going to bring a gun to school and shoot us all because he was sick of bitchy preps." Sadie showed the note to Katie Spittle, another classmate. During the lunch period, Sadie and Katie asked Zach whether the contents of the note were true, and he allegedly told them they were, a point that Zach disputes. After lunch, Sadie and Katie told school officials about the threat. They first told Julie Orsini, the guidance counselor, about the note that Kayla had written. Orsini notified Vice Principal William Howell about the matter and relayed her impression that the girls were "visibly shaken up [and] . . . feeling threatened."

Howell met with Sadie and Katie individually, and later called Kayla to his office as well. All three girls spoke to Howell about what had happened, then wrote statements in which they described the events of that morning and their interactions with Zach. In Kayla's statement, she said the following:

I talked to Zach on the phone Wednesday night & he said he was sick of everybody, everyone was getting on his nerves & he & Rhys Williams were talking about bringing a gun to school & he was

(continues)

Williams ex rel. Allen v. Cambridge Bd. of Educ. (Continued)

very serious about the matter[.] [H]is other option was planting a bomb & taking everyone out on the first (one) shot. But he had made very clear he would spare Katie Spittle because he liked her. This morning I [said] to Sadie LePage I had spoken to Zach & she asked what about & that is when I wrote Sadie telling her about our (mine & Zach's) conversation. Half of the note is now gone.

Sadie said the following in her statement:

I was sitting in first period today and Kayla Hollins wrote me a note that said Zach Durbin was going to bring a gun to school and shoot us all because he was sick of bitchy preps and he was going to start with me because he hated me so much. Then it said that he said it would just be easier to plant a bomb because he could get us all at once. Then in band (second period) I showed Katie Spittle the note because I was scared and she took the note to him at lunch and he said that it was really true, that he was talking to Rhys and they were seriously thinking about it. Zach hates me so much because I broke up with him 1–2 months ago. And he said he was going to spare Katie of all of this because he likes her.

And Katie said the following in her statement:

This morning in 2nd period (Band) Sadie LePage showed me the note. At lunch I asked Zach if it was really true, and he said yes. He said him and Rhys were talking about it. He pointed to Sadie and said she's going first. He said he was going to spare me, because he liked me.

After his meetings with the three girls and after obtaining their statements, Howell [began] the emergency removal process with respect to Zach. In an effort to release Zach to an adult, Howell initially tried to reach Zach's mother, but she was unavailable. He then called Zach's probation officer, Jeffrey Hayes, who came to the school.

When Hayes arrived at the school, Howell briefed him about the situation, told him that the police had been notified and showed him the three girls' written statements. Hayes asked Howell "whether these [girls] were reputable students" because he wanted to determine "whether it was somebody trying to get even with Zach or that type of thing." Howell confirmed the credibility of the girls' statements on the basis of their reputations as students.

At this point, Howell removed Zach from study hall and told him about the girls' allegations. In response, Zach confirmed that he knew about the note, but denied the rest of Howell's accusations. After the interview, Howell asked Hayes to escort Zach from the school. While Hayes claims that he did not arrest Zach at this point, he acknowledges that Zach was not at liberty to leave and that he handcuffed Zach in conformity with the probation department's policies. Hayes [spent the weekend at the] Jefferson County Juvenile Detention Facility.

On Monday, April 26th, the earliest day they could appear in juvenile court, Zach and Rhys were returned to Guernsey County.

A. Fourth Amendment Claim

As a general rule, a law enforcement officer may not seize an individual except after establishing probable cause that the individual has committed, or is about to commit, a crime. Probable cause means the "facts and circumstances within the officer's knowledge that are sufficient to warrant a prudent person, or one of reasonable caution, in believing, in the circumstances shown, that the suspect has committed, is committing, or is about to commit an offense." Once "probable cause is established," this Court has added, an officer is under no duty to investigate further or to look for additional evidence which may exculpate the accused.

(continues)

Williams ex rel. Allen v. Cambridge Bd. of Educ. (Continued)

In fact, law enforcement "is under no obligation to give any credence to a suspect's story [or alibi] nor should a plausible explanation in any sense require the officer to forego arrest pending further investigation if the facts as initially discovered provide probable cause."

At the same time, officers must consider the totality of the evidence "known to them" when considering probable cause, and in cases where they have both inculpatory and exculpatory evidence they must not ignore the exculpatory evidence in order to find probable cause. A "mere suspicion" of criminality will not suffice.

The rub in this case is whether probation officers Hayes and Steven—the two primary defendants with respect to this claim—had probable cause to take Zach and Rhys into custody on Friday, April 23, 1999. In the district court's view, the "information conveyed in the girls' written statements was sufficient for the Defendants to have had more than a 'mere suspicion' of Williams' and Durbin's alleged criminal activities." In response to this conclusion, plaintiffs argue that because Hayes and Stevens relied on vague statements the girls made to Vice Principal Howell and did not test the reliability of the statements themselves, they did not have probable cause to detain either of them.

The problem with this argument is that Hayes and Stevens did not merely accept the girls' three statements at face value. After two of the girls spoke to the guidance counselor, Julie Orsini, about the threats, she passed along the information to Vice Principal Howell and explained that the girls "were visibly shaken up; that—that they were feeling threatened because they had had a correspondence with Zach Durbin concerning threats to them." Howell in turn spoke to all three girls, then asked each of them to write statements about what had happened. The three girls all conveyed the same essential information to Howell, and their written statements matched their oral statements.

Only after Howell vouched for the girls' credibility, and indeed only after Hayes queried whether the girls could be trusted, did Hayes credit this version of the events. In view of Howell's position as Vice Principal, Hayes was justified in trusting Howell's assessment of the three girls' credibility and in respecting Howell's superior position for doing so. On top of this information, Howell separately met with Zach, who confirmed that he knew about the original note.

On this record, the officers' investigation sufficed for the task at hand. The question is not whether Zach made these threats but whether the defendants had probable cause to believe that he had made them. In the aftermath of Columbine, the corroborated statements of three girls whom Vice-Principal Howell deemed trustworthy permissibly cemented the probation officers' probable cause determination—regardless of whether the concern was a shooting/bomb threat or criminal menacing and regardless of whether the suspect himself denied making those threats. At a minimum, the acknowledged statements established probable cause of aggravated menacing, particularly in the environment of that sobering week.

III. For the foregoing reasons, the district court's decision is affirmed.

The judge can consider other factors in deciding whether to continue detention after an initial determination of probable cause. While the factors vary among jurisdictions, generally courts will detain juveniles where:

- The court determines that detention care is necessary to protect the child from doing physical, emotional, or psychological harm to himself;

- The court determines that the child is an immediate danger to the community;
- There is a significant danger that the child will fail to appear for the subsequent juvenile proceedings;
- The child has no parent, guardian, or responsible adult to care for him.

Juvenile court judges should not detain a child based solely on the seriousness of the delinquent act, although where a child has committed a particularly heinous or grievous offense the judge will be likely to decide in favor of commitment based on the child's potential danger to the community or himself.

PROCEDURAL SAFEGUARDS

Juvenile detention proceedings are subject to some procedural safeguards even if they are less formal than adult proceedings. The court must notify the juvenile's parent or guardian of the detention as soon as is practicable. The detaining authority must allow the parent or guardians to see and confer with the child.

The court must allow the parent or guardians to engage counsel on behalf of the child. If the family is indigent and cannot afford an attorney, the court must appoint an attorney at its expense. This attorney will be a local public defender or a private attorney who is qualified and authorized to take cases on the state's behalf.

SIDEBAR

PRIVATE PUBLIC DEFENDERS

All jurisdictions have a bank of private attorneys whom the state can appoint to represent indigent juveniles. In some cases, private attorneys help lessen the public defender's caseload. The state must engage private attorneys to avoid a conflict of interest where there are two or more defendants in a case. Since all of the attorneys in the public defender's office are part of the same office a conflict of interest would result if one co-defendant turned against the other, as often happens.

The court must give the juvenile full notice of the charges against him and inform him of his constitutional rights. His parent or guardian may accompany him to all hearings, as may counsel. The juvenile may call witnesses and offer evidence in his defense.

If the court finds probable cause, it will assess whether there are other factors favoring detention. If so, the court will commit the juvenile to a detention facility.

Separation of Juveniles and Adults

Federal guidelines mandate total separation between adults and juveniles. Juveniles may not be kept in a prison or jail with adult inmates except when it cannot be avoided. In such cases, the jailer must take particular care to keep the child separate from adults and must get the child out of the adult facility as soon as practicable. States that do not comply with these guidelines risk losing federal juvenile justice funds.

The Office of Juvenile Justice and Delinquency Prevention (OJJDP), the juvenile justice arm of the United States Department of Justice, defines separation as the total segregation of youth and adult facilities. Shared facilities must be designed in such as way as to prevent all contact, intentional or otherwise, between adult and juvenile populations or staff. Adult and juvenile populations must not share treatment facilities or staff.

At any given time, the juvenile detention facility will house:

- Youths who are awaiting a detention hearing after an arrest
- Youths whose parent or guardian is not available
- Youths who are awaiting disposition after an adjudication of delinquency
- Youths are awaiting transport to a long-term detention facility after sentencing

DUE PROCESS CONSIDERATIONS

There are two due process clauses in the Constitution. The Fifth Amendment Due Process clause applies to the federal government and provides, in part, "No person shall be . . . deprived of life, liberty, or property, without due process of law." The Fourteenth Amendment says, in part, "No State shall . . . deprive any person of life, liberty, or property, without due process of law." The Fourteenth Amendment makes the Fifth Amendment's provisions applicable to the states.

There are two different types of due process. **Procedural due process** dictates what processes the courts and the state must follow in order to preserve the constitutional rights of detainees and defendants. **Substantive due process** describes the content of the constitutional rights that procedural due process protects. We consider procedural due process in this chapter.

procedural due process
The processes the courts and the state must follow in order to preserve the constitutional rights of detainees and defendants

substantive due process
The content of the constitutional rights that due process protects

Procedural Due Process

The constitutional guarantee of procedural due process mandates that criminal and juvenile defendants possess:

- The right to notice of the charges against them
- The right to a fair trial
- Immunity from compulsion to testify against themselves in criminal trials or delinquency hearings
- The right to call witnesses to a testify on their behalf at trial
- The right to confront their accusers
- The right to cross-examine adverse witnesses at trial
- Immunity from **double jeopardy,** or having to stand trial for the same act more than one time

In practice, these rights govern the way in which the state may or may not proceed against a juvenile defendant in court.

double jeopardy

Having to stand trial in the same forum more than once for the same act

AMENDMENT V

No person shall be held to answer for a capital, or otherwise infamous crime, unless on a presentment or indictment of a grand jury, except in cases arising in the land or naval forces, or in the militia, when in actual service in time of war or public danger; nor shall any person be subject for the same offense to be twice put in jeopardy of life or limb; nor shall be compelled in any criminal case to be a witness against himself, nor be deprived of life, liberty, or property, without due process of law; nor shall private property be taken for public use, without just compensation.

The Supreme Court has held that preventive detention prior to adjudication is not a violation of due process. Such preventive detention serves the legitimate state objective of protecting both the juvenile and society from the hazards of pretrial crime. That objective is compatible with the "fundamental fairness" demanded by the due process clause in juvenile proceedings. The court has held that pretrial detention is not punishment and therefore does not violate juveniles' constitutional rights. The court will allow pretrial detention of juveniles if procedural safeguards are in place to protect against erroneous or unnecessary detentions. The court considers the procedural requirements outlined above sufficient safeguards.

OJJDP STATISTICS REGARDING DETENTION

Exhibit 5-1 illustrates that the number of delinquency cases involving detention increased 11 percent between 1990 and 1999, the most recent date for which reliable statistics are available.

Exhibit 5-2 shows that increases in the number of cases involving detention occurred in three of the four offense categories, with drug offense cases showing the sharpest increase between 1990 and 1999, the most recent date for which reliable statistics are available.

EXHIBIT 5-1 Detained Delinquency Cases, 1990–1999

Year	Number of Juvenile Detentions
1990	302,800
1991	292,800
1992	297,600
1993	289,800
1994	316,100
1995	295,400
1996	302,400
1997	323,900
1998	331,200
1999	336,200

EXHIBIT 5-2 Detained Delinquency Cases by Offense, 1990–1999

Cases	Person	Property	Drugs	Public Order
1990	67,800	146,900	26,800	61,200
1991	70,000	145,300	24,100	53,300
1992	73,300	143,500	24,900	55,400
1993	75,800	129,100	25,700	59,100
1994	84,100	133,200	32,400	66,400
1995	83,800	116,200	34,400	60,900
1996	88,000	112,500	36,300	56,500
1997	91,000	118,100	38,600	76,200
1998	89,300	119,000	44,300	78,600
1999	89,500	115,200	43,500	88,100

CASE PROBLEM

Police took custody of Martin on December 13 and charged him with first-degree robbery, second-degree assault, and criminal possession of a weapon based on an incident in which he allegedly hit a youth on the head with a loaded gun and stole his jacket and sneakers. The incident occurred at 11:30 p.m. and Martin lied to the police about where and with whom he lived. He was consequently detained overnight.

The state filed a petition of delinquency and Martin made his initial appearance in Family Court on December 14. His grandmother accompanied him. The Family Court Judge, citing the possession of the loaded weapon, the false address given to the police, and the lateness of the hour as evidencing a lack of supervision, ordered Martin detained. The court held a probable cause hearing five days later and found probable cause for all the delinquent acts charged. At the fact finding hearing, held December 27–29, the court found Martin committed the acts of robbery and criminal possession. The court adjudged him a delinquent and placed him on two years' probation. He had been in detention for a total of 15 days.

The court detained Martin under a New York statute that authorized pretrial detention of an accused juvenile delinquent based on a finding that there is a "serious risk" that the juvenile "may before the return date commit an act which if committed by an adult would constitute a crime." Martin brought a **habeas corpus** action in Federal District Court seeking a **declaratory judgment** that the statute violated the due process clause of the Fourteenth Amendment. Habeas corpus, literally, "you have the body," is a legal tool that people can use to contest their imprisonment on the ground that it violates the Constitution or other law. A declaratory judgment is a statement from the court concerning the rights or status of a party or parties.

The District Court agreed with Martin and struck down the statute as permitting detention without due process and ordered his release. The Court of Appeals affirmed, holding that since the vast majority of juveniles detained under the statute either have their cases dismissed before an adjudication of delinquency or are released after adjudication, the statute is administered not for preventive purposes but to impose punishment for unadjudicated criminal acts, and that therefore the statute is unconstitutional as to all juveniles.

What is the result in the United States Supreme Court?

ROLE-PLAY PROBLEM

Thirteen-year-old Jackie was inside a crack house at 11:00 p.m. when police knocked on the door and entered. Police found rocks of crack on the tabletops and observed people smoking crack. They arrested the adults and took the juveniles, including Jackie, into custody.

habeas corpus
Literally, "you have the body." The name given to a class of writs whose primary objective is the release of the petitioner from confinement

declaratory judgment
A binding adjudication of the rights and status of litigants. The court grants no consequential relief other than a declaration of the petitioner's rights

Jackie did not have any drugs, money, or criminal property in her possession. She did not resist arrest or cause trouble. She appeared to be under the influence of drugs and was dirty, underweight, and inappropriately dressed for the weather, wearing only a tank top, jeans, and sandals on a cold November night.

The police brought Jackie and the others to the police station, where Jackie gave the officer on duty her mother's cell phone number. The police called Jackie's mother, Diane, at12:30 a.m. Diane sounded drunk or high, because she was slurring her words, and it took the officer several tries before he was able to make her understand what was happening. Diane agreed to come to the station immediately. Two hours later Diane had not arrived. Police called her again. She seemed not to remember having received the first call, but said she would go to the police station immediately. By 4:00 a.m. Diane had not arrived.

The police decided to take Jackie to the juvenile detention facility and commit her for the night. The police later decided not to bring any delinquency charges against Jackie.

The next morning at 9:00, the prosecutor charged Jackie with curfew violation and drug abuse. Detention center personnel called Diane at 10:00 a.m. Again, she sounded impaired and acted as though she was hearing about Jackie's detention for the first time. She said she would come to the station immediately.

At 7:30 p.m. Diane showed up, demanding that the detention center release Jackie to her. Detention center personnel refused. They told her that the detention hearing would be at 8:30 a.m. the following day, and they gave her the information she needed to attend the hearing.

Diane did not show up at the detention hearing. The judge appointed an attorney and a guardian ad litem for Jackie and continued the detention hearing until 8:30 a.m. the next day. The attorney contacted Diane who said she would be at the hearing. The attorney gave Diane all the information about the hearing—the time of the hearing, the location of the courthouse, directions to the courthouse, directions to the courtroom, his office phone number, cell phone number, e-mail address, and the phone number of the courthouse.

The next morning Diane failed to show up for the hearing. The judge agreed to wait until 1:30 p.m. The attorney called Diane several times. Diane showed up at 2:30, offering contradictory explanations for her late arrival.

You are the judge:

1. What factors do you consider important? Weigh and analyze these factors.

2. What do you ultimately decide to do with Jackie—do you release her to her mother?

3. Do you commit Jackie to detention care?

4. Do you take some other action?

5. What additional facts do you want?

You are Jackie's attorney:

6. How do you advocate for Jackie's release in the face of Diane's actions?

7. How do you advocate in the face of Jackie's actions?

You are the guardian ad litem:

8. How will you investigate this case on behalf of your ward?

9. Whom will you interview?

10. What documents will you ask to see?

11. How will you formulate your opinion?

12. What would you recommend based upon what you know right now?

guardian ad litem

Latin for "guardian for the case." A person, often a lawyer, appointed by the court to advocate for the best interest of the child

HYPOTHETICAL PROBLEM

Police took Barry into custody on suspicion of burglary at midnight on a Saturday. They brought him directly to the youth detention facility, and the intake worker decided to hold him. The detention center held Barry for more than two weeks while they tried unsuccessfully to locate a responsible adult. Detention personnel located a distant relative on the 17th day. The young man, a second cousin, went to the detention center and took custody of Barry.

The cousin accompanied Barry to his hearing. After a full hearing on the issues, the judge found that Barry had committed the burglary. She adjudged Barry delinquent and ordered him detained until disposition. The court held the disposition hearing 22 days later. The state presented evidence that during his preadjudication and predisposition detentions Barry was highly disruptive and violent in the detention facility. Based upon this, the judge committed Barry to the Department of Youth Services detention facility for a period of two years.

1. Is it legitimate for the judge to base a commitment decision upon a juvenile's behavior in a detention facility while the juvenile is awaiting hearing?

2. Would it make a difference if the only reason the court was detaining the juvenile was that it could not locate a responsible adult to take custody of him?

3. Are there procedures or safeguards that the court can put into place to ensure that juveniles are detained for legitimate reasons and reasonable amounts of time?

ETHICAL CONCERNS

Juvenile court judges sometimes confront situations where the juveniles before them have not committed serious crimes, nor are they particularly dangerous to themselves or to society, but they have no one to care for them and no safe place to go. Then these judges must decide whether to release the juveniles, as they should based upon the facts, or detain them for their own safety and well-being.

States do not intend for their detention facilities to double as foster homes, but they often do. For some children, the juvenile detention facility is the safest, cleanest, most structured environment they have ever known. For these juveniles, the detention facility is less a punishment than a salvation.

DISCUSSION QUESTIONS

Some juvenile advocates and scholars are urging the legal community to regulate detention hearings more closely. They assert that the detention experience is so traumatic for a child that there should be clear parameters to which the courts must strictly adhere before subjecting a child to it.

1. Do you believe the state should regulate detention hearings more closely? Or should the state allow the juvenile court judges ample leeway to tailor the proceedings to the needs of each individual child?

2. If you were a state legislator and you were called upon to write the rules for juvenile detention hearings, what would you write?

3. What might account for the rise in juvenile detentions over the period from 1990 to 1999?

4. Is it ever acceptable for a juvenile court judge to commit a child to a detention facility simply because there is no other acceptable place to put that child?

5. In the Williams case, what factors did the court consider particularly important in deciding whether probable cause to detain the juveniles existed?

6. How did the surrounding facts and circumstances affect the court's decision-making process?

7. How would you have weighed the girls' statements? Was their demeanor important?

KEY TERMS

attorney general	petition
declaratory judgment	probable cause
double jeopardy	procedural due process
guardian ad litem	substantive due process
habeas corpus	warrant
intake worker	

Chapter 6

DELINQUENCY HEARINGS

OBJECTIVES

By the end of this chapter, the student should know:

- The steps of a delinquency proceeding, beginning with arraignment and ending with disposition
- How the courts conduct arraignments
- How to prepare for an arraignment
- The bail system
- The role of the guardian ad litem
- How courts decide whether to release or detain juveniles prior to hearing
- The plea-bargaining process
- The parameters of the adjudicatory and dispositional phases of a hearing
- The dispositional options available to juvenile court judges
- How to prepare for the dispositional phase of a juvenile proceeding

INTRODUCTION

Judges must consider the best interests of the children in juvenile proceedings. Unique to delinquency hearings is that judges may weigh the best interests of the children before them against the interests and safety of the community.

The majority of delinquency cases settle through the **pretrial** process, just as they do in criminal court. The plea bargain, which is explained in detail below, can take place any time from arraignment to pretrial to adjudication. The disposition generally takes place at a different time from the adjudication. This can be anywhere from 24 hours to several days after the adjudication.

pretrial
An informal meeting among the parties to a case that occurs before the scheduled trial date

arraignment
A proceeding at which the accused criminal or delinquent offender enters a plea of guilty or not guilty to charges against him, and at which the magistrate sets bail for the defendant

magistrate
A judicial officer who can perform many of the functions that a judge performs, but who has less authority than a judge has. The magistrate makes recommendations that do not become binding upon the parties until the judge signs them.

master
A judicial officer whom the court appoints to assist in performing judicial duties in a specific case. Like a magistrate, the master can perform judicial functions but the master's recommendations are not binding upon the parties until a judge signs them.

bail
The release pending hearing of a juvenile defendant in exchange for the payment of a sum of money

bond
The sum of money that secures the release of the juvenile

bail bondsman
A person who is in the business of posting bond for a juvenile defendant in exchange for a fee

ARRAIGNMENT

The **arraignment** is the first step in the juvenile delinquency proceeding. In keeping with the less formal tone of juvenile proceedings, **magistrates** often conduct arraignments, often in chambers rather than in courtrooms. Magistrates are judicial officers who can perform many of the functions that judges perform, but who have less authority than judges or **masters,** who are judicial officers the court appoints to assist in performing judicial duties in specific cases.

The purpose of the arraignment is to give juveniles an opportunity to admit or deny the allegations against them. The court will either release juveniles to their parent or guardian or detain them following the arraignment. If the court releases the juvenile, it can do so on the strength of a written pledge to return or, if the state allows it, the court can set bail.

SIDEBAR

BAIL

Bail is the release of a juvenile or criminal defendant pending hearing or trial. Courts allow defendants to secure their release through payment of a **bond,** which is a sum of money that the defendant pays to the court directly or through a bail bondsman. A **bail bondsman** is a person who is in the business of posting defendants' bail for them.

Defendants pay the bondsmen a percentage of the bond and the bondsmen pay the rest. If the defendants fail to appear, they forfeit the bond. Bail is intended to secure the defendant's appearance at trial and is not intended to be punitive in nature. Therefore, courts set the amount of bail based upon how great a flight risk the offender presents, not upon the seriousness of the charges.

The juvenile defendant, the judge, master, or magistrate conducting the arraignment, the juvenile's attorney if there is one, the juvenile's parent or **guardian ad litem,** and the prosecutor will be at the arraignment.

SIDEBAR

THE GUARDIAN AD LITEM

A guardian ad litem, or GAL, is a person whom the court appoints to advocate for the best interests of the child in a proceeding. Guardians ad litem appear

(continues)

in delinquency proceedings, abuse-neglect-dependency proceedings (See Section III, Abuse-Neglect-Dependency), judicial bypass proceedings (See Chapter 12, Parental Notification of Abortion and Judicial Bypass), and **parentage proceedings,** which are proceedings involving such issues as paternity, custody, child support, and visitation that take place in juvenile court or domestic relations court.

They conduct independent investigations of the facts, history, and law surrounding a their cases, formulate opinions as to the best interests of the children they represent based upon that investigation, and make recommendations to the court. GALs are independent of all the parties involved in a case and of the court; therefore courts afford great weight to their recommendations.

Some jurisdictions require that GALs be attorneys, while other jurisdictions do not. In either event, GALs must undergo extensive training before they are qualified to work as GALs and must participate in regular continuing education throughout the course of their careers.

It is important to distinguish between advocating for what a child wants, which is the attorney's job, and advocating for what is in the best interests of the child, which is the GAL's job. What children want is often very different from what is in their best interests, as when teenagers want to live with the parent who supervises them the least and provides the least discipline. Often children beg to remain with parents who have abused them.

If the delinquency charges involve acts that took place at a school, such as a fight, or if the charges involve acts that directly impacted the school, such as vandalism or theft, then a school board representative will attend the proceedings.

PRETRIAL RELEASE OR DETENTION

The court bases its decision whether to release or detain the juvenile upon the risk of harm releasing the juvenile will pose to the juvenile and to the community. A number of factors inform this decision-making process. It will be your role as paralegal to amass the evidence so that your attorney can use it to achieve your client's goal. If you are working for the defense, your client is the juvenile. If you are working for the prosecution, your client is the state.

The defense will portray the juvenile in a flattering light in terms of the juvenile's personal life, school life, family life, and community involvement and seek to minimize the negative aspects of the home, school, and family. The judge will look to quality of the juvenile's home life to determine whether the child has enough of a support system, or safety net, in place to prevent the juvenile from reoffending while awaiting adjudication. The defense will also seek to minimize any aggravating factors related to the event.

guardian ad litem

Latin for "guardian for the case." A person, often a lawyer, appointed by the court to advocate for the best interest of the child. In delinquency cases where there is no parent or legal guardian present the court will appoint a guardian ad litem for the duration of the proceedings. Guardians ad litem also serve in abuse-neglect-dependency cases.

parentage proceedings

Proceedings involving such issues as paternity, custody, child support, and visitation that take place in juvenile court or domestic relations court

The prosecution will do the opposite, focusing on the damage the juvenile has inflicted and the potential for more damage if the court releases the juvenile. The prosecution will emphasize the harm that the juvenile inflicted and the victim's suffering. The prosecution might also attempt to persuade the judge that pre-adjudicatory detention is in the juvenile's best interest because the juvenile's home life is chaotic or otherwise potentially harmful to the child.

PLEA BARGAINING

There will be at least one pretrial before the adjudication. The pretrial is an opportunity for the defense attorney and the prosecutor to meet, share information, and handle such matters as scheduling and discovery. It also provides an opportunity to plea-bargain.

In a plea-bargain, the prosecutor agrees to reduce or eliminate some of the charges against the defendant in return for the defendant's agreement to admit to the remaining charges. This occurs in virtually all criminal and delinquency cases; exceptions are rare.

The courts actively encourage the parties to plea-bargain. Plea-bargaining benefits the courts by moving cases through the system quickly. It benefits the prosecutor, who obtains a certain adjudication of delinquency. It benefits the defendant, who can anticipate a certain outcome and perhaps some leniency from the judge.

Many judges view a voluntary admission of guilt to be the first step on the road to rehabilitation and will take that progress into account during disposition. Judges often ask prosecutors for recommendations as to disposition. Defendants can extract promises from sprosecutor to make favorable recommendations in exchange for pleas.

If the prosecutor and the defendant reach a plea agreement, they notify the judge who will take the defendant's plea at that time. The judge takes the plea in open court on the record. A court reporter, the bailiff, and the judge's clerk will be present. The clerk will tape the proceedings if there is no court reporter.

The prosecutor addresses the court and says the parties have reached an agreement. The prosecutor makes a motion to amend the charges against the defendant in order to reduce some of the charges and **nolle** others. To nolle a charge is to decline to prosecute it, or to drop it.

The judge will grant or deny the motion after determining that the defendant does not object to the motion and that the defendant is knowingly, intelligently, and voluntarily admitting to the charges. To make this determination, the judge addresses the defendant personally to ensure that the defendant is capable of understanding the proceedings. The judge will ask whether the defendant speaks and understands English, is under the influence of drugs or alcohol, and how much education the defendant has had.

nolle

The shortened version of the phrase *nolle prosequi,* Latin for "I will no further prosecute." It means that the prosecutor will drop the charges against the defendant.

The judge then outlines the defendant's constitutional rights—the right to a trial, the right to bring witnesses to that trial and present evidence, the right to question the state's witnesses, and the privilege against compelled testimony. The judge will ascertain that nobody has coerced the defendant into admitting to the complaint and that nobody has promised the defendant anything in exchange for a plea.

The judge will allow the defense attorney to speak after the defendant answers the questions to the judge's satisfaction. The attorney will affirm that in his professional opinion the defendant is giving the plea knowingly, intelligently, and voluntarily. The judge will accept the defendant's plea if he determines it is appropriate, and will adjudge the defendant delinquent.

In re Phibbs
Slip copy, 2005 WL 2206746
Ohio App. 7 Dist., 2005

Appellant, Walter Phibbs, appeals from a decision adjudicating him a delinquent child for trafficking in drugs, corrupting another with drugs, theft, and involuntary manslaughter.

Appellant took two Kadian pills from his mother. Kadian is a morphine drug. He sold one pill to Paul Graham, Jr., for three dollars and gave him the other pill. The next day, Graham was discovered dead at home. An autopsy revealed the presence of morphine, cocaine, amphetamines, and marijuana in the decedent's body. The coroner concluded that the cause of death was arrhythmia due to combined drug toxicity.

A complaint alleged that appellant, who was 16 at the time, was a delinquent child based on one count of trafficking in drugs; one count of corrupting another with drugs; one count of theft; and one count of involuntary manslaughter.

Appellant entered into stipulations that illegally obtained morphine tablets from his mother and that he furnished them to Graham. The court subsequently held a hearing and determined that probable cause existed to believe that appellant committed an act that would be involuntary manslaughter if committed by an adult.

The trial court found that appellant committed the offenses as charged and adjudicating him a delinquent child. It subsequently committed him to the Ohio Department of Youth Services. Appellant filed a timely notice of appeal.

Appellant assignment of error states:

THE TRIAL COURT VIOLATED WALTER PHIBBS' RIGHT TO DUE PROCESS WHEN IT ADJUDICATED HIM DELINQUENT WITHOUT CONDUCTING AN ON-THE-RECORD COLLOQUY ACCORDING TO JUV.R. 29. FIFTH AND FOURTEENTH AMENDMENTS TO THE UNITED STATES CONSTITUTION, ARTICLE I, SECTION 16 OF THE OHIO CONSTITUTION, AND JUVENILE RULE 29.

Appellant argues that the trial court accepted his admission without affording him his due process rights. He contends that the court failed to comply with Juv. R. 29(D) because it did not address him personally to determine whether he made his admission voluntarily with an understanding of the allegations against him and the consequences of an admission.

(continues)

In re Phibbs (Continued)

Appellant asserts that the court failed to address him personally at all during the hearing.

In pertinent part, Juv. R. 29 (D) provides:

"The court may refuse to accept an admission and *shall not* accept an admission without addressing the party personally and determining both of the following:

"(1) The party is making the admission voluntarily with understanding of the nature of the allegations and the consequences of the admission;

"(2) The party understands that by entering an admission the party is waiving the right to challenge the witnesses and evidence against the party, to remain silent, and to introduce evidence at the adjudicatory hearing." (Emphasis added.) In examining the juvenile court's compliance with Juv. R. 29, this court has stated:

"Juv. R. 29(D) imposes a positive obligation upon the trial court to make certain determinations before accepting an admission from a party. The court cannot accept an admission without first addressing the juvenile personally and determining that he or she is making the admission voluntarily, with an understanding of the nature of the allegations and the consequences of entering the admission. Furthermore, the court must determine that the juvenile understands that by entering an admission he or she is waiving the right to challenge the witnesses and evidence against him or her, as well as the right to remain silent and to introduce evidence at the adjudicatory hearing. The juvenile court's failure to substantially comply with the requirements of Juv. R. 29 constitutes prejudicial error that requires reversal of the adjudication in order to permit the party to plead anew.

At appellant's probable cause hearing, his attorney informed the court that appellant was stipulating to the charges of trafficking in drugs, corrupting another with drugs, and theft. After an off-the-record conference with counsel, the court stated: "[T]his hearing will deal with evidence being presented on the involuntary manslaughter offense, . . . Trafficking in drugs and corrupting another with drug charges have been stipulated to." Subsequently, appellant and the prosecuting attorney filed joint stipulations. The stipulations included admissions that appellant illegally obtained morphine tablets from his mother and that he furnished the morphine to Graham.

The trial court failed to comply with any of Juv.R. 29(D)'s requirements. There is no indication on the record that the court ever personally addressed appellant regarding his admission. It never inquired of appellant to determine whether he understood the nature of the allegations against him or the consequences of his admission. Furthermore, the court never determined whether appellant was aware that by admitting his actions, he waived the right to challenge witnesses and evidence against him, the right to remain silent, and the right to introduce evidence at an adjudicatory hearing. Thus, appellant's assignment of error has merit.

Judgment reversed.

ADJUDICATORY PHASE

motion

A application by a party to the court asking the court to do something

Defense attorneys file a number of **motions,** or requests for action by the court, before the hearing. The most common is the **motion to suppress,** which asks the court to disallow the admission of certain evidence because it is tainted. The basis for the taint will be that the police obtained the evidence in a manner that was contrary to the law or the dictates of the Constitution. A confession that the police obtained through coercion or physical evidence that the police obtained through an illegal search are examples of tainted evidence.

Exhibit 6-1 is a sample motion to suppress:

EXHIBIT 6-1

IN THE COURT OF COMMON PLEAS
JUVENILE DIVISION
CUYAHOGA COUNTY, OHIO

IN THE MATTER OF	)	CASE NUMBER 05 JV 521205
J.R.	)	
	)	JUDGE MORGAN HOPE
	)	
	)	MOTION TO SUPPRESS

Now comes the defendant, J.R., by and through her undersigned attorney, and pursuant to Amendments IV, V, and IV of the United States Constitution, and Section III, Art. 6, of the Ohio Constitution, does hereby move this Honorable Court for an Order suppressing the statements she made while in the custody of the City of Cleveland Police Department.

The grounds for this Motion to Suppress are contained in the Brief in Support attached hereto and incorporated by reference herein.

Respectfully submitted,
Anne Helen, Esquire
Helen Naomi & Midori LLP
Attorney for the Minor Defendant
1492 Gabriella Drive, Suite 1
Cleveland, Ohio 44114

The case proceeds to the adjudicatory phase if the parties do not successfully plea-bargain. This is the equivalent of a criminal trial. Just as in a criminal trial, in a juvenile adjudication there are two sides—the prosecution and the defense.

Juvenile hearings are less structured and formal than criminal proceedings. The judge may ask questions of the participants and the participants may sometimes address each other. The rules of evidence and procedure are relaxed and there is no jury.

The order of hearing is the same in a juvenile hearing as in a criminal trial. The state always goes first because it bears the **burden of persuasion.** The party with the burden of persuasion must convince the court of of something. The party who does not have the burden of persuasion does not need to do anything except refute what the other party has attempted to prove.

motion to suppress

An application to the court asking the court to disallow the admission of certain evidence into the record or at a hearing in the case

burden of persuasion

The obligation to convince the court of the truth of the matter at hand

opening statement
A nonargumentative narrative of the chronology of the case, including which witnesses will appear and an outline of the testimony they will offer

element
One of the constituent parts of a crime. For example, the constituent parts of the crime of robbery would be (1) the taking (2) by force (3) of the property of another (4) from the person of the victim. If any of these is missing, a robbery has not occurred, although another crime may have occurred

chain of custody
A detailed and accurate accounting of where the evidence has been and what precautions the parties holding the evidence have taken to prevent tampering, alteration, loss, or removal of the evidence, from the moment of its discovery until the moment of its introduction in court

closing argument
Remarks that the parties present to the court at the end of the trial in which they seek to tie together and persuasively present all of the evidence that the parties have presented at trial

findings of fact and conclusions of law
The findings of fact are those things that the court adjudges the parties to have proven. The conclusions of law are the legal conclusions that the court has drawn from applying the statutes and case law to the facts at hand.

The hearing begins with **opening statements.** An opening statement is a non-argumentative chronology of the case including which witnesses will appear and what testimony they will offer.

The state presents its case through testimony and physical evidence. The state must prove every **element** of the criminal act beyond a reasonable doubt, just as in a criminal trial. The elements of the criminal act are the constituent parts that comprise the crime.

The parties must provide a **chain of custody** for every piece of physical evidence they wish to admit into the record. The chain of custody a detailed and accurate accounting of where the evidence has been and what precautions the parties holding the evidence have taken to prevent tampering, alteration, loss, or removal of the evidence, from the moment of its discovery until the moment of its introduction in court. This ensures that the evidence is dependable and authentic.

At the end of the evidence each party gives a **closing argument.** The closing argument is where the parties have an opportunity to recall the evidence they presented at trial, weave that evidence in with their legal theories, and attempt to persuade the finder of fact that they have proven their case. After this, the judge retires to consider the evidence. The judge may rule immediately or may take the matter under advisement and issue a ruling later. The judge is required to accompany the ruling with **findings of fact and conclusions of law** in some actions. The findings of fact are those things that the court adjudges the parties to have proven. The conclusions of law are the legal inferences that the court has drawn from applying the statutes and case law to the facts at hand. Judges often ask the parties to submit proposed findings of fact and conclusions of law.

SIDEBAR

HEARING ORDER

State's Opening Statement
Defendant's Opening Statement
State's Witnesses
    Direct examination **(state)**
    Cross-examination **(defense)**
    Re-direct examination **(state)**
        Limited to matters brought up during cross-examination
    Re-cross-examination **(defense)**
        Limited to matters brought up during re-direct examination

(continues)

The state uses witnesses to lay foundations for, and introduce, physical evidence and moves the court to admit the evidence into the record. The other party may object to the admission. If so, the judge will rule to admit or exclude the evidence based upon the Rules of Evidence.

State rests its case

Defendant moves to dismiss on the grounds that the **State** has not met its burden of persuasion. If the court grants the motion to dismiss the judge dismisses the case and it is done. If the court denies the motion, the case proceeds with the **defendant** presenting his refutation of the State's case. The motion to dismiss is an oral motion.

Defendant's Witnesses

    Direct examination **(defense)**

    Cross-examination **(state)**

    Re-direct examination **(defense)**

        Limited to matters brought up during cross-examination

    Re-cross-examination **(state)**

        Limited to matters brought up during re-direct examination

The defendant uses witnesses to lay foundations for, and introduce, physical evidence and moves the court to admit the evidence into the record. The other party may object to the admission. If so, the judge will rule to admit or exclude the evidence based upon the Rules of Evidence.

    Closing argument **(state)**

    Closing argument **(defense)**

    Rebuttal **(state)**

DISPOSITION

If the court adjudges the defendant delinquent, the case will proceed to disposition. The possible dispositions are dismissal, heard and submitted, basic probation, intensive probation, restitution, community service, house arrest, electronic monitoring, suspension of driving privileges, curfew, school and work requirements, drug assessment, drug monitoring, drug treatment, and commitment.

Dismissal

The judge can dismiss a complaint against a juvenile defendant even where the state has proven the charges if the judge determines that a dismissal is in the best interest of the child and the community.

Heard and Submitted

The judge can mark the case "heard and submitted," which means the state has proven the case against the defendant. Now the judge will put the case on hold for a period of time, usually one year, and if the defendant does not re-offend within that time, the judge will dismiss the case. Judges only use this device where it is the juvenile's first offense and it is a nonviolent offense.

Basic Probation and Intensive Probation

The judge imposes a period of commitment and then suspends execution of that commitment while imposing requirements upon the juvenile. These requirements range from occasional reporting to a probation officer to frequent, regular reporting, along with drug monitoring or other requirements. Curfew, school, and work requirements are often part of the probation order.

Restitution

The judge orders the juvenile to pay the victim for any financial damage the juvenile inflicted.

Community Service

The court orders the juvenile to perform a number of hours of community service. Often the judge will specify the organization or type of organization where the juvenile must perform the service.

Drug Assessment, Monitoring, and Treatment

The court orders the juvenile to submit to a drug abuse assessment. If the assessment indicates a drug abuse problem the court can order a combination of monitoring and treatment services to help the juvenile recover from the drug abuse problem and to monitor whether the juvenile remains drug free.

Commitment

The court orders the juvenile to serve a sentence in a commitment facilities, which can range from minimum security treatment facilities to high-security punitive institutions.

The defense will try to minimize the juvenile's sentence by convincing the judge that the child has a support system at home, at school, or through a religious institution, and by minimizing the grievousness of the acts that made up the charges against the defendant.

The state may have no objection to the court releasing the juvenile. But if the state wants the court to detain the juvenile, the prosecuting attorney will have to convince the judge that the defendant is a flight risk with insufficient support, little or no ties to the community, and little to lose by fleeing or failing to appear in court and that the juvenile is a danger to himself and/or the community, and that harm to the juvenile or others is likely to result if he is released to the community.

SIDEBAR

DEATH PENALTY FOR JUVENILES

The United States Supreme Court ruled in March 2005 that the death penalty as applied to juveniles was unconstitutional. Justice Anthony Kennedy wrote the opinion for the 5–4 majority of the justices. The two bases for the decision were those cited in Atkins and the Stanford dissent: "'the evolving standards of decency that mark the progress of a maturing society' to determine which punishments are so disproportionate as to be 'cruel and unusual'" led to the conclusion that the death penalty imposed against people who offended as juveniles is disproportionate, and empirical evidence that juveniles lack the mental ability to give proper thought to their actions, resulting in impulsive and often destructive behavior.

The first execution of a juvenile in America took place in 1642 in Plymouth Colony, Massachusetts, when 16-year-old Thomas Graunger was executed for the crime of bestiality. The youngest child executed in America was 10-year-old James Arcene who was killed in Arkansas in 1885. Hannah Ocuish was 12 years old when she was hanged in Connecticut in 1786. Fourteen-year-old George Stinney was the youngest child to be killed after the World War era. The state of South Carolina executed him in 1944 after he confessed to murdering two young girls, ages 8 and 11.

The modern era of the American death penalty began in 1973. The Supreme Court ruled in Furman v. Georgia, 409 U.S. 902 (1972), that the death penalty statutes as they were then being applied were a violation of the Eighth Amendment's prohibition of cruel and unusual punishment. Following that decision, state legislatures enacted new death penalty statutes in accordance with Furman. These statutes attempted to eliminate the opportunity for caprice, passion, or prejudice in the imposition of the death penalty.

The Supreme Court reversed the death sentence of a 16-year-old boy in Eddings v. Oklahoma, 470 U.S. 1051(1985). The Court held that the lower court should have considered the defendant's young age and his state of mental and emotional development in reaching its decision, declaring that such factors should be **mitigating factors** of great weight. Mitigating factors are those facts and circumstances that do not excuse or justify an offense, but which a court or jury in fairness and mercy may consider as extenuating or reducing the degree of moral culpability.

(continues)

mitigating factors
Those facts and circumstances that do not excuse or justify an offense, but which a court or jury in fairness and mercy may consider as extenuating or reducing the degree of moral culpability

The court further observed that adolescents are less mature, responsible, and self-disciplined that adults and are less able than adults to consider the long-range implications of their actions.

The Eddings court never specifically addressed the issue of whether applying the death penalty to a 16-year-old violated the Eighth Amendment prohibition of cruel and unusual punishment. It did address the question whether the death penalty violated the eighth amendment when imposed upon a 15-year-old in 1988 in Thompson v. Oklahoma, 487 U.S. 815 (1988), holding that it constituted a violation of the Eighth Amendment, which states, "Excessive bail shall not be required, nor excessive fines imposed, nor cruel and unusual punishments inflicted."

The Supreme Court held in Atkins v. Virginia, 536 U.S. 304 (2002) that the death penalty was an unconstitutional imposition of cruel and unusual punishment when applied to mentally retarded defendants. The reasoning the court used in reaching that decision is closely analogous to the reasoning the court was urged to apply in assessing the constitutionality of applying the death penalty to juveniles.

Four months later, in October 2002, the Supreme Court declined to hear In re Stanford, 123 S. Ct. 715 (2002). That case that would have given the court the opportunity to debate the constitutionality of the death penalty as imposed upon 16- and 17-year-olds in light of the Atkins decision. In the widely read and frequently quoted dissent, Justices Stevens, Souter, Ginsberg, and Breyer expressed their dismay that the court declined to consider an appeal relating directly to the constitutionality of the execution of people for crimes they committed while juveniles, concluding, ". . . offenses committed by juveniles under the age of 18 do not merit the death penalty. The practice of executing such offenders is a relic of the past and is inconsistent with evolving standards of decency in a civilized society. We should put an end to this shameful practice."

In March 2005, the Court did.

PREPARING FOR THE DISPOSITION

The parties can present a wide variety of evidence at disposition. Any information that will help the court decide what is in the child's best interests is admissible. Whichever side you work for, look at all relevant evidence and focus on both the child and the event.

The Child

Begin preparing for disposition by focusing on the defendant. Explore all aspects of the juvenile's life outside of the criminal event. The goal for the defense is to humanize the defendant and make him appear as childlike as possible, while also demonstrating to the court that there is an ample family- and community-based safety net for the child.

The prosecution is going to focus more on the facts of the event, the extent of the violence, the extent of the damage the defendant caused, and the likelihood of the defendant re-offending.

School Performance

Obtain a signed release from the child's guardian authorizing the school and its employees to speak to you about the child. Remember that the state or county may be the child's guardian. Some schools and other institutions will accept only their own forms. Contact the institution and ask them whether they will accept your release or whether they require that you use their form. (See Exhibit 9-1, Release and Authorization form.)

You can speak to the child's teachers, principal, assistant principal, school counselor, social worker, nurse, coaches, and other school personnel And examine the child's grades, standardized test scores, attendance records, and disciplinary reports once you have secured a signed release.

The court will be interested to know whether the child is attending school regularly, what kind of grades the child is earning, and what kind of disciplinary record the child has.

Problems at school or the child having dropped out this will have a negative impact. If you are defending the juvenile the best strategy is to be proactive in formulating a plan for the child at school before you go to court. Talk to school personnel and establish what the child needs to do to get back into compliance with school regulations and involve the parents in helping the child to follow the plan.

If you are working for the prosecution, the defendant's poor school record will be a powerful piece of evidence. If possible, bring in the school employee who is most familiar with the defendant's disciplinary issues. This person's testimony will be quite persuasive.

A representative of the school board may be present at some or all of the proceedings if the child is having major problems at school such as chronic truancy or major disciplinary problems involving suspension or expulsion.

Employment

Speak to the juvenile's employer and ask the employer appear on behalf of the child if that is practicable.

Home Life

Identify the number of people living in the home and their relationships to the juvenile. Determine whether the people in the home can provide further support for the child or whether they are a distraction or even a danger.

The Event

The next area of focus is the event. The defense and prosecution will have divergent goals here. The defense will attempt to minimize the violence of the event, the damages that the defendant caused, and the likelihood of such an event recurring. The prosecution will ensure that the court does not overlook any particular of the event, including the harm to the victim, the danger to society, and the likelihood of recurrence.

The Description of the Event

attorney-client privilege
The legal doctrine that prevents lawyers from disclosing anything that their clients tell them about crimes they have committed

The juvenile defendant or the victim of a crime may not be a reliable source of information. Criminal defendants in general and juveniles in particular often entertain the notion that if they can fool their lawyer they can fool the court. Be sure the juvenile understands that as a paralegal you are bound by the **attorney-client privilege.** Attorney-client privilege is the legal doctrine that prevents lawyers from disclosing anything that their clients tell them about crimes they have committed. If the juvenile is still reluctant to speak ask, "What will the police tell me about what happened?" Often this will elicit a better response.

Victims can be hesitant to speak to attorneys or their staffs because they fear reprisal from the defendant or because they fear they will be prosecuted for their actions. If you need a witness's testimony and the witness will not cooperate with you, you can issue a **subpoena** and compel the witness to appear.

subpoena
A command to appear at a certain time and place and give certain testimony. The sheriff will execute a subpoena by force if necessary.

Obtain the names of all witness and co-defendants and get their contact information. Remember that before you can interview a person who is represented by an attorney you must get that attorney's permission. If you are interviewing someone who does not have an attorney but who may have an interest in the case you must make it clear that you are not disinterested.

SIDEBAR
THE THREE-PART INTERVIEW

When interviewing someone for the first time, whether it is your own client, a co-defendant, or a witness, use the three-part method.

Begin by simply asking what happened. Let the person speak without interruption. You can take notes but do not get too involved in the notes; mostly just listen carefully.

Sometimes people do not tell stories in a clear, coherent manner. Let the speaker ramble and get off track to some extent in this phase of the

(continues)

interview. If the story goes way off track, you can lead the speaker back to the story line, but for the most part, simply listen and try to imagine the scene as you do.

The first phase of the interview gives you a general overview of the facts and allows you to gauge what kind of a witness this speaker will be.

Prod the speaker to follow a narrative thread in the second part of the interview. A time line is usually the best means to accomplish this. At this point you should be firmly in control of the interview—there should be no more rambling. Ask, "What happened then?" "What happened next?" "Where were at this time?" "Who was there?" "Then what happened?" Frequently re-state what you think you heard. Ideally, you should record this session elec-tronically for later transcription. If that is not possible, take extensive notes.

The second phase allows you to get a good picture of the facts. You can go over the story repeatedly with the speaker until you are sure you have all of the facts and can spot gaps in the timeline or contradictions.

Ask specific, pointed questions designed to elicit defenses and theories in the third and final phase. Focus on whether there is enough evidence to support the allegations and whether there exist any plausible defenses.

The Description of the Child's Involvement in the Event

Distinguish between major and minor involvement in the act. Major involve-ment would be holding the gun in a robbery. Minor involvement would be standing in a crowd around a fight. Delinquency law generally holds that all par-ticipants in a delinquent act are equally culpable; nonetheless it is important to make the court aware of the extent of the juvenile's role.

Gun The judge will almost surely detain a juvenile who used or possessed a gun during the commission of the delinquent acts. Some states mandate detention in such cases.

Drugs Ascertain the level of the juvenile's drug involvement if the delinquent act was drug-related. A drug treatment center, psychologist, psychiatrist, or general physician can perform a drug assessment.

The prosecution will have to either obtain a court order for such an assess-ment or ask the defendant to submit voluntarily to it. The state cannot compel the juvenile to submit to drug assessment without an order.

The defense should work with the drug treatment facility to fashion a treat-ment plan if the assessment reveals a drug addiction. It is important to do this as quickly as possible, so that by the time the juvenile will have begun drug treat-ment at the time of the hearing.

Gang Involvement Many states have statutes providing for increased penalties if the defendant is a member of a gang, especially a known gang, or if the defendant committed the act pursuant to gang involvement or activity. (See Chapter 14, Youth Gangs.)

Violence Judges are more likely to order dispositions of commitment where delinquent acts involve extreme violence or result in severe injuries to victims.

The likelihood of commitment will increase if the victim was very young or very old, physically or mentally disabled, pregnant, or a family member.

Review the victim's medical records. There should be documentation available at the time of arraignment if the victim was treated at the scene or taken to a hospital from the scene. Read these records with the help of a medical professional if they are complex.

Property Damage View the property damage as soon as possible. Take photographs and draw diagrams of the property.

Value of Property When theft is involved, you must assess the exact value of the stolen property. The level of the charge in a theft action is based upon the value of the property taken. Obtain a complete description of the property, including brand name, make, model, age, and condition.

SIDEBAR
LIFE WITHOUT PAROLE FOR JUVENILES

People may no longer receive the death penalty for crimes they committed as juveniles. They may, however, receive sentences of life in prison without the possibility of release, or life without parole, for crimes they committed as young as 8 years old in Washington State, and 10 years old in Vermont. Only Indiana, Oregon, and the District of Columbia prohibit the sentence. All other states and the federal system allow it; some states mandate the sentence for certain crimes.

The United States has approximately 2,200 people serving sentences of life without parole for crimes they committed as juveniles. In the rest of the world there are a total of 12 other people serving such sentences: seven in Israel, four in South Africa, and one in Tanzania.

Arguments that a sentence of life without parole for juvenile offenses constitutes a violation of the Eighth Amendment's prohibition of cruel and un-usual punishment have failed. The United States Supreme Court has ruled

(continues)

that the punishment is acceptable if it is proportional, and identified three objective factors courts must consider when measuring proportionality:

- The gravity of the offense vis à vis the severity of the sentence;
- Intrajurisdictional comparisons: the sentences other offenders received for similar offenses in the same jurisdiction;
- Interjurisdictional comparisons: the sentences other offenders received for similar offenses in other jurisdictions.

Federal courts almost never overturn such sentences. State courts, with the exception of California, Kansas, Nevada, and Kentucky, rarely do. Most courts have held that the defendant's age at the time of the act has no bearing on the legitimacy of the sentence.

Arguments that people are considerably different as teenagers than they are as adults, and thus should be held to a different standard of accountability, have had success in the death penalty debate, but have had no success in the debate surrounding life without parole. Some courts hold that while the death penalty is a special kind of punishment that courts are correct in treating differently, a life sentence is merely and outlying point on the continuum of sentences. Other observers hold that people of any age who commit murder forfeit their rights to ever live in society again.

CASE PROBLEM

A juvenile defendant appeared in court and, pursuant to a plea agreement, entered an admission. At that hearing, the following exchange took place between the referee, the defendant, and his attorney:

"The Court: Mr. Hoffman, is that your understanding of the agreement?

"Mr. Hoffman: Yes, it is Your Honor.

"The Court: All right. May I address your client?

"Mr. Hoffman: Yes, you may.

"The Court: [Defendant], do you understand the agreement?

"[Defendant]: Yes.

"The Court: And do you understand that if you admit today to the charges, that you will not be having a trial?

"[Defendant]: Yes.

"The Court: Did anybody threaten you or promise you anything to get you to admit to these charges?

"[Defendant]: No."

The trial court accepted the defendant's admissions and adjudicated him delinquent.

Defendant appealed, arguing that he was entitled to a new hearing because the trial court neglected to advice him "that by entering the admission he was waiving his right to challenge witnesses and the evidence against him, to introduce evidence at the adjudicatory hearing, and to remain silent if he so chose."

Juv. R. 29(D) states, in pertinent part, that:

"(D) Initial Procedure Upon Entry of an Admission. The court may refuse to accept an admission and shall not accept an admission without addressing the party personally and determining that:

"(1) He is making the admission voluntarily with understanding of the nature of the allegations and the consequences of the admission: and

"(2) He understands that by entering his admission he is waiving his rights to challenge the witnesses and evidence against him, to remain silent and to introduce evidence at the adjudicatory hearing."

Does the appellate court affirm or reverse the trial court?

Held:

Judgment reversed and cause remanded.

The court stated:

"The applicable standard for the trial court's acceptance of an admission is substantial compliance with the provisions of Juv. R. 29(D), without which the adjudication must be reversed.

"This court finds that the referee who presided at the time appellant entered the admissions did not address appellant personally in a manner that could provide the basis for a determination that he was 'making the admission voluntarily with understanding of the nature of the allegations and the consequences of the admission' or that he understood that 'by entering his admission he is waiving his rights to challenge the witnesses and evidence against him, to remain silent and to introduce evidence at the adjudicatory hearing."

In re Christopher R., 101 Ohio App.3d 245, 655 N.E.2d 280 (1995)

ROLE-PLAY PROBLEM

The juvenile defendant is a 14-year-old girl named Hannah. She goes to school, but is frequently in trouble. Her offenses have ranged from being tardy to fighting on campus. Most of Hannah's teachers are quite fond of her, even though she misbehaves. They say she is charming, intelligent, and sweet.

She gets very bad grades—mostly Ds and a few Fs. She earned her lone A in music: her music teacher says she sings like an angel. Hannah is in the school choir, although the school may force her to withdraw from the choir if her grades and behavior do not improve.

Hannah lives with her mother, who has had a long succession of boyfriends living in the home. The boyfriends don't stay long. Many have been abusive toward Hannah. The mother blames Hannah for the abuse, asserting that she deserved it for being such an unruly child. Hannah has two younger brothers and a younger sister. Each of the siblings has a different father.

Hannah is very close to her paternal grandmother. Hannah frequently visits her grandmother and spends the night or weekends whenever she can. But the grandmother is ill and lives in a tiny apartment, so it would be impossible for Hannah to live with her grandmother. One of their favorite activities is attending church together on Sundays, where Hannah sings in the choir.

Hannah is sexually active. Her last boyfriend abused her. She had an abortion last year. The father was the abusive boyfriend.

A juvenile court judge has adjudged Hannah delinquent because the state proved that she assaulted her mother. Hannah claimed that she was defending herself against her mother, who was drunk and out of control. The mother claimed that Hannah initiated the violence and that the mother was defending herself.

It is now time for disposition.

1. What will you argue as prosecutor?

2. What will you argue as attorney for the defense?

3. What witnesses will you call and what evidence will you present for each side?

HYPOTHETICAL PROBLEM

Hanford D. has been charged in an Ohio juvenile court with being a delinquent juvenile because he allegedly possessed over two ounces of crack cocaine. This act would have been a felony if an adult had committed it.

At trial, the prosecutor gives her opening statement then calls the state's first witness, Officer Swann. Officer Swann testifies that she was out on patrol on the night in question when she spotted a car being driven erratically. She began pursuit. At first the driver attempted to elude Officer Swann, but after a short while the driver pulled over and stopped. When Officer Swann approached the car, she noticed what looked like a plastic bag protruding from the car seat cushions. The portion of the bag that Officer Swann could see appeared to have white residue inside of it.

Office Swann ordered Hanford to exit his vehicle, which he did. She took out the bag and saw that it was filled with a substance that appeared to be crack cocaine. She took Hanford into custody and sent the bag to the police lab for testing. That was the full extent of Officer Swann's testimony.

The next witness was George Ahmed, the police department lab technician who tested the substance. He testified that he had conducted the standard battery of tests upon the substance and determined that it was indeed crack cocaine. That was the full extent of his testimony.

The state rested it case. Hanford's defense attorney moved to dismiss under Ohio Rule 29. The judge granted the motion. Why?

ETHICAL CONCERNS

Much controversy surrounds the issue of plea-bargaining. Many people view it as a way for criminals and delinquents to beat the system and elude justice. Lawyers, judges, social workers, and others who work in the courts every day know that the courts could not operate without the plea-bargaining system in place. The courts would be so bogged down with trial that it would take years for each one to get through.

Prosecutors and judges often encourage plea-bargaining in delicate cases or cases that will be painful for the victim, such as rape and child abuse cases. Plea-bargaining ensures that the court can convict the offender without having to subject the victim to the painful and frightening prospect of seeing or having contact with the offender.

But even in such cases, especially in such cases, society often resents the plea deal for depriving it of the satisfaction of confronting, accusing, and convicting a particularly egregious offender.

Another problem with the plea-bargaining system is what defense attorneys sometimes call the "Trial Penalty." They assert that judges, who are busy and interested in clearing their dockets, pressure defendants to accept plea-bargains even when it is not in their best interest to do so. These judges will sentence a defendant to a more severe sentence following a trial than they would for a plea deal. Judges defend the more severe penalty following a trial by arguing that defendants who voluntarily admit their guilt have already taken the first step toward rehabilitation.

DISCUSSION QUESTIONS

1. What are the advantages and disadvantages of the three-part interview?
2. Why is it important to follow certain prescribed procedures in court proceedings?
3. What are the benefits and drawbacks of plea-bargaining?
4. Should attorneys continue to use plea-bargaining as much as they currently do, or should they attempt to curtail the practice?
5. Should very young children be allowed to testify in court?

6. If so, should there be a minimum age or a minimum level of comprehension before a child is allowed to testify?

7. Why do you think juvenile hearings do not have juries?

8. Should courts allow juries in juvenile hearings?

9. Should courts open juvenile hearings to the public?

10. Should the media be allowed to record and broadcast juvenile proceedings?

11. Suppose a 15-year-old girl is riding in a car with an 18-year-old boy and an adult man. The 18-year-old pulls out a gun and shoots the adult. The girls stands trial and a jury convicts her as an accomplice to the murder, although the state never establishes that the girl knew about the boy's having the gun prior to the shooting. The judge sentences the girl to life in prison without the possibility of release. Is this proportional? Is it good policy to allow these kinds of sentences?

KEY TERMS

arraignment
attorney-client privilege
bail
bail bondsman
bond
burden of persuasion
chain of custody
closing argument
element
findings of fact and
    conclusions of law

guardian ad litem
magistrate
master
mitigating factors
motion
motion to suppress
nolle
opening statement
parentage proceedings
pretrial
subpoena

Chapter 7

YOUTH COURT

OBJECTIVES

By the end of this chapter, the student should know:

- The definition of youth court, teen court, and peer court
- A short history of youth courts in the United States
- How youth courts operate
- The definition of diversion
- The requirements for participation in youth court
- The roles that youths play in youth courts
- The various youth court models
- How juvenile courts divert juveniles to youth court
- Youth court procedure
- How the youth court process affects the right to a speedy trial
- The various dispositions available to youth courts
- Statutory authority for youth courts

INTRODUCTION

Youth courts, also known as **teen courts or peer courts,** are alternatives to the
traditional juvenile court system. Youth courts allow nonviolent, first-time juvenile
offenders to participate in and be subject to the judgment of their peers rather
than the court. Juvenile offenders who participate in youth courts must
admit to their offenses and agree to abide by the youth court's dispositional decision.

The earliest known youth court began operating in Naperville, Illinois, in
1972, and is still operating. There is anecdotal evidence that an earlier youth
court began operating in 1968 in Horseheads, New York; that court is not
documented conclusively. There were 78 youth court programs operating

in the United States by 1994. There are currently over 940 teen courts operating in 48 states and the District of Columbia.

The Office of Juvenile Justice and Delinquency Prevention (OJJDP) created the National Youth Court Center (NYCC) to serve as a central point of contact for youth court programs across the nation. NYCC serves as an information clearinghouse, provides training and technical assistance to youth courts, and develops resource materials on developing and enhancing youth court programs.

THE OPERATION OF YOUTH COURT

Participation in a youth court is a one-time, voluntary diversion option for first-time, nonviolent offenders. Juvenile offenders can participate in youth court through one of three types of **diversion:** *police diversion, school or other social agency diversion,* or *court diversion.* Diversion is the process by which juvenile offenders can avoid facing charges in the traditional court system by agreeing to participate in alternative forums. Although youth court dispositions can be much stiffer than juvenile court dispositions, juveniles generally welcome the opportunity to participate in youth court because they can avoid a delinquency or criminal record by doing so.

Youth courts exploit the fact that adolescents and teenagers are more susceptible to peer pressure than to pressure from adult authority figures. Research has shown that the more youth involvement there is in the youth court system, the more successful it is.

PARTICIPATION IN YOUTH COURT

Juvenile offenders who wish to participate in the youth court must be first-time offenders accused of committing minor, nonviolent offenses, such as vandalism, shoplifting, or alcohol law violations. They must admit that they committed the offenses and they must agree to be bound by the decisions of the youth court. Their parents or guardians must participate in all phases of the proceedings and adhere to the court's dictates.

YOUTHS' ROLES IN THE COURT

Youths play key roles in the administration of the youth court. They can act as prosecutors, defense attorneys, court clerks, bailiffs, judges, members of the tribunal, or members of the jury. They may also act as court administrators who

youth courts, teen courts or **peer courts**
Legal forums that are an alternative to the traditional juvenile court system

diversion
The process by which a juvenile offender can avoid facing charges in the traditional court system by agreeing to participate in an alternative forum

adult judge model

A youth court in which an adult acts as the judge; youths play all other roles

youth judge model

A youth court in which youths play all roles, including that of judge

youth tribunal model

A youth court in which youths play all roles; there is a multi-person panel rather than a single judge

peer jury model

A youth court in which an adult presents the case to a jury of youths

manage the court's schedule, budget, and other administrative matters. The arrangements vary among courts, but consistent in all youth courts and essential to their success is that youths deliberate the charges and impose the sanctions.

Adults supervise the programs, often handling the more complex budgetary, personnel, and administrative matters. They also supervise courtroom activities and coordinate community service facilities where offenders fulfill their dispositional terms.

YOUTH COURT MODELS

There are four youth court models:

Adult judge model—An adult acts as the judge; youths play all other roles

Youth judge model—Youths play all roles, including that of judge

Youth tribunal model—Youths play all roles; there is a multi-person panel rather than a single judge

Peer jury model—An adult presents the case to a jury of youths

Consistent with the theory that youths are more responsive to peer pressure than to adult authority, the youth judge model and the youth tribunal model, which employ youths in all roles, appear to be the more successful.

SIDEBAR

THE EVALUATION OF TEEN COURTS PROJECT

The Office of Juvenile Justice and Delinquency Prevention, a branch of the United States Department of Justice, contracted with the Urban Institute to conduct the Evaluation of Teen Courts Project. They released their results in April 2002.

The Project studied the Anchorage Youth Court in Anchorage, Alaska; the Arizona Superior Court's Youth Court in Maricopa County, Arizona; the Montgomery County Teen Court in Rockville, Maryland; and the Independence Youth Court in Independence, Missouri. The Alaska court follows the youth tribunal model and the Missouri court follows the youth judge model.

Researchers measured pre-court attitudes and post-court recidivism among more than 500 juveniles referred to teen court for nonviolent offenses, such as shoplifting and vandalism. The study compared recidivism outcomes for teen court defendants with outcomes for youths who went through the traditional juvenile justice system.

(continues)

The researchers concluded:

The findings of the ETC Project suggest that teen courts represent a promising alternative for the juvenile justice system. In Alaska and Missouri, the results indicate that youth referred to teen court were significantly less likely to be re-referred to the juvenile justice system for new offenses within six months of their initial offense.

The success that the Alaska and Missouri courts enjoyed was not quite replicated in the Maryland and Arizona courts, but their success rate was no less than that of the traditional juvenile court.

The researchers noted that the two courts that enjoyed the most success were the two courts that had the heaviest youth involvement.

". . . because they give youth more responsibility for the actual conduct of teen court hearings. One of the strongest prima facie arguments for the use of teen courts is that they expose young offenders to the pro-social influence of nondelinquent peers. When a young person charged with a minor offense appears before a court of similarly aged peers, it may help to counter the notion that criminal behavior is 'cool' and that 'everyone does it.'"

DIVERSION TO YOUTH COURT

Youth court cases begin when youths commit offenses. The police can divert juveniles directly to the youth court instead of referring their cases to the prosecutor. School officials can divert the juveniles who commit offenses at school to the youth court rather than to the juvenile court. Juvenile court intake officials, prosecutors, and judges all can divert juveniles to youth court at any point prior to their hearings.

Procedure

Juveniles proceed through youth court much as they would through juvenile court. The basic steps are the same; the differences are that youths generally move more quickly through youth court than they would through the juvenile court, and that youth courts are run by youths or a combination of youths and adults, rather than all adults.

The process begins with intake. The juvenile, his parents, and court officials review the charges and the prosecutor makes a formal presentation of those charges to the court and the juvenile. Court representatives present and explain the youth court alternative to the juvenile. The juvenile must admit that the charges are true, and agree to be bound by the youth court's decisions and dispositions.

The court does not have to accept the juvenile's decision to participate in youth court, nor must it accept the state or county agency's recommendation that the juvenile participate in youth court. It can reject the recommendation where the juvenile has failed to comply with youth court recommendations in the past, where the offense is in appropriate for a diversionary program, or where the court has other grounds to find that youth court is not appropriate. Most youth courts require juveniles to sign waivers of the **right to a speedy trial.**

right to a speedy trial

A constitutional mandate that criminal and juvenile defendants must stand trial in a speedy fashion

The United States Constitution and most state constitutions mandate that criminal and juvenile defendants must stand trial in a speedy fashion. Most states prescribe the number of days within which a case must come to trial or face dismissal. The defendant has the ability to waive that right, and must do so in order to participate in youth court. If the juvenile opts out of the youth court after beginning the process, or if the juvenile fails to complete the dispositional requirements and is remanded to the juvenile court, the speedy trial waiver remains in effect. The juvenile cannot raise that as a defense in a subsequent juvenile proceeding. The following case illustrates that the speedy trial waiver remains in effect even after the juvenile has left the youth court system.

B.W. v. State
855 So.2d 1266 (Fla.App. 2003)

Because we hold that appellant and his mother executed a general waiver of speedy trial, we affirm the disposition of this case and reject appellant's claim that the speedy trial time had expired.

B.W. was taken into custody on July 26, 2001, for battery on a school employee. So that B.W. could participate in a diversion program, he and his mother signed a document entitled "WAIVER OF SPEEDY TRIAL" on September 7, 2001. The document was provided by the Teen Court program in Broward County.

The waiver document contained three paragraphs on one page. It said that appellant had the right to a trial "within ninety (90) days from the date of [his] arrest." The form stated that in return for being "considered for participation in [a diversion] program, I HEREBY WAIVE MY RIGHT TO A SPEEDY TRIAL within ninety (90) days." The form indicated: "I UNDERSTAND THAT IF I DO NOT SUC-

CESSFULLY COMPLETE THE APPLICABLE PROGRAM TO WHICH I AM ASSIGNED, THE PENDING CHARGES MAY BE FILED AGAINST ME AND I MAY BE BROUGHT TO TRIAL."

B.W. decided on September 17, 2001, not to participate in the diversion program, so the state filed a petition for delinquency. After his July 2, 2002, arraignment, B.W. filed a motion to dismiss the charges, claiming that the speedy trial period had expired. He argued that the waiver of speedy trial should be considered only for the 10-day period from the time he executed the waiver until the day he decided not to participate in the diversion program.

The trial court denied the motion to dismiss, and after a non-jury trial found B.W. guilty of battery. The court withheld adjudication of delinquency and gave B.W. a stern judicial warning.

(continues)

B.W. v. State (Continued)

The Florida Rules of Juvenile Procedure contemplate that a juvenile may execute a waiver of speedy trial. As it applied to this case, rule 8.090(a)(1) required B.W. to be brought to an adjudicatory hearing within ninety days of the date he was taken into custody. Rule 8.090(f)(1) provides that the speedy trial time may be extended "[u]pon stipulation . . . signed by the child. . . ." In circumstances similar to this case, rule 8.075(b), which applies *after* the filing of a petition, contemplates that a plan for a diversion program be signed by the child, the parents (unless ex-cused by the court), and the child's counsel, when represented. Rule 8.075(b)(2) requires a diversion plan to contain a "stipulation that the speedy trial rule is waived."

The WAIVER OF SPEEDY TRIAL document signed by B.W. and his mother was a stipulation within the meaning of rule 8.090(f)(1). It effected a general waiver of B.W.'s speedy trial rights. B.W. did not seek to awaken a speedy trial right by filing a demand under rule 8.090(g). The trial court correctly denied the motion to dismiss.

The youth court administrator schedules a hearing, that can occur anywhere from hours to several days after intake.

The juvenile meets with an attorney or team of attorneys to review the charges, learn about the youth court process, and plan for the hearing. The attorneys explain the process to the juvenile and his parents, and interviews the juvenile to uncover any mitigating facts or circumstances to present to the judge, jury, or tribunal in the juvenile's defense. While the defense team is meeting, the prosecutors are meeting and reviewing the facts.

The prosecution and the defense present their cases to the judge, jury, or tribunal at the hearing. The juvenile offender can address the court and point out mitigating facts and circumstances or simply use the opportunity to apologize.

In some jurisdictions the victim can address the youth court. As the juvenile has already admitted the truth of the charges, the victim will not speak to matters of proof, but rather to matters of the damages or the impact of the juvenile's actions upon the victim.

After all the parties have addressed the court, the judge, jury, or tribunal convenes to discuss dispositional alternatives and decide upon an appropriate disposition. Most youth courts have sentencing guidelines that take into account such matters as the amount of damages, the circumstances of the offense, and the attitude of the offender. These guidelines prescribe the maximum disposition that the court can impose as well as the maximum amount of time the juvenile has to meet the requirements of the disposition. A social worker may take part in this phase of the youth court hearing and help the court fashion an appropriate disposition.

The court presents its decision to the juvenile and his parents verbally and in writing. An adult staff member or administrator meets with the juvenile and his parents to make sure that they understand the disposition and understand the steps they need to take in order to comply with it. They address such logistical issues as where to submit proof of compliance.

DISPOSITIONS

Youth court dispositions tend to be more stringent and rigorous than juvenile court sentences. Because these are relatively minor offenses, the regular juvenile court system would treat these offenders lightly, especially in large cities where juvenile crime can be quite serious. Even relatively minor offenses will result in extensive dispositions in youth courts.

Youth court judges and tribunals can choose from a range of dispositional options. They include restitution to the victim, writing a letter of apology to the offender's parents or to the victim, performing community service, serving on a future youth court, writing an essay on the subject of the offense, and attending classes on a subject relevant to the offense.

Adult supervisors oversee the completion of the terms of disposition. They check with community service facilities to verify that the juveniles have completed their service satisfactorily. They read and approve essays and otherwise certify the juveniles' performance. They inform the juveniles when they determine that the juveniles have satisfied their obligations and then destroy the juveniles' records.

LEGAL AUTHORITY

Local jurisdictions create and implement youth courts with the aid of NYCC and OJJDP. They are, for the most part, self-created, self-governed, and self-regulated. Youth courts follow constitutions or bylaws that the creating committees have drafted at the court's inception.

There are no uniform national or local laws governing youth courts. Some states statutes authorize these courts specifically. The provision for Iowa's youth court is an example of such a statute:

IA ST § 602.6110 PEER REVIEW COURT

1. A peer review court may be established in each judicial district to divert certain juvenile offenders from the criminal or juvenile justice systems. The court shall consist of a qualified adult to act as judge while the duties of prosecutor, defense counsel, court attendant, clerk, and jury shall be performed by persons twelve through seventeen years of age.

2. The jurisdiction of the peer review court extends to those persons ten through seventeen years of age who have committed misdemeanor

(continues)

offenses, or delinquent acts which would be misdemeanor offenses if committed by an adult, who have admitted involvement in the misdemeanor or delinquent act, and who meet the criteria established for entering into an informal adjustment agreement for those offenses. Those persons may elect to appear before the peer review court for a determination of the terms and conditions of the informal adjustment or may elect to proceed with the informal or formal procedures established in chapter 232.

3. The peer review court shall not determine guilt or innocence and any statements or admissions made by the person before the peer review court are not admissible in any formal proceedings involving the same person. The peer review court shall only determine the terms and conditions of the informal adjustment for the offense. The terms and conditions may consist of fines, restrictions for damages, attendance at treatment programs, or community service work or any combination of these penalties as appropriate to the offense or delinquent act committed. A person appearing before the peer review court may also be required to serve as a juror on the court as a part of the person's sentence.

4. The chief judge of each judicial district which establishes a peer review court shall appoint a peer review court advisory board. The advisory board shall adopt rules for the peer review court advisory program, shall appoint persons to serve on the peer review court, and shall supervise the expenditure of funds appropriated to the program. Rules adopted shall include procedures which are designed to eliminate the influence of prejudice and racial and economic discrimination in the procedures and decisions of the peer review court.

Other statutes implicitly recognize the validity of youth courts by authorizing their use or by otherwise acknowledging their legitimacy. These statutes may regulate eligibility, referral procedure, the makeup of the youth court, fees attendant to participation in the youth court, the maximum amount of time offenders have to complete their disposition, and whether judges must approve the program. The Texas statute is an example of such a statute:

TX CRIM PRO ART. 45.052 DISMISSAL OF MISDEMEANOR CHARGE ON COMPLETION OF TEEN COURT PROGRAM

(a) A justice or municipal court may defer proceedings against a defendant who is under the age of 18 or enrolled full time in an accredited secondary school in a program leading toward a high school diploma for not

(continues)

more than 180 days if the defendant:

(1) is charged with an offense that the court has jurisdiction of under Article 4.11 or 4.14, Code of Criminal Procedure;

(2) pleads nolo contendere or guilty to the offense in open court with the defendant's parent, guardian, or managing conservator present;

(3) presents to the court an oral or written request to attend a teen court program; and

(4) has not successfully completed a teen court program in the two years preceding the date that the alleged offense occurred.

(b) The teen court program must be approved by the court.

(c) A defendant for whom proceedings are deferred under Subsection (a) shall complete the teen court program not later than the 90th day after the date the teen court hearing to determine punishment is held or the last day of the deferral period, whichever date is earlier. The justice or municipal court shall dismiss the charge at the time the defendant presents satisfactory evidence that the defendant has successfully completed the teen court program.

Youth courts have no compulsory authority. The only coercive force youth courts possess is the threat of returning offenders to the juvenile court system. Youth courts may not order incarceration, fines, or suspension of driving privileges. Because youth courts do not have authority to incarcerate or otherwise deprive juvenile offenders of their liberty, they are not bound by constitutional requirements of due process. Nonetheless, they generally adhere to due process principles by affording juvenile offenders legal representation, the opportunity to be heard, and the opportunity to be judged by a jury of their peers.

CASE PROBLEM

School officials reported that L.R. stole another student's violin, and the county charged her with grand theft. The county Department of Juvenile Justice (DJJ) recommended that the trial court withhold adjudication and sentence L.R. to a diversionary youth court program.

Previously, L.R. had failed to comply with a previously ordered diversionary youth court program.

The court declined to divert L.R., heard the case, found that the charges against L.R. were true, and ordered her to complete a number of hours of community service, among other things.

L.R. appealed, arguing that the trial court erred in adjudicating her delinquent instead of withholding adjudication as DJJ had recommended.

What is the result?

ROLE-PLAY PROBLEM

Form a tribunal model youth court in class. Assign the following roles:

- Juvenile defendant
- Defense attorney
- Prosecutor

The remainder of the students should play the role of the youth court tribunal. Switch roles as you try the following cases:

- The defendant stole a valuable musical instrument from a classmate
- The defendant is charged with possession of a small amount of marijuana
- The defendant is charged with excessive truancy
- The defendant is charged with vandalizing a neighbor's house by spray painting the brick

Be sure to use the full panoply of available dispositional options, as well as any you can devise.

HYPOTHETICAL PROBLEM

Johnny is a 16-year-old high school student. He is a good student and an athlete. He is charged with blowing up his neighbor's mailbox with firecrackers. It appears that this is a varsity football team hazing ritual.

Johnny has been in the court twice before—once on assault charges, and once on charges of domestic violence, involving an incident where Johnny and his father engaged in a fistfight and Johnny's mother called 911. The court dismissed the assault charges when the victim failed to appear in court, and the domestic violence charges when Johnny's parents appeared in court but refused to testify against him.

Should Johnny be diverted to the youth court on the vandalism charges? Why or why not? If he goes to youth court, what kind of disposition would be appropriate for him?

ETHICAL CONCERNS

It is important that all participants in the youth court are aware of the ethical constraints upon them, including the need for confidentiality and privacy.

Because the youth court is not a part of the juvenile court, and because volunteers hold most of the positions, there is a danger that those running the program may be lax about such matters.

The National Youth Court Center recommends that volunteers working in the youth court have an active role in developing the ethical standards for the court. The center recommends that volunteers develop a code of conduct that addresses such issues as conflicts of interest, the consequences for failing to adhere to the standards, and volunteer's behavior within the court, including a system for maintaining **privacy,** which is the act of keeping proceedings out of the public eye, and of **confidentiality,** which is refraining from divulging secret information.

privacy
The act of keeping proceedings out of the public eye

confidentiality
Refraining from divulging secret information

DISCUSSION QUESTIONS

1. Is it a wise idea to tap into adolescent yearning for peer approval and conformity?
2. What effect do you think it has for a juvenile offender to be ordered to participate in a subsequent youth court?
3. What effect do you think the youth court will have on traditional juvenile court proceedings?
4. What are the pros and cons of youth courts?

KEY TERMS

adult judge model
confidentiality
diversion
peer jury model
privacy

right to a speedy trial
youth courts, teen courts,
   or peer courts
youth judge model
youth tribunal model

END NOTE

See Butts, J. A. et al. (2002). *The Impact of Teen Courts on Young Offenders.* Urban Institute Report. (April)

Chapter 8

TRANSFER TO ADULT COURT

OBJECTIVES

By the end of this chapter, the student should know:

- The three classes of transfer statutes
- The outlines and purpose of a waiver hearing
- The definitions of standard of proof and burden of persuasion
- What due process requirements attend a transfer hearing
- The paralegal's role in a transfer hearing
- The factors courts consider in the amenability phase of transfer hearings
- The paralegal's role in the amenability phase of transfer hearings
- The contents of the court's statement that accompanies a waiver decision
- Youthful offender and serious youthful offender law
- Procedures courts follow in considering motions for treatment as youthful offenders
- The five classes of youthful offender statutes
- The due process requirements at youthful offender hearings

INTRODUCTION

The states developed juvenile courts to allow a more individualized and reparative approach to juvenile offenders than adult courts allowed. Juvenile courts take into account the societal and familial factors that bring a youth to its attention as well as the juvenile's actions. Juvenile courts can thus offer rehabilitative services when they are appropriate, an option that is not readily available to the criminal court judge.

The public perception of juvenile offenders began to change in the late twentieth century. People perceived that juveniles were becoming more violent and dangerous and they demanded that the legislatures and courts adapt the laws accordingly. The

judicial waiver

When the juvenile court relinquishes its jurisdiction over a juvenile and turns the juvenile over to the criminal court for trial

prosecutorial discretion

A doctrine that grants the prosecutor the right to make the decision whether to try a juvenile as an adult or as a juvenile

concurrent jurisdiction

The doctrine that, like prosecutorial discretion, mandates that jurisdiction over certain offenses lies in both the adult criminal court and the juvenile court and leaves it to the prosecutor to choose the forum

mandatory transfer

Statutes that prescribe that certain offenses must come under the jurisdiction of the adult criminal court even if a juvenile commits the offense

exclusion

Statutes that proscribe the juvenile court from having jurisdiction over certain offenses or offenders

judicial waiver

The process whereby a juvenile court decides to give up the juvenile's court's jurisdiction over a case and transfer that case to the adult criminal court

discretionary transfer

Statutes that leave it to the juvenile court judge to decide whether to transfer a case to adult court or keep it in juvenile court

focus of juvenile justice has begun to shift from protection and rehabilitation to punishment and retribution in response to that perception.

States now frequently allow or require the transfer of juveniles from juvenile court to adult criminal court under certain circumstances. The number of juveniles subject to such transfer has steadily increased. From 1992 through 1997, 44 states and the District of Columbia passed laws making it easier for juveniles to be tried as adults.[i] As of 1999, 46 states and the District of Columbia had some form of **judicial waiver,** or device whereby the judicial court could voluntarily give up its statutory jurisdiction over a juvenile or an action.[ii]

CLASSES OF TRANSFER STATUTES

There are three classes of transfer statutes. The first is **prosecutorial discretion** or **concurrent jurisdiction** statutes, which grant prosecutors the discretion to commence actions against juveniles in adult court from the outset. Prosecutorial discretion statutes authorize prosecutors decide where they will bring an action—adult court or juvenile court. Concurrent jurisdiction statutes mandate that certain offenses or offenders are under both juvenile and criminal court jurisdiction, and allow prosecutors to choose their forum.

The second class is **mandatory transfer** statutes, which require the criminal court to take jurisdiction of certain offenses or offenders. This class includes **exclusion** statutes, which proscribe the juvenile court from having jurisdiction over certain cases or offenders. In 1999, 29 states had exclusion or mandatory transfer statutes in effect.

Some exclusion statutes mandate that offenses such as murder, rape, or kidnapping will be excluded automatically. Others exclude actions based upon the offender's age, criminal record, or legal status. Other statutes exclude actions based upon on the crime and mandate exclusion of cases where the offender used a firearm, there was great personal injury, or the victim was particularly vulnerable.

The third class of transfer statutes is **judicial waiver** or **discretionary transfer** statutes, which direct the juvenile court judge to hold a waiver hearing, at which the judge must decide whether to transfer the case to adult court.

THE WAIVER HEARING

The waiver hearing is a two-part hearing. The first part is the **probable cause hearing,** at which the court determines whether there is good reason to believe (1) that a criminal act has occurred, and (2) that the juvenile before the court committed that criminal act. The second part of the hearing is the **amenability phase.** This portion of the hearing is devoted to determining whether treatment or rehabilitation within the juvenile court system can help the juvenile. The court may also consider at this phase whether society will benefit from the juvenile's transfer.

STANDARD OF PROOF AND BURDEN OF PERSUASION

Probable cause is a lower **standard of proof** than usual criminal standard of proof beyond a reasonable doubt. Standard of proof is the level of certainty the courts must recognize before they will rule in favor of the party who has the **burden of persuasion.** The party with the burden of persuasion is the person whose job it is to convince the court to take a certain action. The prosecution, or the state, has the burden of persuasion in criminal and delinquency actions.

Criminal cases require the prosecutor to establish the defendant's guilt beyond a reasonable doubt, which is about 90 percent certainty. Preponderance of the evidence, the standard in civil cases, is 51 percent. Probable cause is not usually quantified, but if it were, it would be below 50%.

The low standard of proof is appropriate at the waiver hearing because it is only a preliminary hearing, not the stage at which the prosecutor must establish the defendant's guilt or delinquency.

The state presents its case at the probable cause hearing as it would at a trial. The prosecutor attempts to establish each element of the crime or delinquent act in question through the use of testimony and physical evidence.

The defense team attempts to rebut or denigrate the state's evidence through the use of cross-examination. The state rests after it has presented its case after which the defense presents its evidence to prevent a finding of probable cause.

The court is likely to make a finding of probable cause because it is such a low standard of proof. The following case illustrates how juvenile courts reach waiver decisions.

Faisst v. State
105 S.W.3d 8 (2003)

Appellant Lindsay Faisst was certified as an adult and was charged with the offense of Intoxication Manslaughter. After certification and transfer to district court, Appellant entered a plea of guilty and was sentenced to confinement for ten years, probated. Appellant appeals the discretionary transfer from juvenile court. We affirm.

(continues)

---

probable cause hearing

A hearing to determine whether probable cause exists to find that a crime was committed or an act occurred and whether a complaint or delinquency petition should follow

amenability phase

The portion or a juvenile transfer hearing that is devoted to determining whether treatment or rehabilitation within the juvenile court system can help the juvenile

standard of proof

The level of certainty required in a particular case

burden of persuasion

The job of proving to the court that something is so

Faisst v. State (Continued)

BACKGROUND

Appellant was driving a vehicle, with Ashleigh McCaa as her passenger, when the Whitehouse police clocked her traveling above the speed limit. She attempted to flee when the police began pursuit of her vehicle. As Appellant was negotiating a curve at a high rate of speed, estimated at 100 M.P.H., she lost control of her car and hit a large tree. She was thrown from the vehicle and sustained minor injuries, but her passenger was decapitated and an arm was ripped off when her side of the vehicle made contact with the tree. Because of the amount of force that had been applied to McCaa's seatbelt, it finally gave way, and she was thrown from the car into a barbed wire fence. At the scene, Appellant asked repeatedly, "Where am I?" and "Is my car o.k.?" Her speech was slurred and hard to understand, although there was no evidence of head trauma. It was later determined that Appellant was intoxicated at the time of the incident.

Appellant was sixteen years old when the accident occurred. An original petition was filed in juvenile court alleging that Appellant had engaged in delinquent conduct. The State then filed its motion for discretionary transfer to district court. By the time of the hearing, Appellant had turned seventeen. After hearing testimony, considering evidence and argument of counsel, the juvenile court certified Appellant as an adult, and transferred this case to the district court.

Appellant was sentenced to ten years of confinement in the Texas Department of Criminal Justice—Institutional Division. Appellant then filed a Motion for Probation after Execution of Sentence, which the trial court granted. This appeal followed.

DISCRETIONARY TRANSFER

In order to transfer a juvenile to adult court, the court must find that (1) there is probable cause to believe that the juvenile committed the offense alleged in the petition (Appellant stipulated to her age and that there was probable cause to believe that she had committed intoxicated manslaughter) and (2) because of the seriousness of the offense alleged or the background of the child, the welfare of the community requires criminal prosecution. To facilitate this decision, the Family Code sets out criteria for the court to consider:

(1) whether the alleged offense was against a person or property, with greater weight in favor of transfer given to offenses against the person;

(2) the sophistication and maturity of the child;

(3) the record and previous history of the child; and

(4) the prospects of adequate protection of the public and the likelihood of the rehabilitation of the child by use of procedures, services, and facilities currently available to the juvenile court.

At the conclusion of the transfer hearing, the juvenile court issued the following findings:

(1) The Court finds that the said act would be a felony under the laws of the State of Texas if committed by an adult.

(2) The Court finds that the alleged offense was against a person.

(3) The Court finds that the Child is of sufficient sophistication and maturity to be tried as an adult. The Court specifically finds that the Child is of sufficient sophistication and maturity to aid an attorney in her defense.

(4) The Court finds that because of the extreme and severe nature of the alleged offense, the prospects of adequate protection for the public and likelihood of reasonable rehabilitation of the Child by the use of procedures, services and facilities which are currently available to the Juvenile Court are in doubt.

(continues)

Faisst v. State (Continued)

Appellant contends, because there is neither legally nor factually sufficient evidence to support the finding, the trial court abused its discretion when it transferred the case to the district court.

Factual Sufficiency

[Juvenile probation officer Joe] Berg stated that Appellant had been issued a ticket for the offense of Minor in Possession in June of 1998, one and a half years before the accident. At that time, she was required to complete, and did complete, six hours of alcohol education. He pointed out that the education obviously had no effect on Appellant's actions. Berg further related Appellant's admission that she had been drinking for six months before the accident, and had been intoxicated on at least six or seven of those occasions. Berg opined that this level of drinking showed that Appellant had a significant problem with alcohol abuse.

James Brown, the owner of Trinity Counseling Associates of East Texas, testified on Appellant's behalf. He stated that he had seen Appellant on two occasions. The first time he simply evaluated her maturity level. During the second interview, he spoke with Appellant about the accident. He opined that because of her remorse, he did not believe that there was a high probability that an incident like the one in question would reoccur. Brown also stated that he was not aware that Appellant had any prior juvenile referrals, any truancy problems or any other criminal violations.

Tom Allen, a psychologist who also interviewed Appellant on two occasions, testified that in regard to the question of whether or not Appellant would be a danger to the community, he saw little to no risk assessment issues. He opined that there was a minimal risk of recidivism because of her profound grief and remorse. He also stated that any concerns which society might have about Appellant could be adequately addressed in an eleven-month period.

Shirley Estes, a dance teacher in the Whitehouse Independent School District, testified that when Appellant was in her class, she had been a good student, was respectful, had a sweet disposition, and interacted well with other students. Additionally, she stated that Appellant was a "normal teenager." Lee Yeager, also a teacher with WISD, agreed with Estes' evaluation of Appellant. He further testified that after the accident, Appellant had a very difficult transition, that she no longer interacted with other students, and that she was sometimes zombie-like.

CONCLUSION

After a thorough review of the record, we find not only legally sufficient, but also factually sufficient evidence to support the juvenile court's fourth finding. The court's finding that because of the severity of the offense, which requires a long period of supervision and probation, the juvenile justice system cannot adequately protect the public or provide for the rehabilitation of Appellant, is not so against the great weight and preponderance of the evidence as to be manifestly unjust. Accordingly, we hold that the juvenile court did not abuse its discretion when it certified Appellant as an adult and transferred her case to the district court. We overrule Appellant's sole issue and affirm the judgment of the trial court.

DUE PROCESS CONSIDERATIONS AT THE TRANSFER HEARING

Due process requirements for a transfer hearing are essentially the same as in a standard juvenile delinquency proceeding.

Jury

There is no jury requirement in delinquency or transfer hearings. The Constitution requires a jury trial only in criminal actions, which American courts have defined as actions that are **penal** in nature. A penal action is one that has the potential to end with the defendant's criminal conviction. Delinquency proceedings are civil, not criminal.

penal
A legal action that carries with it the possibility of punishment or loss of liberty as its consequence

Delinquency hearings and transfer hearings are tried to the judge who hears the evidence and issues a ruling either immediately or within a short time.

Because juvenile cases are tried to judges and not juries it is common for both parties to waive opening statements. Legal arguments concerning such matters as the admission of evidence or the sufficiency of pleadings take place in the courtroom rather than at sidebar, although extensive or lengthy arguments may take place in the judge's chambers.

Right to Transcript

Indigent juveniles have the right to receive transcript of their hearings at the state's expense. Most juvenile cases are mechanically recorded. Live court reporters in juvenile hearings are rare. Courts have held that the right to a transcript includes the right to a transcriber, or court reporter if the juvenile so requests and is indigent. The usual procedure for obtaining a court reporter would be to file a motion with the court requesting one.

Right to Counsel

Juvenile defendants have the right to the effective assistance of counsel at all phases of the delinquency hearing and the waiver hearing. The court must appoint attorneys for indigent juveniles defendants.

Usually the court refers the juvenile to the public defender's office, which is often located in or near the courthouse. The public defender meets with the juvenile and the juvenile's parents and to prepare a defense.

Multiple defendants who were involved in the same event cannot all be assigned to the public defender; that would be a conflict of interest. Even if the public defender's office has a hundred attorneys, they are considered the same attorney because they all work for the same office. No one attorney or one office can represent two or more defendants in the same case.

The courts refer multiple defendants to private attorneys who agree to represent indigent juvenile defendants. The county or the state pays their fees. Court rules or state statutes mandate the amount of the fee based upon the level of offense and he amount of hours spent on the case.

Evidence

Evidentiary standards vary among jurisdictions, but as a general rule the major difference between a transfer hearing and a delinquency hearing is in the way that the Rules of Evidence apply. Generally, the rules strictly apply at the adjudication phase and do not strictly apply during the disposition phase.

Strict rules of evidence do not apply in most transfer hearings. The only requirement as to evidence is that it be reliable.

The Exclusionary Rule

The Exclusionary Rule, discussed in Chapter 3, Taking Custody of Juveniles, applies to waiver hearings. The juvenile will seek to exclude from the waiver hearing evidence that the state has obtained as a result of an illegal detention, search, or seizure.

Burden of Proof

The defendant at a waiver hearing has the burden of proof to demonstrate that he is amenable to and appropriate for the application of treatment, care, supervision, and rehabilitation within the juvenile system. That rehabilitation, treatment, care, and supervision can come from the court, governmental social services agencies, private agencies, or other sources.

SIDEBAR

THE PARALEGAL'S ROLE IN THE PROBABLE CAUSE PHASE

The probable cause phase of a waiver hearing is a mini trial. The state goes first and presents evidence to support a finding of probable cause to believe that the juvenile has committed or participated in a delinquent act.

The paralegal participates in the probable cause phase of a transfer case in much the same as in a criminal or delinquency trial. The extent of the paralegal's role and involvement will depend in large part upon whether the paralegal works for a private firm or a government agency.

The prosecutor's office and the public defender's office generally limit their paralegals' role to drafting documents, managing files, preparing reports, doing research, and gathering information. Small firms give their paralegals much bigger roles. In small firms, the paralegal do much more, limited only by the proscription against the unauthorized practice of law.

(continues)

A paralegal can perform the following tasks in preparing for the probable cause phase of a transfer hearing:

- Interview clients and witnesses, prepare them for trial, and make any necessary arrangements for their appearance, including issuing **subpoenas,** which are commands to appear at a certain time and place in order to give testimony. Subpoenas can include commands to produce documents or other physical evidence;
- Arrange travel reimbursement;
- Visit the scene of the incident for the purpose of mapping, diagramming, or photographing it;
- Conduct legal research;
- Draft preliminary documents such as discovery letters, motions to suppress, and motions for a **Bill of Particulars,** which is a document that states with specificity the time, place, manner, and means of commission of a criminal or delinquent act;
- Locate, research, prepare, and schedule expert witnesses;
- Manage the case file and any case documents;
- Assist the attorney at trial

subpoena

A command to appear at a certain time and place in order to give testimony. It can include a command to produce documents or other physical evidence

Bill of Particulars

A document that the prosecution produces during the discovery phase of a criminal trial seeking specificity as to the time, place, manner, and means of commission of a criminal or delinquent act

THE AMENABILITY PHASE

The juvenile court hears and considers evidence on the issue of whether the juvenile is amenable to rehabilitation and treatment within the juvenile court system in the second phase of the transfer hearing, which is called the amenability phase. The Supreme Court has not ruled on what factors the court may or must consider.

The Ohio statute lists the factors that a court should consider in making an amenability determination, and is typical:

Factors Favoring Transfer (ORC § 2152.12(D))

1. The victim suffered physical, psychological, or serious economic harm;
2. The victim's physical or mental harm was exacerbated by the victim's physical or mental vulnerability or age;
3. The juvenile's relationship with the victim facilitated the act;
4. The juvenile committed the act for hire or as part of a gang or other organized criminal activity;
5. The juvenile displayed, brandished, indicated, or used a firearm;

6. At the time of the act charged, the juvenile as awaiting adjudication for delinquency, was under a community sanction, or was on parole for prior delinquency;

7. The results of previous juvenile sanctions and programs show rehabilitation will not occur in the juvenile system;

8. The juvenile is emotionally, physically, or psychologically mature enough for transfer;

9. There is not sufficient time for the juvenile's rehabilitation in the juvenile system.

Factors Against Transfer (ORC § 2152.12(E))

1. The victim induced or facilitated the act charged;

2. The juvenile acted under provocation;

3. The juvenile was not the principal offender, or, at the time of the act charged, was under the negative influence or coercion of another;

4. The juvenile did not cause physical harm to any person or property, or have reasonable cause to believe such harm would occur;

5. The juvenile has not been previously found delinquent;

6. The juvenile is not emotionally, physically, or psychologically mature enough for transfer;

7. The juvenile is mentally ill or mentally retarded;

8. There is sufficient time to rehabilitate the child in the juvenile system and the level of security available reasonably assures the public safety.

SIDEBAR

THE PARALEGAL'S ROLE IN PREPARING FOR THE AMENABILITY PHASE (DEFENSE)

The amenability phase enables to court to determine whether the juvenile justice system can be help this particular juvenile. Paralegals can perform the following tasks:

• Locate, research, prepare, and schedule special treatment programs for the juvenile, such as psychological counseling, drug treatment, anger management, school tutoring, or religious counseling;

(continues)

- Obtain information regarding the juvenile's behavior during custody and detention;
- Obtain a history of the juvenile's involvement with the state, including school programs, counseling, drug treatment, anger management, residential treatment, or foster care;
- Compile a profile of the juvenile's home and family life;
- Obtain the child's school records, attendance records, disciplinary records, and records of involvement in sports or other extra-curricular activities;
- Investigate the child's religious or spiritual involvement.

THE PARALEGAL'S ROLE IN PREPARING FOR THE AMENABILITY PHASE (PROSECUTION)

The prosecution paralegal will prepare for the amenability phase by focusing on the programs and services that have been available to the juvenile in the past and will seek to determine whether the juvenile has benefited from those programs and services. The prosecution will also examine the juvenile's behavior while in pretrial detention and while in the custody of the police. The prosecution will emphasize that the juvenile has failed to utilize the available resources, including school, church, family support, and other community based support.

The Court's Statement

If the juvenile court issues a waiver order, it must issue a statement setting forth the basis for its decision and demonstrate its compliance with state statutes outlining the factors it must consider. The court must also conduct a full investigation and state that it has done so. It will not suffice for the court to merely assert that it conducted a full investigation without substantiating that assertion with the facts of that investigation.

The court must ensure that the juvenile had adequate legal representation. This means that the juvenile had an attorney at the hearing and that the attorney had a meaningful opportunity to investigate the case and had access to resources adequate to try the case in a meaningful fashion. The court must also ensure that the juvenile had access to his **social service record,** which is the written account of the social services agency's involvement with juveniles and their families.

A failure of the juvenile court to provide such a statement, showing the basis for its decision and demonstrating compliance with the requirement of a full investigation will render the order invalid.

social service record

A written account of the social services agency's involvement with a juvenile and his family

YOUTHFUL OFFENDERS

Sometimes a juvenile will commit an act that is too serious to come under the auspices of the juvenile court but is not serious enough to warrant transfer to adult court. This can happen where older youths outgrow the juvenile court's jurisdiction before the expiration of a sentence, where a juvenile disposition is insufficient or inappropriate to the degree of the offense, or where youths are habitual offenders and the acts for which they are being charged is not serious but gain gravity in light of a lengthy juvenile court record.

Youthful offender and serious youthful offender statutes are a relatively new category of juvenile delinquency statutes that afford courts greater flexibility in dealing with older, more serious, or habitual juvenile offenders by allowing them to impose blended dispositions. Many states have both youthful offender and serious youthful offender statutes, the latter being more egregious than the former.

Courts can use youthful offender statutes to impose juvenile dispositions that emphasize rehabilitation or treatment while simultaneously imposing adult sentences that emphasize punishment, retribution, or restitution. The courts can stay the adult sentences while the youths serve the juvenile dispositions, or can suspend the adult sentences pending the successful completion of the juvenile dispositions.

Request for Treatment as a Youthful Offender

Young offenders who are facing charges in criminal court can petition or move the criminal court to grant them youthful offender status. This allows criminal court judges to dispense blended sentences that incorporate juvenile and adult elements, suspending the adult element pending the successful completion of the juvenile element.

The decision whether to grant such status is within the discretion of the court. The court will consider the juvenile's background and family history, the nature of the crime charged, any prior convictions, the defendant's age, whether the juvenile is amenable to rehabilitation within the juvenile system, and any other matters the court deems relevant. A reviewing court will not overturn such as decision unless there is a clear abuse of discretion on the part of the lower court.

Classes of Youthful Offender Statutes

There are five versions of youthful offender statutes, four of which, in two pairs, are currently in practice in the United States. Under one pair of versions, the adult court holds the trial and imposes the penalties. The adult court has authority under these statutes to impose juvenile dispositions and sanctions as well as adult sentences. Under the other pair, the juvenile court holds the trial and imposes the penalties. Under these statutes, the juvenile court possesses the authority to impose criminal sentences as well as juvenile dispositions and sanctions.

Criminal-exclusive statutes authorize the adult criminal court to impose a juvenile disposition or an adult sentence. The youth serves out one penalty, and is finished. These statutes are law in California, Colorado, Florida, Idaho, Michigan, and Virginia.

Criminal-inclusive statutes direct the adult criminal court to impose both a juvenile disposition and an adult sentence. The court stays the adult sentence upon the youth's successful completion of the juvenile disposition. The court imposes the adult sentence only if the youth does not comply with or complete the juvenile sanctions, causes disruption, or commits violations that render rehabilitation implausible. This is the law in Arkansas and Missouri.

Juvenile-exclusive statutes authorize the juvenile court to impose either a juvenile or an adult sanction. New Mexico uses juvenile-exclusive statutes.

Juvenile-inclusive statutes authorize juvenile courts to impose criminal penalties and juvenile dispositions simultaneously. The court suspends the adult sentence pending the youth's successful completion of the juvenile disposition. The court invokes the adult sentence is invoked if the juvenile causes such disruption or commits such violations as to make rehabilitation implausible. Connecticut, Minnesota, Montana, and Ohio use this approach.

The sentencing commission that designed the various blended sentencing approaches also recommended a fifth approach: the *juvenile-contiguous* approach, which allows juvenile courts to impose juvenile dispositions that go beyond the normal time and age limits attendant to juvenile delinquency statutes. No state has yet adopted this approach.

Due Process at Youthful Offender Hearings

Because the serious youth offender (SYO) statutes involve the possibility of an adult criminal sentence, their use invokes the full panoply of constitutional rights and civil liberties normally attendant to a criminal action.

Alleged serious youthful offenders thus enjoy more extensive due process guarantees than their juvenile delinquent counterparts. Most state statutes guarantee an SYO the rights to a grand jury indictment, a speedy trial, bail, counsel, mental competency proceeding, evidentiary and criminal rules procedures, among others.

Grand Jury Indictment

SYO actions require grand jury indictments, unlike delinquency actions, where prosecutors determine the charges. The grand jury must find that there is probable cause to believe that the youth committed an offense, and that the youth is age eligible for SYO disposition.

Either the adult court or the juvenile court can impanel the grand jury. The SYO grand jury process is the same as it is for a conventional grand jury proceeding. That is, the accused has no right to have counsel present, the rules of evidence are relaxed, hearsay evidence is allowed, and the proceedings are secret.

Speedy Trial

SYO statutes afford juvenile defenders the right to speedy trials. The trial must take place within a certain prescribed time period, or the court must dismiss the charges. The clock begins to run on the day the grand jury returns an indictment or the juvenile court files an SYO complaint or notice. Time limits vary, but 270 days is typical. Every day that the accused spends in detention counts as three days in most states.

Federal law requires that if a youth is in detention, or physically restricted custody, the juvenile court must commence a hearing within 30 days of the beginning of the detention. If the juvenile court does not bring the youth to trial within 30 days, then the court must dismiss the information (the federal version of a juvenile indictment) upon the youth's motion.

Bail

SYO statutes afford juveniles the right to bail. If the state has a bail scheme whereby certain offenses and condition mandate certain bail amounts, then the court must follow that scheme in assigning bail to a serious youth offender. In contrast, juvenile statutes vary on juveniles' rights to bail. Some statutes allow bail, some mandate it, some prohibit it, and others are silent on the issue.

Counsel

Juveniles have the right to attorneys in SYO actions. If they cannot afford one, the court will appoint the public defender or a private attorney whom the state has authorized to represent indigent defendants.

Juveniles cannot waive the right to counsel. If they do not have a parent or guardian who is willing or able to appear in court, the court will appoint a guardian ad litem to fill that role.

Jury

Serious youth offenders have the right to a jury trial. Juvenile delinquency statutes afford no such right; a judge alone hears delinquency cases.

Criminal Code and Rules

Defendants in youthful offender proceedings face possible loss of liberty and criminal conviction. The court, therefore, is bound to adhere to the applicable criminal code, the Rules of Evidence, and Rules of Criminal Procedure, just as in a criminal trial.

Mental Competency Procedures

Juveniles have the right to raise mental competency issues. They can assert their incompetence to stand trial, as well as their incompetence to have formed the requisite *mens rea,* or malicious intent, to commit criminal offenses.

mens rea

Criminal or malicious intent to commit a crime

CASE PROBLEM

Police took Kent, who was 16 years old, into custody in connection with charges of housebreaking, robbery, and rape. As a juvenile, Kent was subject to the exclusive jurisdiction of the District of Columbia Juvenile Court unless that court after "full investigation" should waive jurisdiction over him and remit him for trial to the United States District Court.

Kent moved that the juvenile court should give him access to the social service file relating to the petitioner that the staff of the juvenile court had accumulated during his probation period. This file would be available to the juvenile court judge in considering whether it should retain or waive jurisdiction, and Kent's counsel represented that access to this file was essential to his ability to provide Kent with effective assistance of counsel.

The juvenile court judge did not rule on these motions. He held no hearing. He did not confer with Kent, his parents, or his counsel. He entered an order reciting that after "full investigation, I do hereby waive" jurisdiction of petitioner and directing that he be "held for trial for [the alleged] offenses under the regular procedure of the U.S. District Court." He made no findings. He did not recite any reason for the waiver. He made no reference to the motions filed by Kent's counsel. He denied without comment the motions for a hearing, the recommendation for hospitalization for psychiatric observation, the request for access to the social service file, and the offer to prove that Kent was a fit subject for rehabilitation under the juvenile court's jurisdiction.

The state indicted Kent in the adult criminal court. He moved to dismiss the indictment on the ground that the juvenile court's waiver was invalid. The adult court overruled the motion and tried Kent. A jury convicted him on six counts of housebreaking and robbery but acquitted him on two rape counts.

Kent appealed, challenging the validity of the juvenile court's waiver of jurisdiction; the United States Court of Appeals for the District of Columbia Circuit affirmed, finding the procedure leading to waiver and the waiver order itself valid. Was the juvenile court's order valid?

ROLE-PLAY PROBLEM

Jane and Mickey were lifelong best friends. Jane was pretty, smart, athletic, graceful, and popular, and came from a loving and stable family. Mickey had some problems. She was overweight and ungainly. She struggled at school. Her parents divorced after a long, ugly, and very public proceeding, in which Mickey's mother alleged that her husband had molested Mickey.

Mickey frequently asked her mother for counseling during the divorce, but her mother said it was too expensive. Mickey asked her teacher, then her guidance counselor, then the vice principal for help. None of them provided it. Mickey's pastor expressed a slight interest in helping her, but after two counseling sessions, he became too busy with a church renovation to see Mickey.

In spite of their differences, Jane was a loving and faithful friend to Mickey, and Mickey, with all her problems, was a faithful friend to Jane.

One night the two girls went to a football game together. Jane met up with a group of her friends and brought Mickey along. Some of the boys in the group began to make fun of Mickey, calling her fat and alluding to the molestation issues in her family. Jane stood quietly by, neither joining in the mockery nor defending Mickey. Mickey, in tears, fled the stadium.

Jane followed her. Nobody saw either of them again that night. Neither girl went home that night. The next morning Mickey showed up at home. She told her parents that a man had abducted her and Jane, and after keeping them tied up all night, had killed Jane. It did not take long for the police to debunk her story. Mickey soon admitted that she had killed Jane in a furious, jealous frenzy. Mickey directed the police to Jane's body. She appeared to have been the victim of a brutal attack.

You are representing Mickey in a state with discretionary transfer laws.

1. What argument will you make to prevent the juvenile court judge from transferring Mickey to the adult court?

2. What facts will you rely upon?

3. Whom will you interview and what documents will you review?

4. What other facts would you like to have?

5. Whom will you call as witnesses?

You are the prosecutor:

6. What will you argue to the court in favor of transferring Mickey to the adult court?

7. What facts will you emphasize?

8. Whom will you interview and what documents will you review?

9. What other facts would you like to have?

10. Whom will you call as witnesses?

You are Mickey's court-appointed guardian ad litem:

11. What facts do you consider most significant?

12. What will you recommend to the court?

HYPOTHETICAL PROBLEM

Eduardo is 16 years old. He has two children, ages one and three. He has been living with the mother of his children—not his wife—for the past four years. He is devoted to his children and their mother. His own mother is 29 years old and his grandmother is 46.

Eduardo has an extensive criminal record, having spent many months in juvenile detention facilities. None of his offenses have involved violence. He is a member of a street gang that engages in drug dealing.

The police have taken Eduardo into custody for selling heroin.

Eduardo shows tremendous emotion at his arraignment. Through his tears, he tells the arraigning judge of the serious abuse he suffered at the hands of his young mother, who had suffered, in turn, from abuse and neglect at the hands of her own mother. He tells, too, of the repeated physical, emotional, and sexual abuse he suffered at the hands of his mother's succession of boyfriends and dates.

Crime, promiscuity, neglect, and abuse are all Eduardo has ever known. Eduardo tells the judge of his failed attempts to stay in school, something he found impossible despite his desire to do so.

He begs the arraigning judge not to transfer him to adult court. He knows a jury will convict him and a judge will sentence him to prison, and he is probably right. He correctly asserts that no one has ever tried to help him. He feels if he was just given a chance to rehabilitate himself, he might be able to do it.

What should the judge do in this situation?

ETHICAL CONCERNS

The tension between the desire to rehabilitate delinquent juveniles and the desire to punish them is never so fierce as in cases where the state is attempting to try juveniles as adults. Often the underlying crime is heinous and society wants revenge. Transferring juveniles to adult court seems justified when they are older or have extensive criminal records.

It is difficult in serious or high profile cases for courts to adhere to the laws that juveniles can be bound over to adult court only in cases where they are not amenable to rehabilitation within the juvenile system. The tendency is to inflict severe punishment for a heinous crime, but most laws direct courts to make the bind-over decision based not upon the seriousness of the crime alone, but also upon the juvenile's amenability to rehabilitation.

What does a conscientious juvenile court judge do when faced with a young and vulnerable juvenile who has committed a grievous offense? Judges all over the country are facing such decisions more and more often as the scale of juvenile crime escalates, and society's thirst for revenge escalates accordingly.

DISCUSSION QUESTIONS

Some people involved in the juvenile justice system argue that transfer to an adult court for prosecution can actually work to the advantage of the juvenile because juvenile court proceedings are by definition less formal than adult criminal proceedings. The juvenile courts adhere much less stringently to standards of due process, procedural regularity, evidentiary restrictions, and other formalities than do the adult courts.

Therefore, the argument goes, juveniles stand a better chance for fair hearings in adult court. They have access to bail, juries, and live court reporters record the proceedings.

Further, a criminal act that might loom large in a juvenile court may seem less significant in an adult court. Assault, possession of drugs, receiving stolen property—all of these offenses garner little notice in an adult court and are usually plea-bargained away with probation as the penalty. A juvenile court judge would give such charges much more attention and would be more likely to impose a sentence involving incarceration for the juvenile.

Finally, the adult courts tend to take a more restrictive view of accomplices and accessories than do the juvenile courts. Courts can adjudicate juveniles delinquent under most juvenile statutes if a they were present during the commission of a delinquent act, even if they did not participate, or offer encouragement or aid. The adult criminal statutes require a much greater level of participation in order to find a defendant guilty of a crime.

The downside of this argument for transfer to adult court is that juveniles who are convicted in adult court have adult criminal records. Adult records are easier for employers and licensing agencies to access than juvenile records. They are also more explicit and more difficult to expunge. If the juvenile receives a sentence with that includes confinement, he will serve that confinement in an adult prison, fully integrated with the adult population.

Those who argue that the transfer of a juvenile to adult court is never a good thing point out that the adult criminal court as an institution is ineffective even at what it was designed to do—deal with adult criminal defendants. To extend the reach of an ineffective institution to encompass even more people, especially people who may require special treatment, is illogical and only compounds the ineffectiveness.

Further, they argue that a criminal conviction results in the child acquiring a serious stigma at an early age. This stigma works to prevent the child from becoming a productive citizen, thus depriving him of the opportunity to have a meaningful life and depriving society of that potential citizen's contributions.

Opponents of liberal transfer also argue that the potential penalty of committing a child to adult prison is so great that it is not worth the benefits. Even adult inmates are prey to a toughened, veteran prison population. A child in that environment is in extreme danger.

Proponents, however, argue that juvenile crime has grown worse in the years since the creation of the juvenile court in 1899, when children ended up in juvenile court for stealing apples. Juveniles today are going to court for gun violence, drug dealing, rape, and murder. Different times call for different measures.

Proponents also point to the failure of the juvenile court to adequately deal with the rising tide of juvenile crime and argue that it is time to take the worst offenders out of an ineffective environment. They decry the overreliance on victimhood as justification for the worst acts and assert that society owes its citizens only so much. If they continually fail to avail themselves of the opportunities that exist, it is their problem, not society's.

1. With which set of arguments do you agree? Can you think of others that make sense?

2. Should a juvenile offender receive special treatment? If you believe he should not, would you advocate going even further and abolishing the juvenile court altogether as a forum for juvenile delinquency in favor of sending all juvenile offenders to criminal court?

3. Should the criminal court be eliminated as an option for juveniles? Should all juveniles appear only in juvenile court?

After considering the above questions, read the case below. After reading the case, discuss whether doing so has changed your thoughts about the questions above.

The Lionel Tate Case

Twelve-year-old, 166-pound Lionel Tate beat six-year-old, 46-pound Tiffany to death. Tiffany was lifeless and there was vomit on her clothes when the paramedics arrived. Her skull was fractured, several ribs were broken, and her liver was torn. Evidence showed that Lionel, in addition to beating her with his fists and kicking her, had swung her into a metal spiral staircase and jumped into the air and landed on her stomach several times. Photographs showed more than 30 separate injuries to her body.

While this was going on, Lionel's mother slept upstairs.

Police took Lionel into custody and filed a delinquency petition against him in juvenile court. Juvenile prosecutors offered him a plea deal that would have given him three years in a juvenile detention center followed by 10 years of probation and counseling. He refused the offer.

The juvenile court judge transferred Lionel to adult court. The prosecutor charged him with felony murder with an underlying charge of aggravated child abuse. His defense was that the killing was accidental. He claimed he was only playing with Tiffany and imitating moves he had seen on big-time wrestling. Circuit Judge Joel T. Lazarus rejected Lionel's attorneys' request to subpoena pro wrestler Dwayne "The Rock" Johnson.

The penalty for felony murder with an underlying charge of aggravated child abuse is life in prison without parole under Florida law. The judge could have departed from sentencing guidelines if he decided the facts of the case did not sustain the verdict, but he chose not to do so.

The judge stated, "The jury has spoken loudly and unanimously and I am convinced they were correct." He said it was beyond question that Lionel knew what he was doing on the day Tiffany died. "The evidence of guilt was overwhelming. Lionel Tate's guilt is clear, obvious and undisputed."

The judge said his court had no jurisdiction to rule on the defense's contentions that a Florida law mandating that Lionel be tried as an adult—and sentenced to life in prison on conviction—was wrong. "These are legislative decisions that should be addressed with the legislature, and not judicial decisions," the judge said. The judge also rejected arguments that the sentence constituted cruel and unusual punishment.

As the judge listened to friends, teachers, relatives and clergymen make emotional pleas for leniency he said he was moved by the outpouring of concern for the boy, but fretted over the lack of concern for the girl he killed.

Lionel began serving his sentence in a maximum-security juvenile facility. He was to move to a maximum-security adult facility where he would spend the rest of his life, with no chance for parole when he turned 18.

The appellate court overturned Lionel's conviction in December 2003 because the lower court had not evaluated his mental competency before the trial. Lionel, 16 years old at the time, then struck a plea-bargain that would allow his immediate release. The court sentenced Lionel to the three years in prison he had already served and one year of house arrest followed by 10 years of probation. On January 26, 2004, Lionel left prison.

1. Do you believe the court was right to transfer Lionel to adult court? What factors weighed in favor of transfer? What factors weighed against transfer?

2. Do you believe the original sentence was a fair and just sentence? What factors cause you to believe that it was or was not?

3. Would it make any difference to your thinking if Lionel were 8, 10, 14, or 16 years old instead of 12?

4. Do you agree with the judge that the decisions he declined to make were legislative and not judicial decisions?

5. Do you think Lionel's mother, who was supposed to be baby-sitting Tiffany, was in any way responsible?

6. Was the appellate court's decision to throw out Lionel's conviction because he had not received a mental evaluation a good decision?

[*Author's Note:* In September 2004, Fort Lauderdale, Florida, police arrested Lionel Tate on charges of violating his probation when they found him carrying a knife. In May 2005, Tate was arrested again for robbing a pizza delivery man in Pembroke Park, Florida. In March 2006, Judge Lazarus, saying the 19-year-old Tate had "run out of chances," sentenced him to 30 years in prison.]

KEY TERMS

amenability phase	*mens rea*
bill of Particulars	penal
burden of persuasion	probable cause hearing
concurrent jurisdiction	prosecutorial discretion
discretionary transfer	social service record
exclusion	standard of proof
judicial waiver	subpoena
mandatory transfer	

END NOTES

[i] The following states have changed their laws to make the transfer of juveniles to adult court easier: Alabama, Alaska, Arizona, Arkansas, California, Colorado, Connecticut, District of Columbia, Florida, Georgia, Hawaii, Idaho, Illinois, Indiana, Iowa, Kansas, Kentucky, Louisiana, Maryland, Massachusetts, Minnesota, Mississippi, Missouri, Montana, Nevada, New Hampshire, New Mexico, North Carolina, North Dakota, Ohio, Oklahoma, Oregon, Pennsylvania, Rhode Island, South Carolina, South Dakota, Tennessee, Texas, Utah, Virginia, Washington, West Virginia, Wisconsin, and Wyoming.

The following states have not changed their transfer laws: Maine, Michigan, Nebraska, New Jersey, New York, and Vermont.

[ii] Alabama, Arkansas, Florida, Hawaii, Idaho, Iowa, Maryland, Michigan, Mississippi, Missouri, Montana, Oklahoma, Oregon, South Dakota, Tennessee, Texas, Vermont, Washington, Wisconsin, and Wyoming have discretionary waiver; Alaska, Arizona, California, Colorado, Delaware, District of Columbia, Georgia, Illinois, Indiana, Kansas, Kentucky, Louisiana, Maine, Minnesota, Nevada, New Jersey, New Hampshire, North Carolina, North Dakota, Ohio, Pennsylvania, Rhode Island, South Carolina, Utah, Virginia, and West Virginia have a combination of presumptive, discretionary, and mandatory waiver.

SECTION III

Child Maltreatment

Chapter 9

CHILD ABUSE AND NEGLECT

OBJECTIVES

By the end of this chapter, the student should know:

- The legal definitions of child abuse, sexual abuse, psychological abuse, neglect, and dependency
- The outlines of the Child Abuse Prevention and Treatment Act
- How states define child abuse and address identification the perpetrator of the abuse
- How to recognize child abuse and neglect
- The risk factors, warning signs, and symptoms of physical abuse, sexual abuse, and neglect
- The law regarding reporting of known or suspected child abuse and neglect
- How to report known or suspected child abuse and neglect
- How to investigate a child abuse case
- How to distinguish between child abuse and neglect
- The parameters of educational neglect and the legal status of home schooling
- The parameters of medical neglect and the application of the First Amendment freedom of religion

INTRODUCTION

Child abuse occurs when adults, often the children's parents, maltreat children to such an extent that the courts must intervene to protect them. Criminal prosecutions of the abusers often, but do not always, accompany child abuse proceedings in the juvenile courts.

Child neglect is the failure to provide children with necessities such as shelter, food, medical attention, and access to education. States sometimes, but not always, bring criminal charges against parents who neglect their children.

133

The child who drew this picture was in counseling due to a history of extreme domestic violence between her biological parents.

It is difficult to define child abuse and neglect. Parents are allowed to discipline their children physically. It is not a simple matter to determine exactly when physical punishment crosses from reasonable parental discipline into the realm of abuse. Standards of acceptability have changed over time, and what is acceptable varies among cultures and families.

Reasonable parents and professionals can differ as to what is a necessary and what is a luxury. Poverty can limit the quality of housing, food, and security parents can provide their children, even when parents are loving and devoted to their children's well-being. Reasonable parents and professionals can differ as to what constitutes legitimate religious practice and what is the neglectful or abusive withholding of education or medical care. Courts will honor religious practices that affect children to an extent.

LEGAL DEFINITIONS

The term child abuse encompasses **physical abuse; sexual abuse; emotional, mental, or psychological abuse;** and **neglect.** Physical abuse means causing physical pain or harm to a child to a degree that exceeds the normal bounds of reasonable discipline. Sexual abuse means causing a child to submit to, view, or display sexual behavior. Emotional, mental, or psychological abuse means subjecting a child to excessive verbal discipline or humiliation. Neglect means failing to provide reasonable necessaries to a child who is not in a position to obtain those necessaries without adult assistance.

Children may also come under the court's jurisdiction if the court adjudges them to be dependent. **Dependent children** are those children whose parents,

physical abuse
Hitting, shaking, burning, cutting, throwing, or otherwise purposely inflicting pain or injury upon a child

sexual abuse
Causing a child to perform, view, or submit to a sexual act

emotional, mental, or psychological abuse
Berating, humiliating, denigrating, or otherwise purposely inflicting psychological pain upon a child

neglect
Failing to provide necessary care in the form of supervision, clothing, food, shelter, medical care, education, or guidance

through no fault of their own, cannot care for them, as when parents are too mentally or physically ill to care for their children.

State statutes regarding child abuse, sexual abuse, and neglect vary among the states because they are all based upon the Child Abuse Prevention and Treatment Act, 42 U.S.C. 5101, et seq. (CAPTA). This federal law mandates that states have certain "minimum definitions" for child abuse, sexual abuse, and neglect in order to receive federal funds. Most states' definitions, therefore, are essentially the same as those prescribed by CAPTA.

CAPTA defines child abuse or neglect as any act or failure to act:

- Resulting in imminent risk of serious physical or emotional harm, death, sexual abuse, or exploitation
- Of a child under a certain age
- By a parent or caretaker who is responsible for the child's welfare

CAPTA defines sexual abuse as:

- Employment, use, persuasion, inducement, enticement, or coercion of any child to engage in, or assist any other person to engage in, any sexually explicit conduct or any simulation of such conduct for the purpose of producing any visual depiction of such conduct; or
- Rape, and in cases of caretaker or inter-familial relationships, statutory rape, molestation, prostitution, or other form of sexual exploitation of children, or incest with children.

Abusive or neglectful behavior is defined in terms of how the behavior affects the child in most states. It does not necessarily constitute child abuse if a parent is addicted to drugs. But if the parent is addicted to drugs and leaves a toddler home alone while the parent goes out and uses drugs, that constitutes child abuse.

Some statutes require that a parent, guardian, custodian, or other household member be the perpetrator of the child abuse. The Maryland statute is an example of these.

dependent children

Children over whom the court assumes jurisdiction because they are in need of care through no fault of their parents

MD. FAMILY § 5-701.1 DEFINITIONS

(a) Except as otherwise provided in § 5-705.1 of this subtitle, in this subtitle the following words have the meanings indicated.

   (b) "Abuse" means:

(1) The physical or mental injury of a child by any parent or other person who has permanent or temporary care or custody or responsibility for supervision of a child, or by any household or family member, under

(continues)

circumstances that indicate that the child's health or welfare is harmed or at substantial risk of being harmed; or

(2) Sexual abuse of a child, whether physical injuries are sustained or not.

(q) "Mental injury" means the observable, identifiable, and substantial impairment of a child's mental or psychological ability to function.

(r) "Neglect" means the leaving of a child unattended or other failure to give proper care and attention to a child by any parent or other person who has permanent or temporary care or custody or responsibility for supervision of the child under circumstances that indicate:

(1) That the child's health or welfare is harmed or placed at substantial risk of harm; or

(2) Mental injury to the child or a substantial risk of mental injury.

(w)(1) "Sexual abuse" means any act that involves sexual molestation or exploitation of a child by a parent or other person who has permanent or temporary care or custody or responsibility for supervision of a child, or by any household or family member.

(2) "Sexual abuse" includes:

(i) Incest, rape, or sexual offense in any degree;

(ii) Sodomy; and

(iii) Unnatural or perverted sexual practices.

Other statutes define abuse in terms of what the child has experienced, rather than in terms of who perpetrated the abuse. Ohio's statute is one of these.

OH ST § 2151.031 "ABUSED CHILD" DEFINED

As used in this chapter, an "abused child" includes any child who:

(A) Is the victim of "sexual activity" as defined under Chapter 2907 of the Revised Code, where such activity would constitute an offense under that chapter, except that the court need not find that any person has been convicted of the offense in order to find that the child is an abused child;

(B) Is endangered as defined in section 2919.22 of the Revised Code, except that the court need not find that any person has been convicted under that section in order to find that the child is an abused child;

(C) Exhibits evidence of any physical or mental injury or death, inflicted other than by accidental means, or an injury or death which is at variance with the history given of it. Except as provided in division (D) of this section, a child

(continues)

exhibiting evidence of corporal punishment or other physical disciplinary measure by a parent, guardian, custodian, person having custody or control, or person in loco parentis of a child is not an abused child under this division if the measure is not prohibited under section 2919.22 of the Revised Code.

(D) Because of the acts of his parents, guardian, or custodian, suffers physical or mental injury that harms or threatens to harm the child's health or welfare.

(E) Is subjected to out-of-home care child abuse.

Statutes such as Ohio's allow the juvenile court to assume jurisdiction over children who have experienced abuse or neglect even where the court cannot identify who inflicted the abuse.

The definition of child abuse or neglect also encompasses those situations where a child is living in a home where another household member has been a victim of abuse or neglect. The West Virginia statute is an example of such a statute.

WV ST § 49-1-3 DEFINITIONS RELATING TO ABUSE AND NEGLECT

(a) "Abused child" means a child whose health or welfare is harmed or threatened by:

(1) A parent, guardian or custodian who knowingly or intentionally inflicts, attempts to inflict or knowingly allows another person to inflict, physical injury or mental or emotional injury, upon the child or another child in the home;

SIDEBAR

CHILD MALTREATMENT 2000 REPORT

The United States Department of Health and Human Services compiles statistics about child maltreatment every year and releases that information in a report. The latest available report, Child Maltreatment 2000, reveals that in 2000:

- An estimated 879,000 children were victims of abuse and neglect.

- 12.2 children for every 1,000 children in the population were victims of abuse or neglect.[i]

(continues)

- 62.8 percent of victims suffered neglect (including medical neglect); 19.3 percent were physically abused; 10.1 percent were sexually abused; and 7.7 percent were emotionally or psychologically maltreated.
- Neglect, which had the highest reported incidence, had a rate of 7.3 victims per 1,000 children.
- Psychological maltreatment had a rate of 1.0 victim per 1,000 children.
- 48.1 percent of victims were male, and 51.9 percent of the victims were female. The male victimization rate was 11.2 male children per 1,000 in the population compared to a rate of 12.8 female children per 1,000 in the population.
- Children in the age group of birth to three years had the highest victimization rate.

RECOGNIZING CHILD ABUSE AND NEGLECT

Prevent Child Abuse America, a charitable organization dedicated to the prevention of child abuse, lists the following risk factors and warning signs of child abuse:

The National Clearinghouse on Child Abuse and Neglect Information compiled the following list of ways to recognize child abuse by adapting the report *Recognizing Child Abuse: What Parents Should Know,* by Prevent Child Abuse America, © 2003.

The following signs may signal the presence of child abuse or neglect.
The Child:

- shows sudden changes in behavior or school performance.
- has not received help for physical or medical problems brought to the parents' attention.
- has learning problems (or difficulty concentrating) that cannot be attributed to specific physical or psychological causes.
- is always watchful, as though preparing for something bad to happen.
- lacks adult supervision.
- is overly compliant, passive, or withdrawn.
- comes to school or other activities early, stays late, and does not want to go home.
- displays nervousness around adults.
- displays aggression toward adults or other children.
- exhibits low self-esteem.
- has poor hygiene.

The Parent:

- shows little concern for the child.
- denies the existence of—or blames the child for—the child's problems in school or at home.
- asks teachers or other caretakers to use harsh physical discipline if the child misbehaves.
- sees the child as entirely bad, worthless, or burdensome.
- demands a level of physical or academic performance the child cannot achieve.
- looks primarily to the child for care, attention, and satisfaction of emotional needs.

The Parent and Child:

- rarely touch or look at each other.
- consider their relationship entirely negative.
- state that they do not like each other.

Signs of Physical Abuse

Consider the possibility of physical abuse when the **child:**

- has unexplained burns, bites, bruises, broken bones, or black eyes.
- has fading bruises or other marks noticeable after an absence from school.
- seems frightened of the parents and protests or cries when it is time to go home.
- shrinks at the approach of adults.
- reports injury by a parent or another adult caregiver.

Consider the possibility of physical abuse when the **parent or other adult caregiver:**

- offers conflicting, unconvincing, or no explanation for the child's injury.
- describes the child as "evil," or in some other very negative way.
- uses harsh physical discipline with the child.
- has a history of abuse as a child.

Signs of Neglect

Consider the possibility of neglect when the **child:**

- is frequently absent from school.
- begs or steals food or money.
- lacks needed medical or dental care, immunizations, or glasses.
- is consistently dirty and has severe body odor.

- lacks sufficient clothing for the weather.
- abuses alcohol or other drugs.
- states that there is no one at home to provide care.

Consider the possibility of neglect when the **parent or other adult caregiver:**
- appears to be indifferent to the child.
- seems apathetic or depressed.
- behaves irrationally or in a bizarre manner.
- is abusing alcohol or other drugs.

Signs of Sexual Abuse

Consider the possibility of sexual abuse when the **child:**
- has difficulty walking or sitting.
- suddenly refuses to change for gym or to participate in physical activities.
- reports nightmares or bedwetting.
- experiences a sudden change in appetite.
- demonstrates bizarre, sophisticated, or unusual sexual knowledge or behavior.
- becomes pregnant or contracts a venereal disease, particularly if under age 14.
- displays an unusual interest in or avoidance of all things of a sexual nature.
- exhibits depression or withdrawal from friends or family.
- make statements that their bodies are dirty or damaged, or fear that there is something wrong with them in the genital area.
- refuse to go to school.
- have conduct problems.
- exhibit secretiveness.
- include aspects of sexual molestation in drawings, games, fantasies.
- exhibits unusual aggressiveness, or suicidal behavior.
- reports sexual abuse by a parent or another adult caregiver.

Consider the possibility of sexual abuse when the **parent or other adult caregiver:**
- is unduly protective of the child or severely limits the child's contact with other children, especially of the opposite sex.
- is secretive and isolated.
- is jealous or controlling with family members.

Signs of Emotional Maltreatment

Consider the possibility of emotional maltreatment when the **child:**
- shows extremes in behavior, such as overly compliant or demanding behavior, extreme passivity, or aggression.

- is either inappropriately adult (parenting other children, for example) or inappropriately infantile (frequently rocking or head-banging, for example).
- is delayed in physical or emotional development.
- has attempted suicide.
- reports a lack of attachment to the parent.

Consider the possibility of emotional maltreatment when the **parent or other adult caregiver:**
- constantly blames, belittles, or berates the child.
- is unconcerned about the child and refuses to consider offers of help for the child's problems.
- overtly rejects the child.

Risk Factors

The National Clearinghouse on Child Abuse and Neglect Information has determined that while child abuse and neglect occur in every segment of society, the risks are greater in families where parents
- Seem to be having economic, housing, or personal problems
- Are isolated from their family or community
- Have difficulty controlling anger or stress
- Are dealing with physical or mental health issues
- Abuse alcohol or drugs
- Appear uninterested in the care, nourishment or safety of their children

The art therapist told this child, a victim of sexual abuse, to draw himself as a boat. He said his drawing was of the *Titanic*. It had hit an iceberg and was sinking.

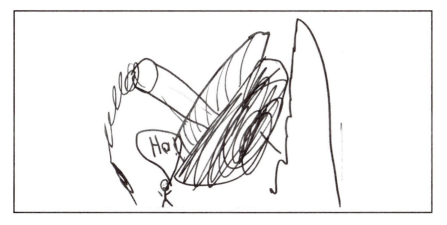

REPORTING CHILD ABUSE AND NEGLECT

If you suspect that a child is the victim of abuse or neglect you must report it to the local police department or child protection services agency. The Child Abuse Prevention and Treatment Act (CAPTA) mandates that all 50 states require certain people to report suspected child abuse. Legal professionals, including paralegals, are included in that group. To neglect to do so is a crime.

CAPTA also requires all states to enact legislation providing immunity from prosecutions for people who report suspected child abuse. Reporters enjoy absolute civil and criminal immunity when they act in good faith.

The Nevada statute is a typical reporting statute:

NEVADA REVISED STATUTES—PROTECTION OF CHILDREN FROM ABUSE AND NEGLECT

NRS 432B.220. Persons required to make report; when and to whom reports are required; any person may make report; report and written findings if reasonable cause to believe death of child caused by abuse or neglect.

1. Any person who is described in subsection 3 and who, in his professional or occupational capacity, knows or has reasonable cause to believe that a child has been abused or neglected shall:
   (a) Except as otherwise provided in subsection 2, report the abuse or neglect of the child to an agency which provides child welfare services or to a law enforcement agency; and
   (b) Make such a report as soon as reasonably practicable but not later than 24 hours after the person knows or has reasonable cause to believe that the child has been abused or neglected.

2. If a person who is required to make a report pursuant to subsection 1 knows or has reasonable cause to believe that the abuse or neglect of the child involves an act or omission of:
   (a) A person directly responsible or serving as a volunteer for or an employee of a public or private home, institution or facility where the child is receiving child care outside of his home for a portion of the day, the person shall make the report to a law enforcement agency.
   (b) An agency which provides child welfare services or a law enforcement agency, the person shall make the report to an agency other than the one alleged to have committed the act or omission, and the investigation of the abuse or neglect of the child must be made by an agency other than the one alleged to have committed the act or omission.

3. A report must be made pursuant to subsection 1 by the following persons:
   (a) A physician, dentist, dental hygienist, chiropractor, optometrist, podiatric physician, medical examiner, resident, intern, professional

(continues)

or practical nurse, physician assistant, psychiatrist, psychologist, marriage and family therapist, alcohol or drug abuse counselor, advanced emergency medical technician or other person providing medical services licensed or certified in this state;

(b) Any personnel of a hospital or similar institution engaged in the admission, examination, care or treatment of persons or an administrator, manager or other person in charge of a hospital or similar institution upon notification of suspected abuse or neglect of a child by a member of the staff of the hospital;

(c) A coroner;

(d) A clergyman, practitioner of Christian Science or religious healer, unless he has acquired the knowledge of the abuse or neglect from the offender during a confession;

(e) A social worker and an administrator, teacher, librarian or counselor of a school;

(f) Any person who maintains or is employed by a facility or establishment that provides care for children, children's camp or other public or private facility, institution or agency furnishing care to a child;

(g) Any person licensed to conduct a foster home;

(h) Any officer or employee of a law enforcement agency or an adult or juvenile probation officer;

(i) An attorney, unless he has acquired the knowledge of the abuse or neglect from a client who is or may be accused of the abuse or neglect;

(j) Any person who maintains, is employed by or serves as a volunteer for an agency or service which advises persons regarding abuse or neglect of a child and refers them to persons and agencies where their requests and needs can be met; and

(k) Any person who is employed by or serves as a volunteer for an approved youth shelter. As used in this paragraph, "approved youth shelter" has the meaning ascribed to it in NRS 244.422

4. A report may be made by any other person.

SIDEBAR

INVESTIGATING A CHILD ABUSE CASE

When working on a child abuse case, get as much background information as possible before you interview the parents, the child, witnesses, caregivers, or others. The best place to obtain background information is from the police reports, the social services files, and court records.

(continues)

EXHIBIT 9-1 Release and Authorization Form

This will authorize you to release any and all information that you, your agents, or employees possess concerning [Client's Name] to my attorney, [Attorney's Name], her agents, or employees.

You are directed to accept a photocopy or facsimile of this Release and Authorization as though it were an original.

This Release and Authorization is to remain in effect until [a date six months from the date of signing].

[Signature of Juvenile's Parent or Guardian]   [Date]

It is imperative that, if you are not an attorney, you get permission from your attorney before making any contact with parties, witnesses, or workers on a case. It is also imperative that you conduct your investigation under the close supervision of your attorney.

You will need a release to obtain medical records, school records, or other information. Below is an example of a simple, legally binding release. Many institutions, however, will not accept any releases but their own, so check with the institution first to see if that is the case.

Exhibit 9-1 is a sample release and authorization form.

INTERVIEWING CAREGIVERS

Caregivers include relatives, noncustodial parents, friends who are caring for the child, or foster parents. For the most part these people will readily offer valuable assistance. Always contact the caregiver immediately upon becoming involved with a case.

Visit the child at the caregiver's home, if possible. It is particularly useful to compare the child's interaction with the caregiver to his interaction with his parent.

INTERVIEWING THE CHILD

Interview children carefully. Children in abuse cases may not be reliable witnesses for the following reasons, among others:

- The abuser may have warned them not to tell, and accompanied the warning with threats
- They may believe that if they tell what happened, they will pay for it later
- They may be afraid that if they report the abuse, they will be removed from their family and taken to a place that is much worse
- They may have experienced abuse all of their lives and do not realize it is abuse
- They may feel they deserve the abuse because they are bad
- They may have convinced themselves that the abuse is not so bad, and will get better

(continues)

When you interview a child, the tone and content of the interview will depend upon the child's age. Children have varying levels of comprehension and ease of expression. They may not understand your questions or have the words to express what they experienced. With very young children, your meeting may consist of merely looking at the child to assess his general physical condition.

Do not attempt to interview a child too deeply or broach the subject of abuse unless you have received training. If the child shows signs of distress, you should cut off the interview, but not without reassurance to the child and an immediate report to the caregiver. Especially do not discuss sexual abuse with a child unless you have received specialized training in that area.

INTERVIEWING SIBLINGS

In addition to interviewing the child who is the subject of the investigation, you may also interview the child's siblings. Siblings can corroborate or refute allegations of abuse.

OBTAINING RECORDS AND INFORMATION

You must have a signed release when seeking confidential records, such as school records or medical records. The child's legal guardian must sign the release. Remember that the child's legal guardian is often not the parent. Check with the institution to see whether it will accept your release or whether it has its own. (See Exhibit 9-1 for Authorization and Release.) Social workers, foster parents, relatives, and family friends can talk to you without a release.

OTHER METHODS OF GATHERING INFORMATION

Exercise great care and discretion when interviewing people outside the immediate family. Be sure to obtain the permission of your attorney before approaching outsiders.

The foster parent is the first person you should speak to if the child is in a foster home. Ask about the child's behavior immediately before and immediately after a parental visit in addition to the usual line of questions. This can be an important piece of information.

Interview the physician or other medical personnel who have treated or witnessed the child's injuries in a physical or sexual abuse case. Many states' laws allow or require those treating injuries that are the result of suspected abuse to photograph and X-ray those injuries without first obtaining the permission of the child's parent or guardian, as in the following Nevada statute.

NEVADA REVISED STATUTES—REPORTS OF ABUSE OR NEGLECT

NRS 432B.270 Interview of child; photographs, X-rays and medical tests.

1. A designee of an agency investigating a report of abuse or neglect of a child may, without the consent of and outside the presence of any person responsible for the child's welfare, interview a child concerning any possible abuse or neglect. The child may be interviewed at any place where he is found. The designee shall, immediately after the conclusion of the interview, if reasonably possible, notify a person responsible for the child's welfare that the child was interviewed, unless the designee determines that such notification would endanger the child.

2. A designee of an agency investigating a report of abuse or neglect of a child may, without the consent of the person responsible for a child's welfare:

(a) Take or cause to be taken photographs of the child's body, including the areas of trauma; and

(b) If indicated after consultation with a physician, cause X-rays or medical tests to be performed on a child.

Examine all photographs as well as emergency room reports, treating physician's reports, and nursing reports. Interview the social worker who initially removed the child from the home or who made the initial investigation.

intake worker

A social worker who initiates a child abuse case, taking physical custody of the child if necessary, starting a file for the child, and initiating legal proceedings

There are often several workers involved in a case. The **intake worker** is usually the first agency contact with the family. The intake worker is the county social services worker who will receive the initial report and conduct the initial investigation.

An *ongoing worker* takes over for the intake worker and acts as the continuing contact with the family, checking on the family's and the child's progress. The ongoing worker formulates the *case plan* and monitors the family's progress in completing the case plan. The case plan is the series of goals and processes that the family must attain and complete in order to end the state's and the court's jurisdiction over the child. (*See* Chapter 10, Abuse-Neglect-Dependency Hearings.)

social services agency

A county organization charged with overseeing issues involving the health and welfare of its constituents

The family will have a history with the **social services agency** in many cases. Ask the current worker if other workers have been involved in the case. Ask to see the entire case file, not just the current working file, which may be a condensed version of the full record.

Speak to any professionals who are providing counseling or therapy. You will need a release. (*See* Appendix for a sample release.)

Interview the police if the police were involved, and ask to see the police report.

Teachers can tell you whether the child has appeared at school with suspicious bruises or injuries, and how the child behaves and whether the child's grades or behavior have changed. Examine all grade reports, standardized test scores, attendance records, and disciplinary records.

When interviewing witnesses, do not suggest answers or disclose confidential information. Keep questions neutral and open-ended.

(continues)

REPORTING TO AN ATTORNEY

The result of your investigation will be a written report to an attorney. Outline the steps of your investigation and summarize each step. List all the people you interviewed, where you interviewed them, and the date, time, and duration of each interview.

Write a complete, fair, and accurate summary of your interview with each person. Include your observations and any significant statements that person made. If you visited a home, describe the home. Describe the interviewee's appearance and demeanor, and include any other details you find significant, including the efforts the person made to make himself available to you, and whether the person was regular and punctual in meeting appointments.

Most jurisdictions require a written report from the guardian ad litem if there is a possibility that parental rights may be permanently terminated. The GAL files the report with the court, and it part of the case record. Your report to the attorney will form the basis of that written report.

SEXUAL ABUSE

Medical professionals and the legal system define sexual abuse in virtually identical ways. Both define it as physical contact of a sexual nature or exploitation of a child for sexual purposes. Both require that the participants be asymmetrically

The child who drew this was a victim of sexual abuse from the ages of three to six. The perpetrator was his mother's live-in boyfriend, who watched him and his brother while his Mom worked evenings. The art therapist asked him to draw what he would like to do to the perpetrator.

related, that is, one of the participants has physical, emotional, or situational power over the other.

The sexual abuser can be a person from within the child's family, such as a parent, sibling, stepparent, grandparent, or cousin, or from without the family, such as a teacher, childcare provider, or neighbor. It is both legally and medically possible for a child to sexually abuse another child if there is sufficient disparity in their ages or in their physical or mental capacity.

There is little difference between sexual abuse and other forms of abuse in the context of the adjudicatory hearing. All require the state to prove that the child suffered abuse. Some states require the prosecuting agency to prove who perpetrated the abuse; others do not.

There is greater difference, however, in the dispositional phase of hearings involving sexual abuse and other kinds of abuse. The court will avail itself of a greater array of treatment, counseling, and other therapeutic options for the child victim in sexual abuse cases. The court will also require more strenuous and rigorous types of treatment for the offender before it will allow contact between the offender and the victim than in other types of abuse cases.

PSYCHOLOGICAL ABUSE

Psychological abuse, also known as emotional, mental, or verbal abuse, occurs where a child is subjected to harassment, isolation, humiliation, nonphysical torture, name-calling, or terrorizing. It also includes extreme or bizarre forms of punishment such as confining children to cages, small rooms, or closets, tying or chaining children, forcing children to wear signs or masks, and other such punishments.

Psychological, emotional, or mental harm necessarily accompanies any child abuse or neglect, whether it is primarily physical, sexual, or some combination of the two. The federal child abuse statutes, CAPTA, includes emotional harm in its definition of child abuse and neglect, which includes "any recent act or failure to act on the part of a parent or caretaker, which results in death, serious physical or emotional harm, sexual abuse or exploitation, or an act or failure to act which presents an imminent risk of serious harm. . . ."

CAPTA defines the term "child abuse crime" as a "crime committed under any law of a State that involves the physical or *mental injury,* sexual abuse or exploitation, negligent treatment, or maltreatment of a child by any person . . ." (emphasis added).

Psychological abuse is particularly difficult to define because it leaves no visible marks or scars. Just as the line between reasonable physical discipline and physical abuse is difficult to demarcate, so is the line between acceptable criticism and psychological abuse.

SIDEBAR

DOMESTIC VIOLENCE AS PARENTAL NEGLECT

In December 2004, the New York City Administration of Children's Service (ACS) settled a long running case, *Nicholson v. Scoppetta,* in which the issue was whether being a victim of domestic violence constituted parental neglect.

The ACS had a policy of removing children from their mothers if their mothers were victims of domestic violence, even where the mothers had committed no violence and the children had never been, nor were in danger of becoming, victims of the violence.

The policy was based upon ACS's allegations that the mothers, as victims of domestic violence, had "engaged in domestic violence," which constituted one of the grounds for removal of a child on the basis of neglect under New York law.

Sharwline Nicholson, a mother whose children ACS removed under the law, sued ACS in federal court under **42 USC § 1983,** a federal statute that allows citizens to sue the federal government for constitutional violations.

The court granted a **preliminary injunction,** or order temporarily barring ACS from carrying out its policy, concluding that the city "may not penalize a mother, not otherwise unfit, who is battered by her partner, by separating her from her children; nor may children be separated from the mother, in effect visiting upon them the sins of their mother's batterer."[ii]

New York Eastern District Senior Judge Jack B. Weinstein, who wrote the opinion, called the ACS policy "pitiless double abuse" whereby mothers were victimized twice—first by their batterers and second by the state authority that removed their children. The judge alleged that the policy was based upon ACS's desire to protect themselves from liability and criticism following a horrific case where a mentally ill mother tortured and murdered her child, Elisa Izquierdo, after the state returned the child to the mother in spite of repeated incidents of substantiated abuse and no evidence that the mother had remedied the situation.

The judge observed that victims were more likely to suffer the legal consequences of the violence than the batterers were, noting, "[o]f the cases involving domestic violence where ACS files [a petition to remove a child due to neglect], the petition explicitly charges the victim with having failed to protect the child from witnessing domestic violence in 23.1 percent of cases. The abusive partner, by contrast, is charged with causing harm to the child by engaging in domestic violence in only 15.4 percent of the cases."

42 USC § 1983
A federal statute that allows citizens to sue the federal government for constitutional violations

preliminary injunction
An order temporarily barring a party from carrying out a certain action

(continues)

certify

To send a case from one court to another

ACS appealed the ruling, and the federal appellate court sent the case to the state appellate court, or **certified** the case, on the grounds that it was a case of first impression, and that in such cases state law should take precedence over federal law.

The state court considered the question whether it was neglect for a victim of domestic violence to allow her children to witness the violence. The New York Family Court Act defines a neglected child as one whose "physical, mental or emotional condition has been impaired or is in imminent danger of becoming impaired as a result of the failure of his parent or other person legally responsible for his care to exercise a minimum degree of care. . . ." The court interpreted this to require a showing of harm as a consequence of the parent's inaction or improper supervision or care.

This unfavorable preliminary ruling prompted the settlement under which ACS acknowledged that automatic removal of children from parents who are victims of domestic violence is not justified. The agency did not, however, state what course of action it would take in the future.

ABUSE AND NEGLECT DISTINGUISHED

The main criteria for distinction between abuse and neglect are intent and degree. If a family member intentionally and maliciously causes harm to a child, it is abuse. If the adult inflicts harm through lack of care and attention rather than malicious intent, it is neglect. If neglect is severe enough, it becomes abuse.

Neglect

Neglect occurs where children experience harm because of their parents' failure to act or protect them, or where parents willfully fail to provide necessaries such as food, clothing, shelter, medical care, education, or supervision where they have the ability to do so.

There must be a showing of harm and a showing that the harm resulted from the parents' action or failure to act before a court will find parental neglect. Injury without parental wrongdoing or parental wrongdoing without injury generally will not constitute legal neglect. For instance, if a child is swinging on a backyard swing set and falls off, severely injuring himself, there is no parental neglect. If a parent abuses drugs and alcohol, but nonetheless feeds, clothes, supervises, and protect her child, there is no parental neglect.

The following case, *In re MN,* cited above, is an example of neglect so severe it becomes abuse.

In re MN
2003 WL 22415752 (Wyo., 2003)
LEHMAN, Justice.

The mother of MN, a minor child, appeals the district court order terminating her parental rights. Mother primarily asserts that the district court erred when it found clear and convincing evidence upon which to terminate her parental rights. Upon review, we affirm.

DISCUSSION

Termination of Parental Rights

Termination of parental rights pursuant to Wyoming law initially requires the establishment of parental abuse or neglect by clear and convincing evidence. "Abuse" means inflicting or causing physical or mental injury, harm or imminent danger to the physical or mental health or welfare of a child other than by accidental means, including abandonment, excessive or unreasonable corporal punishment, malnutrition or substantial risk thereof by reason of intentional or unintentional neglect, and the commission or allowing the commission of a sexual offense against a child as defined by law. "Neglect" means "a failure or refusal by those responsible for the child's welfare to provide adequate care, maintenance, supervision, education or medical, surgical or any other care necessary for the child's well being."

The evidence presented to the district court showed that in 1996, when MN was two years old, the State received information that Mother was giving MN alcohol in an infant cup and shaking out and re-using diapers. In July 1997, the State received a report that MN was being watched by inappropriate male caregivers who were drinking and driving with MN and bringing her to the local bar, that MN's teeth had rotted, and that she was being fed a diet of only soda and candy. Statements were also made which gave concerns that MN may have also been sexually abused.

It was also reported that MN was left playing on the road while Mother was passed out in her car, that MN was being left on numerous occasions unattended in a bar while Mother drank, and MN was being transported in an unsanitary vehicle full of rotted food and garbage. In October of 1997, law enforcement contacted the State again with concerns regarding MN's teeth. In December of 1997, Mother took MN to visit her mother in Las Vegas, Nevada, and, although MN was then three and a half years old, fed her primarily Coca Cola and sweets. Mother also failed to monitor MN in the bathroom, which led to MN smearing feces all over a restroom.

In January and February 1998, MN's daycare provider made two referrals to the State reporting that MN was arriving at the daycare hungry, dirty, and smelling like urine. The daycare also reported that MN often had caked food on her, expressed concerns about her teeth, and reported that the only food Mother brought to the daycare were sweets. MN was also developmentally behind other children of her age, had difficulty interacting with her peers, and would have lengthy screaming fits. On May 28, 1998, the State received a report that Mother and MN were living in a hazardous, filthy apartment filled with dog feces. The State investigated and found the apartment filled with flies, feces, garbage, and rotting food. However, by then Mother and MN had vacated the apartment. The State formally substantiated this claim. In August of 1998, the State received complaints that Mother's campsite was a mess and that all MN was eating was candy, soda, and other sugary foods.

In February of 1999, the State received another complaint that Mother had dropped off MN on the doorstep of a co-worker's home without making any previous arrangements and drove off before anyone

(continues)

In re MN (Continued)

answered the door, leaving MN overnight. It was also reported that MN's underwear was black with dirt, her sleeping bag was "filthy," and that Mother's apartment was filled with junk and had no food. The State formally substantiated these claims, leading to the instigation of neglect proceedings and Mother voluntarily placing MN with her aunt, Ms. Griffin.

When MN, then almost five years of age, was placed at Ms. Griffin's home, she was unfamiliar with eating utensils, did not know what toilet paper was or how to use it, hoarded food despite being given sufficient food, and would go up to strangers to hug them and sit on their laps. In December of 1999, MN was moved to a foster family home in Osmond, Wyoming, approximately five miles from Afton, Wyoming. Mother could not be contacted regarding this change because she had moved and did not provide the State with contact information. When MN arrived at the new foster home, she had no top teeth, had bridges on her bottom teeth, and preferred to eat only sweets. She would also scream for hours without any tears when she did not get her way, struggled with peer interaction, was underdeveloped, and preferred to be with adults all the time. She continued to go up to strangers and hug them.

Mother criticizes the evidence presented at trial and characterizes it simply as a showing of five unsubstantiated reports of alleged neglect and two reports of neglect that were substantiated at low risk. Therefore, Mother concludes that this factual foundation is insufficient to terminate her parental rights to MN. We have previously recognized that in the ordinary parental rights termination case consideration must be given to a combination of factors, incidents, and conditions that demonstrate the neglect required to justify termination of parental rights. Rarely do we find a single condition or incident that, standing alone, would justify termination. Rather, neglect is usually manifested by numerous incidents and conditions extending over a considerable length of time.

The neglect in this case extended over a long period of time and is apparent by the occasions and conditions described by the witnesses and in the exhibits. The record discloses long-term general neglect, and the detailed instances are adequate to show by clear and convincing evidence the failure to provide adequate care necessary for MN's well being. Thus, at a minimum, neglect, if not abuse, is presented.

Educational Neglect

Educational neglect occurs where parents allow school age children to be truant from school, fail to register school age children for school, or keep children home from school for non-legitimate reasons, such as to work, to care for siblings, or because the parents are too busy or tired to wake the children.

The National Clearinghouse of Child Abuse and Neglect defines it in the following way. (Source: Unites States Department of Health and Human Services, Administration for Children and Families, National Clearinghouse for Child Abuse and Neglect Information.)

Permitted Chronic Truancy

Habitual truancy averaging at least 5 days a month was classifiable under this form of maltreatment if the parent/guardian had been informed of the problem and had not attempted to intervene.

Failure to Enroll/Other Truancy

Failure to register or enroll a child of mandatory school age, causing the school-aged child to remain at home for non-legitimate reasons (e.g., to work, to care for siblings, etc.) an average of at least 3 days a month.

Inattention to Special Education Need

Refusal to allow or failure to obtain recommended remedial educational services, or neglect in obtaining or following through with treatment for a child's diagnosed learning disorder or other special education need without reasonable cause.

The rising popularity of home schooling has brought increased attention to the issue of educational neglect. Many home-school information websites are devoted to helping parents avoid charges of educational neglect.

Home-schooling laws vary among the states. Some states, such as Alabama, do not recognize home schooling as an educational option. Parents in these states who wish to home school their children must find a sponsoring private school to oversee the home school process. Other states, such as Alaska, recognize home schooling as a legal option subject to state regulation. In these states, parents must adhere to state educational standards and outcomes, submit paperwork on a regular basis to state authorities, maintain records, meet instructor qualifications, and submit results of periodic testing, including standardized testing. Other states, such as Massachusetts, have no statewide policy concerning home schooling. State educational authorities review home-school requests on a case-by-case basis.

Medical Neglect

Medical neglect is depriving children of necessary medical care, including vaccinations, booster shots, and other preventative and curative medical treatments where parents are able to afford and have access to such medial care.

Whether parents can choose faith healing over standard medical care for their children remains a subject of some debate and controversy. Some religious groups deprive their children of medical care because of their religious beliefs. The United States Supreme Court ruled in *Prince v. Massachusetts,* 321 U.S. 158 (1944) that:

> The right to practice religion freely does not include the right to expose the community or the child to communicable disease or the latter to ill-health or death. Parents may be free to become martyrs themselves. But it does not follow they are free, in identical circumstances, to make martyrs of their children before they have reached the age of full legal discretion when they can make that choice for themselves.

Traditionally, courts have held that the free exercise clause of the First Amendment does not confer an absolute right upon parents to deprive their children of crucial medical care.

The Court ruled in 1972, in *Wisconsin v. Yoder,* 406 U.S. 233–234, that "The power of the parent, even when linked to a free exercise claim, may be subject to limitation under Prince if it appears that parental decisions will jeopardize the health or safety of the child. . . ."

SIDEBAR

ASSER-SWAN STUDY OF CHILD FATALITIES IN FAITH-HEALING RELIGIOUS GROUPS

Dr. Seth M. Asser, of the Department of Pediatrics, University of California, San Diego, School of Medicine, San Diego, California, and Rita Swan, president of Children's Healthcare Is a Legal Duty (CHILD), an Iowa-based nonprofit organization that works to protect children from abusive religious and cultural practices, especially religion-based medical neglect, conducted a study designed "[t]o evaluate deaths of children from families in which faith healing was practiced in lieu of medical care and to determine if such deaths were preventable."

Asser and Swan reviewed cases of 172 children who died between 1975 and 1995 while their parents were members of faith healing sects. They identified the children through referrals and record searches. Criteria for inclusion were evidence that parents withheld medical care because of their reliance on religious rituals and documentation sufficient to determine the cause of death. They then estimated the probability of survival for each based on expected survival rates for children with similar disorders who receive medical care.

The researchers found that one hundred forty fatalities were from conditions for which survival rates with medical care would have exceeded 90%. Eighteen more had expected survival rates of >50%. All but three of the remainder would likely have had some benefit from clinical help.

Pediatrics, 101, No. 4 (April 1998), 625–629.

Some states provide a mechanism whereby the state or a hospital seeking to provide critical medical care to a child whose parents withhold consent to such medical care for religious reasons can petition for the right to provide medical care without the parents' consent. Pursuant to such a petition, the court can find that a child is in need of medical care and that the parents do not consent to medical care. They may not, however, adjudge such children to be abused or neglected. In such cases, the court may appoint the hospital a temporary guardian of the child, thus allowing the hospital to provide the medical care its doctors deem crucial to the life and health of the child.

DEPENDENCY

Dependency, like neglect and abuse, means a child is living under a set of circumstances that make it necessary for the court to assume jurisdiction of that child. Some states make no distinction among abused, neglected, or dependent children. In the states that do make a distinction, a dependent child is defined as one whose parents are unable to provide for the child's needs through no fault of their own. For example, a county would file a dependency action in a case where a parent was terminally ill, mentally disabled, imprisoned, or suffering from a disability that prevented the parent from caring for the child.

REMOVAL OF CHILDREN

State or county authorities, social workers, or police may remove children from their parents where there is an emergency situation. In such cases, the removing authority must act within a very short period of time—usually 24 to 72 hours—to begin official proceedings in the juvenile court. (*See* Chapter 10, Abuse Neglect-Dependency Hearings.)

Emergency Seizure

Authorities have sufficient grounds for emergency removal where there is an immediate danger that serious harm will come to the children if they are not removed. Emergency removal is also allowable where an infant is born addicted to drugs, tests positive for drugs, or suffers from **fetal alcohol syndrome.** Fetal alcohol syndrome is a condition where a child displays symptoms known to be associated with the mother having consumed intoxicating substances while she was pregnant with that child.

fetal alcohol syndrome
A condition where a child displays symptoms known to be associated with the mother's having consumed intoxicating substances while she was pregnant with that child

CASE PROBLEM

H.S. and L.S. were twin boys. Prior to their birth, they experience twin-to-twin transfusion syndrome, whereby the twins' circulatory systems were joined at the placenta, causing the blood to flow preferentially to one twin, L.S., and causing H.S. to become anemic. Doctors were able to perform a natural, in utero, blood transfusion by massaging the umbilical cord. Despite this, H.S. was stillborn. Doctors revived him seven minutes later, although he remained in critical condition until, several days later, his platelet count dropped to such a degree that his physician believed his life was in danger if he did not receive a blood transfusion, to which there was no medical alternative.

H.S.'s parents were members of the Jehovah Witness church, which objects to all blood transfusions. The hospital was aware of this. Nonetheless, the hospital performed the transfusion. H.S. remained critically ill. The hospital petitioned for temporary guardianship of both H.S. and L.S., pursuant to Nevada law. The hospital based the petition on "the substantial and immediate risk of physical harm, potential death, and the emergency circumstances surrounding the health and well being" of both children and requested a "special" guardianship to "provide for the medical care of the twin children." An attached affidavit of Dr. Barry Perlin stated that a significant probability existed that H.S. and L.S. would require a blood transfusion within the next 30 days to survive. Furthermore, if a transfusion were needed, the hospital would need to initiate the transfusion in less than two hours after the emergency arose.

The court granted temporary guardianship on an emergency basis for the purpose of consenting to blood transfusions and to other medical care as deemed necessary by the hospital for both children. The order required that Jason and Rebecca be given notice "as soon as practical."

The court awarded the hospital temporary guardianship, over the parents' objections, and the parents appealed. What is the result?

ROLE-PLAY PROBLEM

Social workers and police visited a home after receiving reports of a severely abused child in the family. Upon entering the home, the authorities found a family of two parents and three children. Two of the children, 10-year-old Jane and 8-year-old Laura, appeared healthy and well developed mentally, emotionally, intellectually, and physically.

The third child, 12-year-old Robbie, was lying in bed alone in the attic. He was severely underdeveloped and tiny for his age. Later examination revealed that he was four-feet-four-inches tall and weighed 60 pounds. He barely spoke, and he was dirty—his hair was matted, his teeth were rotten, and he was covered with sores, scratches, and scars.

Workers removed all three children from the home and placed them in three different foster homes. The parents insisted that Robbie refused to eat, scratched himself until he bled, threw himself against the wall and onto the floor, refused to clean himself, and would not go anywhere but the room in the attic. Jane confirmed her parents' account.

Laura, however, said that this information was not true—she said that her parents hurt Robbie, would not allow him to eat, and made him stay in the attic. She said that Robbie cried all the time, and she tried to sneak food to him, but if her parents caught her they punished her. She still tried, nonetheless.

After being in foster care for a month, Robbie was clean and calm, and had gained 10 pounds. He shrieked at the sight of his parents and Jane, and would see only Laura. The foster mother reported that Robbie was an extremely difficult child.

Jane begged to return to her parents. Laura asked to return to her parents. Both girls wanted to live with their parents and Robbie.

The county filed an action in juvenile court seeking custody of all three children on the grounds of child abuse and neglect.

The court has appointed you to work as the guardian ad litem to investigate the case and make a recommendation to the court as to which action will serve the best interests of the children.

1. How will you investigate this case?

2. Whom do you want to interview?

3. What questions would you ask those people?

4. What documents or records would you like to see?

5. What do the facts as you currently understand them lead you to believe?

6. Which facts do you find most significant?

7. What more do you want to know?

HYPOTHETICAL PROBLEM

A young, single mother and her two daughters, ages six and four, were living together in an apartment with a month-to-month lease. The mother lost her job as a bagger at a local supermarket when the market closed. She found another job as a clerk at a convenience store, but the pay was much lower than she had been earning at the supermarket, and she soon fell behind in her rent. The landlord evicted the family.

The mother rented a six-by-ten foot storage unit in an industrial section of town, close to the convenience store. She paid the $25 monthly rent and bought a $10, 24-hour access card to the unit and moved into it with her daughters. She left the girls locked in the unit while she went to work every day.

This continued for about a week, until one day the manager was walking by the unit and heard children's voices inside. He called out, "Who's there?" There was no answer, so he called the police.

Police arrived and cut off the padlock. They initially did not see the children inside the unit, which held some furniture and boxes. They discovered the two little girls hiding underneath a table after searching.

The girls appeared healthy, clean, and well fed. They were not afraid of people and answered questions in an age-appropriate manner.

The girls had been using a plastic bowl as a toilet and had no food, soap, water, or light inside the unit, which was solid metal and unheated.

Police went to the convenience store and arrested the mother, who cooperated with them. She told them of losing her job and apartment, and explained that she had no friends or relatives. Asked why she did not seek help from social services, she answered that she did not trust them not to remove her children.

1. Has the mother neglected her children?

2. Should she have made a better effort to find an appropriate living facility before resorting to living in a storage unit?

3. Would your assessment of the situation change if there had been a fire in the unit, and the girls had died while padlocked inside of it?

4. Was the mother justified in her belief that if she sought help from social services, they would remove her children from her?

5. Are children better off living in a bad situation with a mother who loves the than in a good situation with strangers?

Later investigation revealed that on several of the nights that the three were living in the storage unit, the mother left the girls and stayed at her own mother's house. On those occasions, she told her mother the girls were at a friend's house.

6. Does this fact change your opinion?

7. Why or why not?

ETHICAL CONCERNS

Almost all communications between attorneys and clients are privileged, and the privilege belongs to the clients, not the attorneys. This means that attorneys may not divulge secrets or confidences that they receive from their clients, even if those secrets and confidences involve criminal acts. Clients can waive the privilege if they break the confidence by telling others, by speaking in such a way as to allow others to hear them, or by expressly giving their attorneys the right to divulge the information.

The only exceptions to this privilege are where clients tell attorneys of *prospective* criminal actions and where attorneys must divulge confidences to prevent clients from committing fraud upon the court. The most attorneys can do when they learn their clients have committed crimes is attempt to persuade them to go to the authorities—the attorneys themselves may never divulge information regarding a past crime.

The attorney-client privilege extends to all the employees of an attorneys office—paralegals, secretaries, word processors, private investigators, law clerks, and other employees who have access to client communications.

At the same time, clients, paralegals, and other professionals are required by state law to report cases of known or suspected child abuse. This leaves attorneys in an ethically awkward position when they learn their clients have abused children.

Generally, the privilege prevents attorneys from reporting child abuse they learn of in the course of representing clients. Attorneys may be required to report of child abuse they discover or suspect where they learn of the abuse while representing children in child abuse cases. Paralegals should report known or suspected child abuse to their attorneys.

DISCUSSION QUESTIONS

Consider the case of *Nicholson v. Scoppetta* above.

1. Do you believe that witnessing abuse is inherently harmful to a child?

2. If you do believe that it is harmful, do you believe that a mother who allows her children to witness the abuse is responsible for the harm they suffer?

3. Recall that under the December 2004 settlement, ACS agreed not to automatically remove children from their mothers on the basis of the mother's being a victim of domestic violence, but they did not specify how they would proceed in the future. If you were writing the new ACS policy, how would you fashion it?

A woman left her two-year-old child alone for nearly three weeks while she was in jail. The child survived by eating mustard, ketchup, rice, and raw pasta. The child's father, who was separated from her mother, said he talked to the mother by phone at the jail and she told him their daughter was with neighbors. The mother never told anyone at the jail that she had a child at home alone.

The father went to the mother's apartment and found his daughter watching cartoons. When he got into the apartment, the youngster had dragged food and toys into her mother's bedroom and was lying in a baby's bathtub, covered with dried ketchup.

When she saw her father, she grabbed him and would not let go. She was suffering from malnutrition and required hospitalization.

4. Did the mother's actions constitute abuse or neglect?

5. If you believe the mother's actions constituted abuse, at what point did her behavior cross the line between abuse and neglect?

6. Would your opinion of this case be different if the mother had left the toddler alone for three days rather than three weeks? Three hours?

7. If the child had died as a result of being left alone for three weeks should the state charge the mother with a crime? **Murder? Manslaughter?** Murder is the intentional killing of a human being with **malice aforethought,** which is the desire to bring about the death of a human being and acting to do so. Manslaughter is the unintentional killing of a human being as the result of neglect.

You are a state legislator and you are charged with the task of writing a new legal definition of child abuse and neglect.

murder
The intentional killing of a human being with malice aforethought

manslaughter
The unintentional killing of a human being through negligence

malice aforethought
Wishing to bring about the death of another human being and acting to do so

8. What elements will you incorporate into your definition?

9. Will you write a restrictive definition or an amorphous one?

10. How will abuse differ from neglect?

11. Will you distinguish among physical, sexual, psychological, and emotional abuse?

12. How will you define each?

13. How will you approach the issue of parents withholding medical care for religious reasons?

14. How will you address the issue of home schooling or nontraditional schooling for religious or other reasons?

KEY TERMS

42 USC § 1983	manslaughter
certify	murder
dependent children	neglect
emotional, mental, or psychological abuse	physical abuse
	preliminary injunction
fetal alcohol syndrome	sexual abuse
intake worker	social services agency
malice aforethought	

END NOTES

[i] A child was counted each time he or she was found to be a victim of maltreatment.

[ii] *In re Nicholson,* 181 F Supp 2d 182, 188 [ED NY Jan. 20, 2002]; see also *Nicholson v. Williams,* 203 F Supp 2d 153 [ED NY Mar. 18, 2002] [108-page elaboration of grounds for injunction].

Chapter 10

ABUSE-NEGLECT-DEPENDENCY HEARINGS

OBJECTIVES

By the end of this chapter, the student should know:

- The two phases of abuse-neglect-dependency (a-n-d) hearings
- What comprises a case plan and how case plans apply to a-n-d cases
- The issues parties can contest at a-n-d hearings
- The procedural requirements and time limits attendant to a-n-d hearings
- Juvenile court policies regarding juries, notice, open hearings, and evidence
- Who has the burden of proof in a-n-d hearings
- The standard of proof at a-n-d hearings
- The basis for appealing a-n-d decisions
- How courts evaluate children's testimony and other evidence at a-n-d hearings
- The dispositions available to juvenile courts
- The parameters of protective supervision, legal custody, temporary custody, long-term foster care, planned permanent living arrangements, and termination of parental rights
- The grounds for termination of parental rights (TPR)
- The basis for appealing TPR orders

INTRODUCTION

Abuse-neglect-dependency (a-n-d) hearings, like delinquency hearings, are two phase hearings. Constitutional protections exist to guard the rights of the parents and to ensure the regularity of the proceedings, although the number and scope of constitutional protections attendant to a-n-d hearings do not equal those of criminal or civil trials.

adjudicatory phase
The phase of a juvenile hearing where the court determines whether the facts the county has alleged are true

dispositional phase
The phase of a juvenile hearing where the court determines which course of action will be in the children's best interests

The first phase of an a-n-d hearing is the **adjudicatory phase.** Juvenile courts weigh the facts and determine whether they indicate the child is an abused, neglected, or dependent child in this phase. The level of proof necessary depends upon the jurisdiction. Some jurisdictions require clear and convincing evidence, while others require the state to prove its case by a preponderance of the evidence. The result of this phase will determine whether the court can assume jurisdiction over the child. If the court determines that the child is abused, neglected, or dependent, it will assert jurisdiction over the child.

The second phase is the **dispositional phase.** Juvenile courts determine a course of action in the dispositional phase. Juvenile courts are concerned only with the children's best interest this phase. They do not consider the interests of society at large in these hearings, as they do in delinquency hearings.

Juvenile court hearings are generally informal. In the words of California's statute, which is typical:

> . . . Except where there is a contested issue of fact or law, the proceedings shall be conducted in an informal nonadversary atmosphere with a view to obtaining the maximum cooperation of the minor upon whose behalf the petition is brought and all persons interested in his or her welfare with any provisions that the court may make for the disposition and care of the minor . . .[i]

Some states, however, require that juvenile hearings be "conducted in a formal manner."[ii] South Carolina's statute is an example of these:

SECTION 20-7-755 CONDUCT OF HEARINGS

All cases of children must be dealt with as separate hearings by the court and without a jury. The hearings must be conducted in a formal manner and may be adjourned from time to time. The general public must be excluded and only persons the judge finds to have a direct interest in the case or in the work of the court may be admitted. The presence of the child in court may be waived by the court at any stage of the proceedings. Hearings may be held at any time or place within the county designated by the

(continues)

judge. In any case where the delinquency proceedings may result in commitment to an institution in which the child's freedom is curtailed, the privilege against self-incrimination and the right of cross-examination must be preserved. In all cases where required by law, the child must be accorded all rights enjoyed by adults, and where not required by law the child must be accorded adult rights consistent with the best interests of the child.

THE ADJUDICATORY PHASE

The adjudicatory phase of an a-n-d hearing begins when a state or county agency—usually the social services agency or the county prosecutor—files a complaint charging that a child or children are abused, neglected, or dependent. The charging party bases the complaint upon things the children's parents or guardians have done or failed to do that have resulted in harm to the child.

In abuse complaints, the filing party charges that the parents have caused physical, sexual, or emotional harm to the children through their actions, or have allowed such harm to come to their children through inaction.

In neglect complaints, the filing party charges that the parents have allowed harm to come to their children through their failure to provide basic necessaries, such as food, clothing, shelter, medical care, education, or supervision.

In dependency complaints, the filing party charges that the parents have a physical, mental, or other disability, such as a severe mental or physical illness, a physical limitation, imprisonment, or other indisposition, that has prevented or will prevent them from properly caring for their children. Dependency complaints are no-fault complaints, insofar as they do not place the blame for the children's status on the parents, but rather on circumstances beyond the parents' control.

Case Plans

A **case plan,** or social services plan, is a document that the social services agency workers devise in conjunction with the parents. It identifies the specific problems that the parents have that prevent them from providing proper care, or cause them to harm, their children, and outlines a plan to address each of the issues. Case plans generally contain assessment, therapy, education, and life management components.

For example, the case plan will direct parents who physically abuse their children to attend anger management classes, parents who are neglectful to attend parenting classes, and parents who have failed to provide adequate housing to obtain housing. The parents must sign the case plan and indicate that they are in agreement with it, or file specific objections to it.

case plan
A document that the social services agency workers devise in conjunction with the parents

The social services agency submits the case plan to the juvenile court at the adjudicatory hearing. If the court agrees with the case plan, it will accept the plan and enter it into the record. Once it becomes part of the record, it serves as a guidepost for the parents' progress in meeting the requirements to get their children back.

The social services agency must assist the parents in working on their case plans. If the parents fail to comply with the case plans, or fail to make significant progress in completing the goals, they must offer a reasonable explanation for that failure. If they cannot, their failure to comply with the case plan will become evidence against them in the adjudication. The court will consider the parents' failure or success in meeting the case plan in its dispositional decisions.

The case plan assumes that reunification of the family is the ultimate goal. The components of the plan are aimed at eliminating the problems that caused the court to intervene in the family and separate the children from their parents. The social services agency can move to withdraw the plan where there are significant problems in the family and the agency believes that the family either will not or cannot remedy those problems, and that termination of parental rights will be in the children's best interests.

The following case illustrates a typical social services plan, and demonstrates how the courts use case plans, and the parents' progress in complying with them, to make decisions regarding termination of parental rights.

In re C.F.C.
— S.W.3d —, 2005 WL 288681 (Mo.App. 2005)

A.D.S. (hereinafter, "Mother") appeals from the judgment terminating her parental rights to her five-year-old son, C.F.C. (hereinafter, "Child"). She challenges the trial court's finding that three grounds for termination exist. We reverse and remand.

Between June and December of 2001, the Division of Family Services (hereinafter, "DFS") received three separate reports that Child's 1-year old sister, E.R.M. (hereinafter, "Sister"), had unexplained injuries. DFS questioned Mother after the first two reports. She responded that Child hit, scratched, and bit Sister, as well as other children. Mother also confirmed an additional report that Child overdosed on

his prescription medication. DFS suspected Mother neglected her children. Upon receiving the third report about Sister's injuries, DFS contacted the police, who took Child and Sister into protective custody on December 10, 2001. The next day, DFS placed Child in Our Little Haven, a residential facility for children with special needs, where he currently resides.

At the request of DFS, Mother underwent a psychological evaluation on February 12, 2002. In his evaluation report, Dr. Robert Schlitt opined that Mother had significant learning disabilities and functioned overall in the mild mental retardation range. He questioned whether she could function without

(continues)

In re C.F.C. (Continued)

having another responsible adult in the household and whether she had even minimal parenting skills and judgment. He recommended that she receive treatment from a clinical therapist, a family therapist, and a psychiatrist. DFS also referred a social worker, Michael Mehan, to her and he counseled her weekly in her home for at least the next two years.

After a hearing on April 22, 2002, the trial court found Child lacked proper care. The court took jurisdiction over him and assigned DFS legal custody. The court also ordered Mother to begin family counseling and to continue seeing a psychiatrist and participate in Parents as Teachers. That same day, Mother and DFS signed, and the court later approved, a written social service plan for family reunification. The plan ordered DFS to help Mother comply with the following requirements: (1) visit Child twice a month; (2) make financial contributions to his support; (3) obtain a psychological evaluation; (4) obtain and maintain housing; and (5) participate in psychological counseling and parenting classes.

Over the next year, Mother performed most of the tasks to some extent, and therefore, she did fail to completely comply. Specifically, she failed to pay for Child's support, although she did provide gifts and food for Child during her visits, even though some of the gifts were inappropriate, according to DFS. She consistently visited Child twice a month as allowed by the court. A DFS worker testified that during the visits Mother usually engaged in appropriate activities with Child, such as singing songs, reading books, and playing with Legos. Mother obtained a psychological evaluation and participated consistently in her psychological counseling. She participated in Parents as Teachers more sporadically. She completed parenting classes in July 2003 after the termination petition was filed.

Later, the court also ordered her to use the parent aide services of the St. Louis Regional Center and to continue taking GED classes. Again, Mother performed most of the assigned tasks to some extent. However, she did not utilize the Regional Center's housing services because she refused to share an apartment with another mother, as the Center would require. She also turned down the employment services offered by the Center because she already had a job and felt capable of finding another one on her own in the future, if necessary.

On three occasions after the trial court assumed jurisdiction over Child, the court reviewed the progress Mother and DFS made regarding the social service plan and the court updated the permanency plan for the placement of Child. After the third permanency hearing on May 23, 2003, the court cancelled the social service plan and referred the matter to the Juvenile Officer for termination. The court explained that further efforts by DFS to reunite Mother and Child would be fruitless and inconsistent with establishing a permanent placement for Child. The Juvenile Officer then filed a petition to terminate Mother's parental rights. The trial court held a bench trial. At the time of the termination hearing, Mother lived at her grandmother's house with her young son (half-brother to Child). Child still lived in a residential care facility, did not have a foster family, and there was no permanent placement available for him.

On December 4, 2003, the court entered a judgment terminating Mother's parental rights to Child. The court found that termination was in Child's best interest and that three separate grounds for termination existed. Mother appeals the trial court's judgment, arguing that there was insufficient evidence to support any of these grounds for termination.

(continues)

In re C.F.C. (Continued)

The court's findings regarding the social services plan do not cure the other deficiencies in the judgment. The court did make specific findings about what the service plan required, how Mother complied, and Mother's failures [but] the findings are insufficient. A parent's failure to comply with a written service plan does not, in itself, constitute a ground for terminating parental rights. Non-compliance is merely a factor to consider in deciding whether the grounds [to terminate parental rights] exist. The statute requires the trial court to consider "the extent to which the parties have made progress in complying with [the service agreement's] terms," not whether the compliance was full or substantial.

Here, the trial court did not discuss how Mother's progress, or lack of progress, with the social services plan impacted on her future ability to parent Child. These findings alone are insufficient to support termination and additional findings are necessary.

[Reversed and remanded.]

Contested Hearings

There are two ways in which an adjudicatory hearing can proceed: by agreement or as a contested hearing. A hearing proceeds by agreement when the parent and the state agree upon the truth of the allegations. Abuse-neglect-dependency cases begin with the state making a series of allegations that it contends constitute grounds for taking custody of a child. The state serves the complaint and a notice of hearing upon the parent. The state also sends the parents information on how to contact the public defender's office.

The parents and their attorneys review the charges in the complaint and decide which of them are true as written, which would be true with slight changes, and which are completely false. The parents' attorneys and the state's attorneys then begin the negotiation process, through which they attempt to reach an agreement on language that will satisfy both parties.

Exhibit 10-1 is a sample complaint that demonstrates the kinds of changes a complaint may undergo.

Lucinda's mother and her attorney would confer and negotiate with the prosecuting attorney, softening the language on some allegations, eliminating others, and perhaps adding others, so that eventually it might look like the sample amended complaint in Exhibit 10-2.

The resulting complaint contains enough substance to support an adjudication that Lucinda is an abused or neglected child, but the language is slightly less severe than that of the original complaint. Joanne will admit to the allegations, and the case can proceed to disposition without a full hearing.

If the parents and the prosecutor cannot agree upon language, the case will proceed to a full adjudicatory hearing. The purpose of the adjudicatory hearing is to determine whether there exist sufficient grounds for the courts to adjudicate the subject children abused, neglected, or dependent, thereby affording them

EXHIBIT 10-1 Complaint

Lucinda James is a three-year-old child.

Lucinda's father is unknown.

On many occasions, most recently on August 25, 2005, Lucinda's mother, Joanne James, left Lucinda home alone for at least eight hours while she went to work.

On many occasions, most recently on August 27, 2005, neighbors saw Lucinda wandering the neighborhood alone, dirty and inappropriately dressed, during the day while Joanne slept.

On many occasions, most recently August 28, 2005, neighbors noticed a number of suspicious bruises on Lucinda's arms, legs, and neck.

EXHIBIT 10-2 Complaint

Lucinda James is a three-year-old child.

Lucinda's father is unknown.

On ~~many occasions, most recently on~~ August 25, 2005, Lucinda's mother, Joanne James, left Lucinda home alone ~~for at least eight hours~~ while she went to work ∧but Joanne asked a neighbor to check on Lucinda

On ~~many occasions, most recently on~~ August 27, 2005, neighbors saw Lucinda wandering the neighborhood alone, ~~dirty and inappropriately dressed~~, during the day ~~while Joanne slept~~.

On many occasions, most recently August 28, 2005, neighbors ∧reported ~~noticed~~ a number of suspicious bruises on Lucinda's arms, legs, and neck.

grounds to take legal custody of those children. If the court so determines, it can move on to the dispositional phase wherein the court decides which placements are best for the children.

The parties contest issues of fact at adjudicatory hearings. Each side presents witnesses, testimony, and photographic and documentary evidence addressing the matters contained in the complaint. Evidence consists of testimony, medical records, photographs of injuries, photographs of a home, and anything else that would document the conditions that the state contends constitute the abused, neglected, or dependent status of a child.

Procedural Requirements

Abuse-neglect-dependency hearings are subject to essentially the same procedural requirements as other juvenile hearings. The Supreme Court has held that the constitutional guarantee of due process requires certain procedures and elements to be in place in juvenile proceedings, although the number and scope of those procedures and elements are more limited than in non-juvenile hearings.

Time Limits

The prevailing philosophy regarding children is to favor stability and permanence. Courts do not like to leave children languishing in temporary living arrangements while their cases drag through the legal system. They also do not like to move children more than they absolutely must. Once a child is in a placement, courts want to leave him there, and will disturb him only if the potential harm of remaining in his current placement outweighs the harm of moving him.

To this end, each state has set a time limit whereby the juvenile court must hold the adjudicatory hearing no later than a certain number of days after the filing of the complaint or the seizure of the child, and must hold the dispositional hearing no later than a certain number of days after the adjudication. The maximum time between filing or seizure and adjudication ranges from 48 hours to several days. The maximum time between adjudication and disposition generally ranges from 30 to 60 days.

Courts have the authority to extend the time limits where the extension is in the best interests of the children. Parties involved may also waive the time limits where the waiver is in the best interests if the children.

Notice Requirements

The court must provide the parents written notice of the time and place of all hearings. The court must deliver the notice in accordance with the time, place, and manner of delivery requirements that state statutes prescribe. The state must deliver notice via certified or registered mail, and the notice must contain the date, time, and place of the hearing in most jurisdictions. The notice must also contain contact information for the court, a statement describing the nature of the proceedings, the parents' right to attend the proceedings, their right to counsel, and the consequences if the parents fail to attend.

Juries

The Supreme Court has held that while the Constitution guarantees jury trials in adult court, it does not so provide the right to jury trials in juvenile court. Some states provide for jury trials; most do not.

Public Observation

Some states allow the public to attend and witness juvenile proceedings, but many do not allow such public witness. The conflict is between benefits that attend transparency in legal proceedings and the children's interest in privacy.

Public hearings create less opportunity for oppression, abuse, prejudice, and bias, and more opportunity for a party to appeal to the community at large. Further, open hearings help to educate the public about the juvenile justice system, providing for a more informed and reasoned discourse on the issue. Open hearings may also act as a deterrent to potential offenders. The publicity, however, may harm the children involved, who will bear the stigma that might attend such hearings.

Most state statutes provide that the only parties who may be present at juvenile court hearings are the children, their parents, and any necessary witnesses but grant juvenile court judges the authority to admit other witnesses, the general public, or even allow media coverage of juvenile proceedings. Some states do not allow the public to witness juvenile hearings under any circumstances.

Evidence

The Rules of Evidence apply at adjudicatory hearings. Because much of the testimony at a-n-d hearings is in the form of parents' admissions, social workers' reports, foster parents' reports, medical records, police reports, and school records, the rules governing **hearsay, admissions, privilege,** and **authentication of records** are especially relevant.

hearsay
An out of court statement that a party is attempting to offer to prove the truth of the matter stated therein

admissions
A statement against one's interest

privilege
A class of communications that society values enough to afford special protections

authentication of records
The process by which a party seeking to introduced written records into evidence can prove to the court that the records are genuine, trustworthy, and what they purport to be

SIDEBAR

THE RULES OF EVIDENCE

Hearsay is any out of court statement that a party seeks to admit into evidence in order to prove the truth of the matter contained therein.

Example: The County is trying to remove a child from her mother, Arliss, because, the state alleges, the mother left the child home alone for three days. The mother disputes this. She puts her sister, Esther, on the stand. Esther will testify that her mother said, "Arliss was home all that time."

The statement is an out of court statement. The content of the statement is "Arliss was home all that time." Arliss is attempting to introduce the statement in order to prove that she was home all the time. Therefore, we have an out-of-court statement being introduced in order to prove the truth of the matter contained there. It is classic hearsay.

Admissions are statements that people make against their own interests.

Example: In the story above, the county wants to put Arliss's next-door neighbor on the stand. The neighbor will testify that Arliss said, "I left my

(continues)

baby home alone all last week." This looks like hearsay because it is an out-of-court statement. The county is using the statement "I left my baby home alone all last week" to prove that Arliss left her baby home alone all last week, so the county is introducing it in order to prove the truth of the matter contained therein. But, because it is Arliss's own statement, and it is against Arliss's interests, it is not hearsay. Therefore, it is admissible.

Privilege refers to a class of communications that society values enough to afford special protection. Examples are *attorney-client privilege,* which protects communications between lawyers and their clients; *priest-penitent privilege,* which protects communications between a priest and a person who has gone to the priest to make a confession; the *doctor-patient privilege,* which protects communications between a doctor and a person who seeks treatment from the doctor; and the *marital privilege,* which protects communications between a husband and wife.

   Authentication of records refers to the process by which a party seeking to introduce written records into evidence can prove to the court that the records are genuine, trustworthy, and what they purport to be.

Burden of Proof

burden of proof

The responsibility to prove to the court that something is so

standard of proof

The degree of certainty that a party must establish

preponderance of the evidence

A level of proof that establishes a certainty of 51 percent or greater

beyond a reasonable doubt

A level of proof that establishes a certainty of approximately 90 percent or greater

The **burden of proof** is the responsibility to prove to the court that something is so. The state has the burden of proof in a-n-d cases. This means the state must prove to a specific degree of certainty, or **standard of proof,** that the child is an abused, neglected, or dependent child. In most states, the standard of proof is clear and convincing evidence. In some states the standard or proof is a **preponderance of the evidence.**

   Preponderance of the evidence is otherwise stated as "more likely than not." Courts quantify this standard at 51 percent certainty. Clear and convincing evidence is higher than preponderance. Courts generally quantify clear and convincing evidence as approximately 75 percent certainty.

   Clear and convincing evidence is lower than the criminal standard of **beyond a reasonable doubt,** which courts typically quantify as approximately 90 to 95 percent certainty. The reason that a-n-d cases have a lower standard of proof than criminal cases is that if there is to be an error, the states would rather the error is in favor of protecting the child rather than protecting the parents.

   If the parents refuse to testify at a-n-d hearings, the court will draw the strongest case against them that the opposing evidence will allow. The weight of these inferences against non-testifying parents is part of the total weight of the evidence the courts can consider.

Appeals

Parents often appeal lower courts' decisions on the basis of the weight of the evidence, alleging that the verdicts were against the manifest weight of the evidence. These parents contend that the evidence that the states' attorneys presented at trial did not rise to the mandated standard of proof.

These challenges are common because, especially in sexual abuse cases, there are rarely witnesses. If sexual abuse occurred, there were likely only two people present during the event: one of them is the abuser and the other one is the child. There are many problems with children's testimony: vagueness, children's difficulty in distinguishing between fact and fantasy, and the ease with which adults can coerce children into saying and even believing that what occurred was permissible, or if not permissible, then the child's fault.

Courts, however, give great weight to children's testimony in abuse cases, especially where other witnesses corroborate the children's testimony or where the children's testimony is consistent and reasonable. The case below illustrates the manner in which courts weigh children's testimony, witnesses' testimony, and the fact that when parents refuse to testify in abuse cases the courts will draw every inference against the parents that the opposing evidence will allow.

In re Nathaniel II
18 A.D.3d 1038, 795 N.Y.S.2d 780 (2005)

Appeal from an order of the Family Court of Chemung County which granted petitioner's application to adjudicate Dakota II. to be an abused child.

Respondent is the father of three children, two boys (born in 1998 and 2001) and a girl (born in 1999). A fourth child, a boy (born in 1990), who is the legal ward—but not the biological child—of respondent, also resided in the household. In December 2003, petitioner commenced this proceeding alleging, among other things, respondent's sexual abuse of the girl (then four years old). Following a fact-finding hearing, Family Court sustained the abuse petition as against respondent, finding that he had committed the offense of sexual abuse in the first degree. Respondent appeals.

We affirm. Respondent's primary contention is that Family Court's decision is against the weight of the evidence. In a Family Court proceeding, parental misconduct must be established by a preponderance of the evidence. Thus, it was petitioner's burden to present evidence which, taken as a whole and given its appropriate weight, shows that it was more probable than not that respondent committed the acts alleged (*see* Black's Law Dictionary 1182 [6th ed. 1990]).

In the instant case, we find that the girl's statements to her teacher, police investigators and the family's caseworker, which were corroborated by the statements of two of the other children, were sufficient to support Family Court's findings. The abuse was first revealed when, unsolicited, the girl told her

(continues)

In re Nathaniel II (Continued)

preschool teacher that respondent had been coming into her bedroom, pulling her pants down and sleeping on top of her. The school contacted police and, when questioned, the girl consistently repeated her description of respondent's behavior and, without prompting, lay on the floor and demonstrated how respondent would move back and forth. The girl also stated that respondent always sleeps with her, drew a picture of a penis which she described as respondent's "bug," and said that "wet stuff" came out of his "bug" and went on her stomach and pillow.

The girl's five-year-old brother also told the caseworker that respondent had always slept with his sister. In addition, the 13-year-old testified that he observed respondent sleeping in the girl's bed. Although, when questioned, respondent explained to the police that on that occasion he slept with the girl because she had awakened crying in the middle of the night, that description was inconsistent with the description provided by the teenager who testified that respondent, without prompting, got up while they were watching a movie and went to sleep in the girl's bed with her. Further, respondent's failure to testify allowed " 'Family Court to draw the strongest inference against him which the opposing evidence would allow.' "

In our view, the evidence submitted at the hearing, combined with the allowable inference against respondent, was sufficient to support Family Court's finding of abuse.

Nor do we find merit in respondent's contention that the girl's out-of-court statements were not sufficiently corroborated. "It is well settled that a child's unsworn, out-of-court statements relating to abuse or neglect may be introduced into evidence at a fact-finding hearing and, if sufficiently corroborated, will support a finding of abuse or neglect." An out-of-court statement "may be corroborated by any evidence tending to support its reliability, and a relatively low degree of corroborative evidence is sufficient in abuse proceedings."

Family Court also has broad discretion in assessing credibility when there is inconsistent testimony. Here, the girl's explicit and consistent age-inappropriate knowledge of sexuality, her brother's statement and the testimony of the teenager corroborated the girl's out-of-court statements. In addition, we find that Family Court properly considered respondent's apparently false explanation to police as additional evidence in support of its finding. Finally, we reject respondent's contention that the girl's stories about, among other things, monsters in her bedroom undermine the credibility of her statements. We agree with Family Court's assessment that these fabrications reflect a child's natural imagination, and in no way detract from the reliability of the girl's detailed, spontaneous and consistent statements implicating respondent. We therefore decline to disturb Family Court's determination of abuse. We have considered respondent's remaining claims and find they are without merit.

ORDERED that the order is affirmed, without costs.

THE DISPOSITIONAL PHASE

If the court decides at the adjudication hearing that the children are abused, neglected, or dependent, and thus assumes jurisdiction over them, it must then decide where to place the children, what restrictions to place upon the parents, whether and how to proceed toward reunification of the family, what kind of visitation to allow among the parents and children, and what timeframe to impose.

Among the several alternatives available to juvenile courts are protective supervision, temporary custody, long-term foster care, legal custody, and permanent custody, or termination of parental rights. Most statutes have the stated goal of seeking to preserve the family unit whenever possible, to seek the least intrusive intervention, to keep siblings together, to keep children within their extended families when they cannot remain within their nuclear family, and within their communities when they cannot remain within their families, and to provide as much stability for the children as possible. States also instruct their courts to move children's cases through the system quickly, avoiding situations where children remain in limbo for extended periods of time.

Protective Supervision

Protective supervision allows the parents to retain legal and physical custody of their children while they work on their case plan. The court retains jurisdiction over the children, and uses that jurisdiction to allow the social services agency to send social workers, therapists, counselors, or other service providers into the home to monitor the situation in the home and to gauge the child's well-being.

> **protective supervision**
> A disposition that allows the parents to retain legal and physical custody of their children while they work on their case plan

Social services workers provide assistance on such issues as proper nutrition, hygiene, discipline, play, or education. When the court determines that the family has resolved its problems, or when the family has achieved all of the goals and completed all of the processes that the case plan has stipulated, the court will end the protective supervision.

Protective supervision is appropriate where the abuse was mild or appeared to be a result of ignorance or a belief that conflicts with mainstream American beliefs. For instance, in many cultures physical discipline of children in a manner that most Americans would consider abusive is a normal, accepted practice and is not considered abusive. In such a case, simply educating the parents on accepted American means of discipline and providing support and follow-up while the parents assimilate the new practices may be sufficient to protect the children.

Neglect is also often a matter of parental ignorance and easy to remedy. Many young parents, for instance, have incorrect ideas of what constitutes proper nutrition or an acceptable level of hygiene. Some parents neglect to provide medical care to their children because they are unaware of the requirements, or they do not know how to make appointments and follow through with them. In cases such as these, education, follow-up, and support may be enough to protect the children.

Protective supervision is the least disruptive disposition and so courts use it as often as they reasonably can without exposing the children to jeopardy. Parents who receive care, education, and support in the home while caring for their children are more likely to remedy their problems, and their children are more likely to recover from the neglect or abuse they experienced.

Temporary Custody

A disposition of **temporary custody** removes the children from their parents' custody, and keeps the children under the juvenile court's jurisdiction for a discrete period of time with a view toward reunification in a relatively short time. The court vests custody of the children on a temporary basis in a social services agency, a private child agency, a parent, a relative, or a state authority.

The children live in a foster home, with a relative, or in an institution while the family works on the case plan.

Temporary custody is appropriate in cases where the neglect or abuse was severe and the parents knowingly or recklessly caused it to happen. In these cases, the court removes the children from the parents for their safety, and the social services system provides education, support, and therapeutic services to both children and parents.

The social services agency schedules regular visits between the parents and the children, unless the agency or the court determines that visitation will be detrimental to the children. The social worker or the GAL often supervises and monitors the visits initially to protect the children, to assure the children that they will be safe, to observe the interaction between the parents and the children, and to ensure that the visits are appropriate. The visits are an important benchmark of progress and a good indicator of whether the parents can care for their children.

The ultimate goal of temporary custody is for the parents to remedy the problems or situations that allowed or caused the abuse and reunite the parents and children. Often, however, parents do not complete the educational programs or avail themselves of the services offered to them, or they do not visit their children during the separation. In these cases the state files an action to terminate parental rights.

SIDEBAR

RELATIONAL THERAPY WITH VERY YOUNG CHILDREN IN FOSTER CARE

Infants and toddlers are particularly vulnerable to abuse and neglect, and they have special needs that older children do not. Parenting very young children is more difficult than parenting older children and teens. Many young parents have never received guidance or instruction on child rearing. Where infants and toddlers are in foster care, and family reunification is the

(continues)

goal, social services agencies must make a special effort to teach parents to tend to their children's needs and to condition the children to view their parents in a positive light.

A Michigan program called Families in Transition has devised a program of relational therapy. Parents are awarded extra visitation sessions with their children that a therapist attends. The therapist guides the parents through the visit, giving them instruction on proper treatment of their children, coaching them as they interact with their children, and asking questions designed to aid them in exploring their experiences with maltreatment. The therapy continues for six months to a year.

The therapists aim to heighten parents' awareness of their children's needs, remove barriers to appropriate responsiveness, shape realistic expectations of parents, and provide insight into the connection between the parents' relationship history and its impact on the child.

Twenty-four families participated in the first run of the program. The children were ultimately returned to their biological parents in twenty-one of those cases, and caseworkers noted substantial positive relational changes in the families. Caseworkers also reported feeling more comfortable in their recommendations of reunification.

Lee, R.E., & Stack, A.M. "In Whose Arms? Using Relational Therapy in Supervised Family Visitation With Very Young Children in Foster Care." *Journal of Family Psychotherapy, Vol. 15(4).*

Legal Custody

Legal custody places the children with a person, usually a relative, who assumes the rights and responsibilities attendant to custody. Legal custodians have the right to determine where the children will live and go to school and have the right to discipline the children. They have the duty to protect them and provide them with food, shelter, clothing, education, medical care, supervision, and other necessaries.

The parents retain residual parental rights, which include the right to determine the children's religion, the right to reasonable visitation with the children, and the right to consent to adoption. When parents wish to regain legal custody of their children, they can file a motion with the juvenile court. The juvenile court may, upon consideration of the motion, vest legal custody of the children with their moving parents.

Legal custody is appropriate where the abuse or neglect was severe enough to warrant a long-term separation of the children from their parents, but there remains some hope that ultimately the parents can improve, and a strong support network is available.

legal custody

A disposition where the court places children with a person who assumes daily rights and responsibilities for the children, while the parents retain some parental rights

Long-Term Foster Care or Planned Permanent Living Arrangement

long-term foster care and **planned permanent living arrangement**
A disposition where the parents retain their parental rights, while the social services agency places the child into a foster home or institutional home on a long-term or possibly permanent basis

Long-term foster care and **planned permanent living arrangement** are essentially the same. The parents retain their parental rights, while the social services agency places the child in a foster home or institutional home on a long-term or permanent basis.

This arrangement is appropriate where the children are unable to function in a family setting and require institutional or specialized care, the child is not a suitable candidate for adoption, or the child is older and objects to adoption. Courts generally disfavor long-term foster care and planned permanent living arrangements because they keep children in a legal and physical limbo, and because courts favor home-like and family-like settings for children.

Termination of Parental Rights

termination of parental rights (TPR)
A disposition the completely and permanently deprives parents of custody and all rights and responsibilities attendant to raising their children

All of the dispositions outlined above have dates certain by which time the court must either terminate its jurisdiction over the children and return them to their families, or move the children into a permanent arrangement by means of **termination of parental rights (TPR).**

Termination of parental rights permanently and completely ends the parent child relationship. This relieves the parents of all duties, and strips them of all rights and privileges regarding their children. Once the court has entered an order of TPR, the children are available for adoption. This is a highly favored where the children are young and readily adoptable, and the parents have severe problems.

Termination of parental rights can occur voluntarily, when parents relinquish their parental rights and duties of their own volition, or involuntarily through an adjudication and disposition process. States have enacted stringent requirements for TPR hearings because it is the most extreme measure that a court can undertake with regard to child custody, and because it is permanent.

States initiate TPR proceedings only when the prima facie presumption that children's welfare will be best served in the care and custody of their parents is overcome by a showing that the natural parents are unfit to have custod, or exceptional circumstances make parental custody detrimental to the best interests of the child.

The petitioning agency bears the burden of proof, and must provide the court with sufficient evidence to form grounds for TPR. All of the states and the District of Columbia have TPR statutes, and all contain a number of grounds that will provide a basis for TPR. Among the most common are:

- Severe or chronic abuse or neglect
- Abuse or neglect of other children in the household

- Abandonment
- Long-term mental illness or deficiency of the parents
- Long-term alcohol or drug-induced incapacity of the parents
- Failure to support or maintain contact with the child
- A felony conviction of the parents for a crime of violence against the child or other family member, or a conviction for any felony when the term of conviction is such a length as to have a negative impact on the child and the only available provision of care for the child is foster care
- Withholding medical treatment for non-religious reasons
- Withholding food

Appealing Termination of Parental Rights Dispositions

A TPR order is a final order that parents may appeal. The requirements for a TPR appeal are generally the same as for other types of appeals—the appellant must file a notice of appeal within a certain number of days, must provide the appellate court with the record of the hearing that they are appealing, must pay a fee, and must comply with other procedural requirements, such as filing a certain number of copies, filing in a certain format, and providing certain forms and paperwork.

CASE PROBLEM

The state charged a father with abusing his four sons. The court held at the hearing that that father had the burden of proof and that the standard of proof was preponderance of the evidence. By this standard, the court found that the father had abused is oldest son.

    The father appealed on the grounds that the preponderance of the evidence standard was too low, and that the court should have applied the clear and convincing evidence standard. What is the result?

ROLE-PLAY PROBLEM

Fred and Mary are the father and mother of three children, ages three, five, and six. They have admitted to the following allegations:

1. Fred abuses alcohol, frequently drinking to the point of losing consciousness.
2. Fred becomes violent when he is drinking and often hits Mary and the children.
3. Mary abuses cocaine and other narcotics.
4. Fred and Mary have left the children home alone for several hours while they were out drinking and using drugs.

5. Fred often brings other women home, in front of Mary and the children.

6. On several occasions, social workers have gone to the home and found no food in the home.

7. The home is filthy, with trash and dirty clothing piled everywhere.

8. There have been several occasions when the water, electricity, and phone were disconnected because Fred and Mary did not pay the bills.

9. You are the social worker. Craft a workable case plan that will address all of the issues in the above allegations.

HYPOTHETICAL PROBLEM

Lillian is six years old. She and her mother, Jane, are HIV positive. Shortly after her birth, doctors determined Lillian's viral load to be 550,000, which is quite high. Doctors placed her on a three-drug regimen, and instructed Jane in detail as to proper administration of those medications. At a medical checkup when Lillian was three years old, her viral load increased to 2,148,000. This indicated to hospital staff that Lillian was not getting all of her medication. Doctors also were concerned with Lillian's height and weight, which consistently were measured at the 25th percentile for children her age.

Doctors got Lillian's viral load back down to an acceptable level through aggressive intervention and a rigorous medication regimen. They released Lillian to her mother. Within two months, her viral load was back up to 1,000,000 and she weighed between 16 and 19 pounds.

Her pediatrician admitted Lillian to a pediatric care facility for children with HIV/AIDS. Within a month, Lillian's viral load was down to 2350. According to medical testimony, these dramatic changes necessarily indicated that Mother had, again, not been properly giving Lillian her medications.

The medical staff continued to monitor Lillian's viral load after she returned to Mother's home. Three months later, her viral load was "out of control" at 360,000. Doctors considered this a life-threatening situation, one that could only be explained if Mother was again failing to administer Lillian's drug regimen. Medical personnel placed a hotline call was placed to the social services agency, which took custody of Lillian immediately. They placed her in a foster home, where she remains to the present day. In the time Lillian has been in the foster home, her height and weight have risen to the ninetieth to 95th percentiles. Her viral loads have fluctuated between a low of 925 and a high of 40,000.

The relationship between DFS and Mother was governed, in part, by a case plan with which Mother failed, in some respects, to comply. Specifically, social services described her as "non-compliant" concerning a requirement that she participate in therapy sessions with a provided counselor, who stopped seeing Mother after six months due to her lack of cooperation. The service agreement required Mother to obtain medical treatment for her own HIV infection, which she resisted for some time. Social services records indicated that Mother was extremely ill at one visit, when she was so weak that "she couldn't even get up and walk." It was the concern of some agency employees at the time that Mother might not "make it." Workers also expressed concerns about the unsanitary condition of Mother's home, with dirty dishes in the sink, food lying out, and clothes in the floor.

The social services agency filed a petition to terminate the parental rights of Mother as to Lillian. As statutory grounds for terminating Mother's parental rights, the agency alleged that Mother had neglected Lillian, as evidenced by Lillian's medical history and mother's noncompliance with the case plan.

In re J.V.O., 133 S.W.3d 570 (Mo.App., 2004)

1. How should the court rule on the petition?

2. What factors are important?

3. Is mother's noncompliance with the case plan more or less significant than the medical evidence?

ETHICAL CONCERNS

An ethical concern arises when parents have been abusive or neglectful enough that it appears unlikely that reunification will be possible, but the abuse or neglect is not extreme enough to warrant the immediate filing of a petition to terminate parental rights. In such a situation, the county should craft a case plan, and aid the parents in complying with it, and provide referrals to social services, education, therapy, drug treatment, and whatever other services they deem necessary. It is difficult, however, to justify spending the county's limited time and resources on such a case plan when it appears unlikely that the parents will ever complete the case plan.

DISCUSSION QUESTIONS

Some counties favor reunification of families at almost any cost. Critics argue that this policy favors parents' rights over children's rights.

1. Do you agree?

2. Do you believe parents' rights or children's rights should take precedence?

3. Should the county remove children first and ask questions later when there is an allegation of abuse or neglect?

One the county removes a child from a home, it will be several weeks at the least before that child returns home, even where the allegations are proven false.

4. Do you think that time apart damages the children?

5. How long should the county allow a child to remain in foster care before they move to terminate parental rights?

6. What should be the grounds for termination of parental rights?

Referring to the sample complaint listed above:

7. What are the differences between the two complaints?

8. Why did Lucinda's mother ask for these changes?

9. Do the changes make a difference legally? Will the amended Complaint support an allegation that Lucinda is an abused child?

Referring to the *Nathaniel II* case above:

10. What was the nature of the evidence?

11. Were there problems with the evidence? What were the problems?

12. If there were problems with the evidence, should they have risen to the level of reversible error?

13. Do you think courts should have different rules or standards when they are evaluating children's testimony?

14. Should those rules apply to all cases involving children, or just abuse cases?

15. Should there be a difference between sexual abuse cases and other abuse cases?

KEY TERMS

adjudicatory phase
admissions
authentication of records
beyond a reasonable doubt
burden of proof
case plan
dispositional phase
hearsay
legal custody

long-term foster care and planned
   permanent living arrangement
preponderance of the evidence
privilege
protective supervision
standard of proof
temporary custody
termination of parental rights

END NOTES

i California Welfare and Institutions Code § 350 (a)(1)
ii South Carolina Code of Laws § 20-7-755

SECTION IV

Current Issues

Chapter 11

EMANCIPATION

OBJECTIVES

By the end of the chapter, the student should know:

- The definition of emancipation
- The types of emancipation
- The difference between express, implied, and constructive emancipation
- The legal requirements for implied or constructive emancipation
- The legal effects of emancipation
- What emancipated minors may and may not do
- The rights and obligations of the parents of emancipated minors
- The law of contracts involving minors
- The procedures for emancipation
- The procedures for rescinding emancipation

INTRODUCTION

Emancipation is the process by which a minor attains majority, or adult, status in the eyes of the law. An emancipated minor may do many of the things legally reserved for adults, such as buy real estate, enter into contracts, or consent to medical treatments.

Parents of unemancipated children can make decisions for them about where they will attend school, what religion they will practice, and in what activities they will participate. They have the right to receive their children's wages and the responsibility to provide for their children's needs.

emancipation

The process by which a minor attains majority, or adult, status in the eyes of the law

The parents of emancipated minors are no longer financially responsible for their children, nor do they have the rights attendant to parenthood, such as the rights to make decisions for their children and to receive their children's wages.

TYPES OF EMANCIPATION

Minors become emancipated automatically when they reach the age of 18. They can seek emancipation prior to that in one of three ways—by means of a legal proceeding, by getting married, or by joining the military. Minors must obtain their parents' consent before joining the military and before getting married, depending upon their states' marriage laws. (*See* Chapter 13, Marriage.)

express emancipation

The conferring of majority status upon a minor by means of the parents' spoken or written consent

Express emancipation occurs by spoken or written parental consent. Parents can explicitly and specifically grant permission for their minor children to live separately from them, free from their control, and without obligation to them and move the court for an order making the emancipation official. The emancipation becomes legal, effective, and public when the court grants the motions and issues the order.

implied emancipation

The conferring of majority status upon minors by means of unspoken parental consent to them living separately and apart from their parents without the parents' or the minors' objection

Implied emancipation occurs by unspoken parental consent where minors live apart from their parents without objection from either the parents or the minors. Minors in these situations must be financially and physically independent. Courts will find implied emancipation where minors are close to the age of majority and have either left the parental home voluntarily or are so unmanageable and unruly that the court terminates the parents' duty to support their children.

Emancipation can occur where minor children have entered into relations that are inconsistent with being subordinate members of their parents' family. The parents' acquiescence to their children's conduct will cause emancipation.

constructive emancipation

The conferring of adult status upon minors by means of a change in the minor's position in the eyes of society, in most instances through marriage or joining the military

Constructive emancipation can occur by a change of the child's status in the eyes of society, as when the minor marries or joins the military. The marriage must be legal in accordance with the laws of the state in which it takes place. The case below demonstrates that minors cannot get married and then claim they are emancipated through marriage if the marriage is not lawful.

Implied and Constructive Emancipation

Implied or constructive emancipation cases frequently arise where courts have adjudicated minors dependent and the county provides care and support for the minor, then seeks reimbursement from the parents for that care and support. Implied emancipation cases also often arise where noncustodial parents seek to

Kingery v. Hintz
124 S.W.3d 875 (Tex.App. 2003)

Appellant Christopher Kingery filed a petition for divorce from appellee seeking dissolution of an alleged informal marriage between the parties. The trial court granted appellee's motion for summary judgment and dismissed appellant's action for divorce with prejudice, finding that the parties never entered into a ceremonial or common-law marriage. In ten issues, appellant claims the trial court erred in granting summary judgment because the elements of a common-law marriage were met. We affirm.

Appellant is presently incarcerated for the offense of sexual assault of a minor—the minor complainant is the appellee in this case. Appellant filed a petition for divorce in an effort to claim the parties had been legally married. In his petition, appellant claims that he and appellee were parties to an informal marriage and states that "the issue of divorce has become a legal priority because of pending . . . criminal issues. . . ." Appellant notes his conviction is still on appeal. Appellant alleges the parties were married on or about October of 1999, and ceased to live together as husband and wife on or about April of 2001. Appellant states the parties conceived a child on Valentine's Day of 2000. At that time, appellant was 36 years old and appellee was 15 years old. Appellant contends the parties agreed to become husband and wife, lived together as husband and wife, and held themselves out publicly as husband and wife. Appellant asserts that appellee's family consented to the union. Appellant now seeks dissolution of the marriage and division of property.

Although the parties did live at the same address, appellant was the live-in boyfriend of appellee's mother. Appellee asserts that any sexual relationship between she and appellant occurred without her mother's consent or knowledge. Around April of 2000, appellee's mother learned that appellee was pregnant and sent her to stay with her grandparents. Appellee terminated the pregnancy. DNA testing conclusively established appellant was the biological father of the child. Criminal proceedings were then brought against appellant. Appellant contends that the marital relationship lasted for another 15 months because, until his trial, appellee performed "spousal duties," such as "sending letters, phone calls, visitation, [and providing] financial help."

After appellant filed for divorce, appellee filed a motion for summary judgment. The trial court granted the motion, finding the parties never entered into a lawful marriage. At no time during the alleged union did appellee reach the age of 18, the age of consent for an informal marriage.

A common-law or informal marriage can be established by showing the parties (1) entered into an agreement to become husband and wife; (2) cohabitated as husband and wife; and (3) held each other out publicly as husband and wife. However, there is a crucial prerequisite: both parties must possess the legal capacity to marry.

To counter arguments concerning appellee's age, appellant claims that appellee was emancipated and that appellee's family consented to the informal marriage. The cases cited by appellant regarding emancipation are general contract cases and do not relate to emancipation in the context of the marriage relationship. Importantly, the Family Code emancipates a minor only after she has been married in accordance with the laws of Texas. Hence, appellee could only have been emancipated after she entered into a legal marriage.

The judgment of the trial court is affirmed.

terminate their child support obligations by claiming that their children are emancipated.

Courts disfavor findings of emancipation on the grounds that parents are primarily responsible for their children and they must not abrogate that responsibility lightly. For this reason, emancipation is never presumed. Rather, the burden is upon the party asserting it to demonstrate the facts proving emancipation.

Legal Requirements for Implied or Constructive Emancipation

Courts reviewing petitions for emancipation examine the circumstances under which the minor left home and the nature of the parents' obligation throughout the period of separation.

No single factor confers emancipated status upon a minor. Rather, the court will examine, among other things, where the minors are living, how dependent they are financially, physically, and emotionally upon their parents, and whether they have children of their own, then they will rule that the minors have been emancipated. Courts will declare minors emancipated where they determine the minors are independent from their parents. Courts will not adjudge minors to be emancipated simply where they have refrained from having contact with their parents or simply because they have given birth to children of their own.

Where minors of employable age and in full possession of their faculties voluntarily abandon their parents' home against their parents' wills for the purpose of avoiding parental discipline and control, they may be deemed to have forfeited their rights to parental financial support.

The court in the following case adjudged a minor to be constructively emancipated where he voluntarily left his mother's home rather than follow her reasonable household rules, thus denying the father's claim for child support.

Donnelly v. Donnelly
2004 WL 3092286 (N.Y.A.D. 3 Dept., Jan. 13, 2005)

Appeal from an order of the Family Court of Albany County entered June 26, 2003, which dismissed petitioner's application, in a proceeding pursuant to Family Ct Act article 4, for modification of a prior order of child support.

Petitioner and respondent were married in 1981 and are the parents of four children. In November 2000, petitioner was removed from the family home after being found guilty, following a trial, of neglect based upon abuse of the eldest child, now emancipated. By order of Family Court, respondent retained custody of the children and petitioner was directed to pay child support and was subject to an order of supervision restricting visitation. In November 2002, the parties'

(continues)

Donnelly v. Donnelly (Continued)

second child, Brandon, moved out of respondent's home on his eighteenth birthday and moved in with petitioner. Shortly thereafter, as relevant to this appeal, petitioner commenced this proceeding to modify the child support order, seeking, among other things, child support from respondent for Brandon.

Following a hearing, the Support Magistrate agreed with respondent's assertion in opposition that Brandon's voluntary abandonment of her home, after failing to comply with the reasonable rules of the household, constituted constructive emancipation and forfeited his right to support from respondent. Family Court issued a written decision which, among other things, affirmed that finding and rejected petitioner's objections. On petitioner's appeal, we affirm.

On the merits, under well-established law, a parent's obligation to support a child until he or she reaches age 21 may be suspended where the child, although not financially self sufficient, abandons that parent's home without sufficient cause and withdraws from the parent's control, refusing to comply with reasonable parental demands, under the doctrine of constructive emancipation. Thus, "a child of employable age and in full possession of his or her faculties who voluntarily abandons his or her parents' home against their will, and for the purpose of avoiding parental

discipline and control, may be deemed to have forfeited his or her right to parental financial support.

Here, there was ample, virtually unrefuted evidence that Brandon's decision to depart his mother's home was voluntary, prompted by her insistence that he follow entirely legitimate and reasonable household rules and standards of acceptable behavior after having failed to do so for a prolonged period of time. Respondent's testimony established that Brandon stole from her, subjected her to acts of violence and verbal abuse, failed to attend school, abused alcohol and drugs, was arrested, barricaded his room and sequestered a girlfriend in his room for days, all in total defiance of respondent's reasonable rules and expectations. Respondent testified that, after his departure, she maintained contact with him despite his continued unacceptable behavior, and she wanted and would allow him to return home if he abided by reasonable household rules. Having chosen to "deliberately flout" respondent's legitimate mandates and voluntarily abandon home to avoid her parental discipline and control, Brandon has forfeited the right to support from her. We thus discern no basis upon which to disturb Family Court's determination in that regard.

Affirmed.

LEGAL EFFECTS OF EMANCIPATION

Emancipation relieves parents of all familial and parental obligations toward the minor and concurrently grants the minor the rights and responsibilities attendant to adulthood.

Emancipated minors may:

- Sign binding contracts
- Buy, sell, and own real and personal property
- Obtain employment
- Keep their earnings

- Consent to medical care and procedures
- Buy insurance
- Sue and be sued
- Establish their own residences
- Enroll in school
- Obtain operators' licenses if they are above the legal driving age
- Own stock
- Make wills, trusts, or other probate arrangements
- Buy, sell, and register motor vehicles
- Execute releases
- Marry
- Enlist in the military
- Disobey their parents
- Be immune from status offenses

SIDEBAR

CELEBRITY EMANCIPATION

Many young actors and musicians begin their careers with their parents as their managers and end up petitioning for emancipation. The child stars often base their petitions on their parents' mismanagement of their careers, but more often they base their petitions on their parents' misappropriation of their earnings.

In the past few years, pop singer Aaron Carter sued his mother for taking money out of his bank account without authorization, country singer LeAnn Rimes sued her father for stealing $7 million while acting as her manager, television actor Taran Noah Smith sued his parents for control of a $1.5 million trust fund, movie actor Macaulay Culkin sued his father for legal control of his assets, tennis player Anna Kournikova filed an action against her parents over title to a house, movie actor Jena Malone sought emancipation from her mother based on her mother's financial mismanagement and failure to pay taxes, and pop star Tiffany filed a petition for emancipation from her mother based on her mother's mismanagement of her career.

Even animated characters are not immune. In an episode of *The Simpson's* entitled "Barting Over," Bart discovers he was the star of a commercial when he was a baby and that Homer has squandered all of his

(continues)

earnings. Bart takes Homer to court and wins emancipation. Bart moves into a loft downtown where he befriends skateboarder Tony Hawk, who lives upstairs. As Bart embarks on a national tour with Tony, Homer appears, attempting to win his beloved Bart back into his life.

The majority of these cases settled out of court, with the minors' funds being placed in a trust fund.

Emancipation does not allow minors to evade:

- School attendance laws
- Purchase of alcohol or tobacco laws
- All child labor laws
- Marriage laws

The parents of emancipated minors:

- Are no longer the minors' guardians
- Have no obligations regarding the minors' school attendance
- Have no legal liability for the minors' actions
- Have no obligation to support the minors
- Have no right to the minors' earnings, support, or services

SIDEBAR
CONTRACTS INVOLVING MINORS

American courts will not compel minors to perform most contracts. This is to protect minors from the folly of their decisions.

There is, however, one notable exception to this principle: minors must perform on contracts involving **necessaries,** or those items that are crucial to their survival. Necessaries include food, clothing, shelter, and transportation to a place of employment. This principle is also intended to protect minors: if merchants knew that minors could escape their obligations to perform under all contracts, they would not enter into any contracts with minors, including contracts to provide necessaries. That would result in minors being unable to secure those items they need to survive. Therefore, the courts compel minors to perform these contracts, thus ensuring that merchants remain willing to provide such items to them.

necessaries

Items that are crucial to a person's survival, such as food, clothing, shelter, and transportation to a place of employment

PROCEDURES FOR EMANCIPATION

The majority of states have statutes that dictate the procedures and requirements for express emancipation. The minimum age varies among the states, but is usually between 14 and 16 years.

Most statutes require an assertion or proof that:

• The minor is living independently of her parents;

• She can demonstrate an adequately managed and lawful source of income;

• Both the minor and her parents are voluntarily seeking the emancipation; and

• The emancipation is in the child's best interests.

The underlying notion of emancipation is that the minor is mature enough to shrug off the mantle of protective juvenile laws. Thus, the courts are supposed to deny emancipation petitions where the minors in question have not demonstrated maturity or the ability to care for themselves. Legislatures did not intend to allow parents to use emancipation to punish unruly children or to rid themselves of burdensome children.

SIDEBAR

SANGER-WILLEMSEN STUDY OF EMANCIPATION IN MODERN TIMES

Law professors Carol Sanger and Eleanor Willemsen studied how parents were using the California emancipation laws. They outlined the results of their study in *Minor Changes: Emancipating Children in Modern Times, 25,* U. Mich. J. L. Ref. 239 (1992). They describe the genesis of the project as the result of an offhand remark at a cocktail party. A woman stated that "in order for her and her new husband to begin their marriage without the complicating presence of stepchildren, they 'had to emancipate' her sixteen year-old daughter."

This prompted the professors to wonder whether parents were using emancipation as a means to abdicate their responsibility rather than as a legal and formal declaration and recognition of as minor's maturity, as it was intended. Their study revealed that this was indeed the case.

After interviewing children of parents who ranged in socioeconomic status from a very poor non-working single mother to an affluent dual professional couple they found a similarity in their reasons for employing the emancipation process. In the majority of cases the idea for emancipation came from the parents. Nonresident parents were using it to avoid paying child support;

(continues)

stepparents were using it to avoid financial responsibility for their stepchildren's care and legal responsibility for their stepchildren's actions.

Once initiated, Sanger and Willemsen found, emancipation was "a procedural snap. Declarations of emancipation are obtained with stunning ease and speed; the ones we studied typically took less than a week from formal start to finish. When parents sign their child's petition, as they did in each of the ninety petitions examined, the parents consent to a declaration of emancipation without a hearing. The few hearings that were held were perfunctory, often taking only five or ten minutes. Thus, despite the statutory requirement that the judge determine that emancipation is not contrary to the minor's best interests, exchange between the judge and minor was minimal at best."

RESCINDING EMANCIPATION

Courts have consistently held that emancipation is not necessarily a permanent, continuing status. The courts can expressly terminate it at the request of the parties or the parties can terminate it implicitly or constructively by their actions.

CASE PROBLEM

Robert and Betty were divorced. A.D.G., the minor child of the parties, was placed in the residential custody of Betty and has remained there to the present time. A.D.G. quit school on her 16th birthday and later became pregnant and gave birth to a child of her own.

Robert filed a motion to terminate his obligation to pay child support on the grounds that his daughter had emancipated herself when she quit school and became a mother. She continued to live with her mother and remain financially dependent upon her.

The trial court terminated Robert's child support obligation, finding "that in as much as she is not attending school and has dropped out of school and is not attending [and] has in essence emancipated herself that support is no longer appropriate."

Betty appeals. What is the result?

ROLE-PLAY PROBLEM

You represent the mother of a 16-year-old girl. The girl's father has abandoned the family and the mother is about to remarry. She wants to petition the court to emancipate her daughter so that she and her husband can "start the marriage off right."

Fashion a petition for emancipation.

HYPOTHETICAL PROBLEM

Fifteen-year-old Ruby Rae is an international pop star who has sold millions of records. Ruby Rae's mother, Pearl, has always been her manager. There have always been whispers that Pearl is domineering, abrasive, and makes poor career decisions on Ruby Rae's behalf. The belief is that only Ruby Rae's phenomenal talent has accounted for her success in spite of her mother's mismanagement.

Pearl was personally responsible for killing a movie deal in which Ruby Rae would have starred as a teenaged pirate in the sequel to *Pirates of the Caribbean*. She killed a deal in which Ruby Rae would have starred alongside Jim Carrey in big budget science fiction film. Ruby Rae's recording contract is in danger because of Pearl's unreasonable and outlandish demands.

Ruby Rae has filed a petition seeking a declaration that she is an emancipated minor. She wishes to be free of her mother's influence, and wishes to keep her earnings. Her mother is vehemently opposing the petition. Pearl asserts that at 15, Ruby Rae is too young to make any decisions for herself, and that Pearl's influence, imperfect as it is, is a product of Pearl's unconditional maternal love for Ruby Rae.

1. Should the court grant Ruby Rae's petition? Why or why not?

2. Can you fashion an acceptable compromise solution to the parties' dispute?

3. Suppose Ruby Rae were a regular 15-year-old working at a fast-food restaurant and she filed her petition because her mother took all of her earnings without giving Ruby Rae any money at all. Would you support Ruby Rae's petition in those circumstances?

ETHICAL CONCERNS

As always, there is an ethical tension between advocating on behalf of your client's wishes and wanting to advocate for what is in a child's best interests. It would be difficult for any compassionate and ethical legal practitioner to file a petition for emancipation of a minor child who is getting in the way of a new marriage. It would be similarly difficult to file a petition for emancipation of a minor child because the child's noncustodial parent does not want to pay to support that child any longer.

The best course in the above cases is to ensure that there are legal grounds to support the petition. If the legal argument is sound, and the legal requirements are in place, the position will be ethically sound.

DISCUSSION QUESTIONS

1. Is there an age below 18 at which courts should presume emancipation is in a minor's best interests?

2. Should marriage or joining the military automatically confer emancipated status upon minors?

3. Are there other circumstances that should automatically confer emancipated status upon minors?

4. Should courts favor petitions for emancipation in cases where parents remarry and wish to start new lives without the complicating factors of dependent children?

5. Should courts grant emancipation petitions where minors voluntarily leave their parents' homes?

6. Should courts grant emancipation petitions where minors are unruly and refuse to follow household rules?

KEY TERMS

constructive emancipation
emancipation
express emancipation

implied emancipation
necessaries

Chapter 12

PARENTAL NOTIFICATION OF ABORTION AND JUDICIAL BYPASS

OBJECTIVES

By the end of this chapter, the student should know:

- A very brief history of American abortion law
- The parameters of states' parental notification of abortion laws
- How states define "minor" for purposes of parental notification laws
- The procedures for obtaining a judicial bypass
- The grounds for obtaining a judicial bypass
- The procedure for appealing a bypass decision

INTRODUCTION

Minor girls, like adult women, have a constitutionally protected right to obtain abortions under *Roe v. Wade*, 410 U.S. 113 (1973). The United States Supreme Court held in that case that the constitution guarantees women a right to privacy, and that right to privacy includes women's right to make decisions about abortion. While *Roe v. Wade* has been under constant attack ever since, it remains the law.

The states have the right to restrict *Roe v. Wade* somewhat by enacting laws that limit its applications. Among the many ways that the states have limited *Roe v. Wade* is through the passage of **parental notification of abortion laws.** These laws require minor girls to either notify or obtain the consent of one or both of their parents prior to obtaining abortions.

The Supreme Court held that minor girls must have the opportunity to appeal directly to a court for permission to obtain an abortion with notifying or obtaining consent from their parents in certain circumstances in the 1979 case

Bellotti v. Baird, 443 U.S. 622 (1979). The Court set out the parameters for this mechanism:

> . . . every minor must have the opportunity—if she so desires—to go directly to a court without first consulting or notifying her parents. If she satisfies the court that she is mature and well enough informed to make intelligently the abortion decision on her own, the court must authorize her to act without parental consultation or consent. If she fails to satisfy the court that she is competent to make this decision independently, she must be permitted to show that an abortion nevertheless would be in her best interests. If the court is persuaded that it is, the court must authorize the abortion. If, however, the court is not persuaded by the minor that she is mature or that the abortion would be in her best interests, it may decline to sanction the operation. 433 U.S. at 647–48.

The process has come to be known as a **judicial bypass,** which is the device that allows a pregnant, unemancipated **minor** to petition the court to allow her to consent to her own abortion in states that have parental notification of, or consent to, abortion statutes. A minor, for purposes of these statutes, is a female ranging in age from 16 to 18 years old. These statutes require the health care provider to either provide notice to, or obtain the consent of, one or both parents of an unemancipated minor before the provider can perform an abortion.

PARENTAL NOTIFICATION STATUTES

Forty-four states currently have laws requiring parental notice or parental consent before minors can obtain abortions.[i] The courts or the attorney general in nine of these states have declared the state's law, or some aspect of the law, unconstitutional or unenforceable on one of three grounds: the law violates the woman's right to privacy, does not contain an adequate judicial bypass procedure, or does not contain an adequate exception for situations where the young woman's life or health is in danger.[ii]

All of the statutes require notice to one or both of the parents and/or consent from one or both of the parents. Notice must be actual notice unless the provider

parental notification of abortion laws
Laws that require minor girls to either notify or obtain the consent of one or both of their parents before they can obtain an abortion

judicial bypass
A device that allows a pregnant, unemancipated minor to petition the court to allow her to consent to her own abortion in states that have parental notification of, or consent to, abortion statutes

minor
In the context of parental notification of abortion laws, an unemancipated girl ranging from 16 to 18 years of age, who has not been married, and is not a member of the armed services

cannot reach the parent to provide actual notice. Providers can give constructive notice by sending a letter via certified or regular mail in those cases.

All of the notice statutes provide for a 24- to 48-hour waiting period between the time of providing notice and the time the provider can perform the abortion. The waiting period in cases of constructive notice begins when the provider mails the notice.

The medical provider must obtain the written consent of both parents, the surviving parent if one parent is dead, or the custodial parent if the parents are divorced, before performing an abortion in states where the statute requires consent. Some states require the provider to furnish written materials to the parents describing the abortion procedure in detail, and containing lists of alternatives to abortion before the state will acknowledge the parents' consent. Some states require the girl and her parents to receive counseling from a pro-life organization.

Some states allow a girl to obtain the consent of, or give notice to, an interested adult other than her parents, such as a grandparent, adult sibling, or another close relative or adult.

EXCEPTIONS

Most statutes do not contain an exception for situations where the pregnancy is the result of rape or incest. This leaves some girls in the position of having to obtain the consent of the father who raped and impregnated them in order to abort the resulting pregnancy.

There are few states that have an exception to the notice or consent requirement where the young woman is the victim of child abuse. This does not refer to sexual abuse described above, but rather to situations where the girl has been the victim of physical abuse in her home, such that she fears further abuse if she tells her parents she is pregnant and considering an abortion. The states that provide exceptions in such cases are the minority. Those states that do have such an exception require the girl to provide clear and convincing evidence of a pattern of abuse.

Most notification statutes contain an emergency exception whereby the provider can avoid the notice or consent requirement in situations where the young woman's life or health is in danger. The statutes vary as to the level of danger that is required in order to avoid the notice or consent requirements. Some statutes, such as North Dakota's, require "grave danger" that will result in the girl's death if she observes the 24-hour mandated waiting period. Wisconsin allows a medical emergency exception where the threatened harm is psychological.

Courts that have ruled the health exception requirement too stringent have granted injunctions against the enforcement of the law.

Exhibit 12-1 shows the state laws on parental notification of or consent to abortion.

EXHIBIT 12-1 State Law Chart

State	Age	Notice of Consent	One Parent or Both	Can Another Adult Provide Consent?	Exception for Rape, Abuse, or Incest	Medical Exception	Judicial Bypass
Alabama	18	Consent	One	No	No[*][iii]	Yes	Yes
Alaska[iv]	17	Consent	One	No	No	Yes	Yes
Arkansas	18	Notice	Both	No	Yes	Yes	Yes
Arizona	18	Consent	One	No	Yes[v]	Yes	Yes
California[vi]	18	Consent	One	No	No	Yes	Yes
Colorado	18	Notice	Both	Yes	Yes[vii]	Yes	Yes
Connecticut	No Parental Notification of Abortion Statute						
Delaware	16	Notice	One	Yes	No	Yes	Yes
District of Columbia	No Parental Notification of Abortion Statute						
Florida[viii]	18	Notice	One	No	Yes	Yes	Yes
Georgia	18	Notice	One	No	No	Yes	Yes
Hawaii	No Parental Notification of Abortion Statute						
Idaho[ix]	18	Consent	One	No	No	Yes	Yes
Illinois[x]	18	Notice	One	Yes	Yes	Yes	Yes
Indiana	18	Consent	One	No	No	Yes	Yes
Iowa	18	Notice	One	Yes	Yes	Yes	Yes
Kansas	18	Notice	One	No	Yes[xi]	Yes	Yes
Kentucky	18	Consent	One	No	No	Yes	Yes
Louisiana[xii]	18	Consent	One	No	No	No	Yes
Maine	18	Consent	One	Yes	No	No	Yes
Maryland	18	Notice	One	No	No	No	No
Massachusetts	No Parental Notification of Abortion Statute						
Michigan	18	Consent	One	No	No	Yes	Yes
Minnesota	18	Notice	Both	No	Yes	Yes	Yes
Mississippi	18	Consent	Both	No	No	No	Yes
Missouri	18	Consent	One	No	No	No	Yes
Montana[xiii]	18	Notice	One	No	No	Yes	Yes
Nebraska	18	Notice	One	No	Yes	Yes	Yes
Nevada[xiv]	18	Notice	One	No	No	Yes	Yes

(continues)

EXHIBIT 12-1 State Law Chart (Continued)

State	Age	Notice of Consent	One Parent or Both	Can Another Adult Provide Consent?	Exception for Rape, Abuse, or Incest	Medical Exception	Judicial Bypass
New Hampshire[xv]	18	Notice	One	No	No	Yes	Yes
New Jersey[xvi]	18	Notice	One	No	Yes	Yes	Yes
New Mexico[xvii]	18	Consent	One	No	No	No	No
New York		No Parental Notification of Abortion Statute					
North Carolina	18	Consent	One	Yes	Yes[xviii]	Yes	Yes
North Dakota	18	Consent	Both	No	No	Yes	Yes
Ohio	18	Consent	One	Yes	Yes	Yes	Yes
Oklahoma	[xix]	Consent	Unclear	No	No	No	No
Oregon		No Parental Notification of Abortion Statute					
Pennsylvania	18	Consent	One	Yes	No	Yes	Yes
Rhode Island	18	Consent	One	No	No	No	Yes
South Carolina	17	Consent	One	Yes	Yes[xx]	Yes	Yes
South Dakota	18	Notice	One	No	No	Yes	Yes
Tennessee	18	Consent	One	No	Yes	Yes	Yes
Texas	18	Notice	One	No	No	Yes	Yes
Utah	18	Notice	Both	No	No	No	No
Vermont		No Parental Notification of Abortion Statute					
Virginia	18	Consent	One	Yes	Yes	Yes	Yes
Washington		No Parental Notification of Abortion Statute					
West Virginia	18	Notice	One	No	No	Yes	Yes
Wisconsin	18	Consent	One	Yes	Yes[xxi]	Yes[iii]	Yes
Wyoming	18	Consent	One	No	No	Yes	Yes

JUDICIAL BYPASS PROCEDURES

All of the parental notice or consent statutes that the state courts have let stand contain a mechanism for bypassing the notice or consent requirement. These allow a girl to obtain a court order from a judge allowing her to get an abortion without the consent of her parents in a consent state, or notice to her parents in a notice state, and without there being a danger to her life or health.

The burden of proof in a judicial bypass proceeding is on the minor girl seeking the bypass. She must establish one of the grounds upon which the court can base a decision to grant a bypass. The standard of proof is **clear and convincing evidence.**

The girl must convince the judge that she is sufficiently mature and well informed to make an abortion decision for herself. In some states she may also obtain judicial bypass by providing clear and convincing evidence that she is the victim of a pattern of abuse in the home, and that providing her parents with notice or obtaining their consent would subject her to further abuse. She may also attempt to prove that the judicial bypass is in her best interests.

THE JUDICIAL BYPASS HEARING

Most local rules mandate that the judicial bypass process be fast, anonymous, confidential, and free to the petitioner. There is usually a requirement that the minor receive assistance in complying with the statute and properly executing the required steps. Court clerks must give minors prompt assistance, including notary services.

To ensure quickness of execution, most states mandate that the court conduct a hearing "promptly" after filing the complaint, usually within 24 hours, but no later than a certain number of days after the filing of the complaint. If the court fails to hold a hearing within the prescribed time, then it will be deemed to have granted the complaint.

To preserve anonymity and confidentiality, many states require that the second page of the complaint, which contains the girl's name, be removed from the file and sealed.

The hearing on the complaint is closed. Only the minor, her attorney, her guardian ad litem, and essential court personnel may attend. Essential court personnel are the judge's clerk, the bailiff, a person to record the proceedings, and the judge.

Proceedings in juvenile court are almost always recorded by means of a tape recorder rather than a live court reporter. Live court reporters only work in juvenile court where there is a particularly difficult, complex, or high profile case or where one of the parties requests a live court reporter and pays that reporter's fees.

Unlike other hearings, the judicial bypass hearing does not require legal notice to the child's parent or guardian. In fact, such notice is specifically prohibited.

Courts must conduct these hearings in such a way as to preserve the anonymity of the minor. The court never uses the girl's real name during the hearing. Rather, participants and court documents often refer to the girl throughout the hearing as "Jane Doe." For this reason, court personnel often refer to these hearings colloquially as "**Jane Doe hearings.**"

clear and convincing evidence
A standard of proof that lies above **preponderance of the evidence** and below **proof beyond a reasonable doubt.** Most legal practitioners quantify preponderance of the evidence as 51 percent certainty, proof beyond a reasonable doubt as approximately 90 percent certainty, and clear and convincing evidence as somewhere between those two numbers.

Jane Doe hearing
A colloquial name for a judicial bypass hearing. The name comes from the fact that in order to preserve the anonymity of the applicant, courts personnel in many states refer to the minor girl as "Jane Doe"

The courts have recognized that the public is entitled to some information regarding these hearings. To preserve the girls' anonymity, however, the public may only have access to the docket number, the name of the judge, and the decision, including a **properly redacted opinion,** in which court personnel have blacked out any language that would tend to identify the participants.

Court personnel must file the complaint promptly on behalf of the minor without cost to her. The court may not assess filing fees or court costs against the minor. If the girl does not have her own attorney, the court must appoint one for her at no cost to her. The court must also appoint a guardian ad litem at no cost to the minor.

properly redacted opinion
An opinion in which court personnel have blacked out any language that would tend to identify the participants

The Complaint

There are typically three different grounds upon which to base a judicial bypass complaint:

- The girl is sufficiently mature and well enough informed to intelligently decide whether to have an abortion without notifying or obtaining the consent of her parents, guardian, or custodian.
- One or both of the girl's parents, her guardian, or her custodian was engaged in a pattern of physical, sexual, or emotional abuse against her.
- Notifying or obtaining the consent of the girl's parents, guardian, or custodian is not in her best interests.

If the court finds that the girl is mature and well enough informed, it can issue an order allowing her to bypass the notice or consent requirement on that basis, and need go no further. If the court determines that the girl is not sufficiently mature and well enough informed to make the decision on her own, then it can consider the other two grounds.

If the court finds either one or both of the other grounds exists—that the girl has been the victim of abuse at the hands of her parent, guardian, or custodian, or that a bypass is in her best interests—it can grant the complaint on either or both of those grounds.

Sufficiently Mature and Well Enough Informed

In assessing the girl's maturity, the courts look at her age, school performance, employment history, her relationship with the father or the child, her relationship with her own parents, her birth control practices, her sexual practices, her demeanor, and other factors.

Age Courts calculate the girls' ages to the month, week, and day. The older the girl is, the more likely the court is to find she is sufficiently mature. As the case below illustrates, however, a girl's proximity to adulthood can work against her in the trial court. The judge may use her advanced age as an excuse to deny the petition on the grounds that soon she will be eighteen and legally able to make the decision for herself without her parents' or the court's intervention.

Consultation   The court will examine whether the girl has consulted with anyone—a medical professional, a therapist, a trusted adult, a school counselor or teacher, or other person. The more consultation the girl has done, and the more appropriate the consultation she has sought, the more likely the court will be to find her mature.

Understanding of the Process   The girl must demonstrate that she has an understanding of pregnancy and the abortion procedure. She must explain how the procedure works and the attendant physical ad psychological risks. She must demonstrate that she is aware of the alternatives to abortion and articulate her reasons for favoring abortion over the alternatives.

School Performance   Courts assess the girls' school records to gauge their maturity. They examine grades, disciplinary records, activities, their plans for future education or military service, and whether they are enrolled in honors courses or other academically challenging programs.

Employment   The court is more likely to find sufficient maturity in a girl who is gainfully and stably employed than in one who is not employed or who has an inconsistent or problematic employment record. The court will examine how the girl uses her income. If she puts her income to good use, such as saving for college or helping to support her family, the court is more likely to deem her mature.

Relationship to the Father   The court will note whether the girl has knows who the father is and whether she has a healthy relationship with him. The court will look more favorably upon a girl who has a steady and long-term relationship with one partner, and who has discussed the pregnancy and the possible abortion with him. Courts will examine the father's record as well—his employment, stability, and maturity as part of its examination of the girl's maturity.

Relationship with Her Parents   The girl's reasons for not wanting to tell her parents will be significant to the court. If she does not want to tell her parents because she fears severe retribution, the court will consider that grounds for a finding of parental, custodial, or guardian abuse rather than part of the maturity argument. If the girl does not want to tell her parents about the pregnancy and proposed abortion because she is afraid it will damage their relationship, destroy their trust in her, disappoint her parents, or hurt a physically weak or sickly parent, the court will consider that in terms of the maturity the girl demonstrates.

The Complainant's Birth Control Practices

A failure to use a birth control method that is adequate and effective is a prima facie case for the girl's lack of maturity. However, that prima facie case can be overcome by a reasonable explanation of why the girl did not, or could not, use birth control. A good birth control plan that failed this one time, or a good birth control plan that was suspended involuntarily by the girl, belies the case for a lack of maturity.

The Complainant's Sexual Practices

A girl who has had multiple pregnancies, who has been with multiple partners, or whom the court perceives to be promiscuous is less likely to convince the court that she is of sufficient maturity to waive the parental notification requirement.

The court will also take note if the girl has had other abortions, and if so, whether the other pregnancies were by the same father, or multiple fathers.

The following case, *In re Anonymous,* demonstrates the factors that a trial court considers in making its determination of maturity. It also demonstrates how an appellate court may intervene where it appears that the trial court is imposing its personal values in a case in derogation of its duty to uphold the law regardless of the judge's personal views. Finally, it demonstrates the depth and strength of emotion on the subject of abortion, especially as applied to minors.

In re Anonymous
2005 WL 19217 (Ala.Civ.App., 2005.)

An unemancipated minor seeks review of the trial court's decision denying her petition for a waiver of parental consent to have an abortion.

The record indicates that the minor is 17 years old and approximately 8 weeks pregnant. The minor has been in a relationship with her boyfriend, the father of her unborn child, for several months. According to the minor, her pregnancy is the result of the first time she had sexual relations with this boyfriend; she testified that they used a condom but that the condom they used broke. The boyfriend is 19 years old and is employed. The minor testified that her boyfriend would support her decision either to have the child or to have the abortion procedure, and she testified that she had discussed the emotional impact of having the abortion procedure with her boyfriend's mother and

(continues)

In re Anonymous (Continued)

sister. The minor testified that she did not want to inform her parents of her pregnancy because they would be disappointed in her and because, in the past, they had threatened to withhold financial support if she were to become pregnant.

The minor is an excellent student who has qualified for or obtained an athletic scholarship to college. The minor has aspirations to graduate college and to work in the medical profession. She testified that she would be unable to attend college if her parents withdrew their financial support, as, she says, they had threatened to do in the event she became pregnant.

The minor talked to her school nurse, a medical professional at a women's clinic, and another medical professional about her pregnancy. The school nurse and at least one of the two medical professionals stressed the alternative of adoption to the minor. The minor did not specifically explain why she rejected the possibility of placing the child for adoption; however, she did state that carrying the child to term would impact the availability of her athletic scholarship.

The minor's testimony before the trial court indicated that the minor was informed regarding the possible risks of the abortion procedure. The minor testified that she has friends who have become pregnant. At least one friend had an abortion when she was 17 years old, and, according to the minor, that friend experienced no negative repercussions from having had the abortion. The minor indicated that she had two other friends who had become pregnant and had kept their children. According to the minor, both of those friends had had a difficult time attempting to go to school and rear a child at the same time.

In its judgment denying the minor's petition for a waiver of parental consent, the trial court determined that the minor was not sufficiently mature to make the decision to have the abortion without her parents' consent and that the abortion would not be in the minor's best interests. The trial court made a number of factual findings in reaching those determinations.

The minor argues that the trial court erred in determining that she was not sufficiently mature to make the abortion decision and in determining that it was not in her best interests to have an abortion.

In the present case, the trial court found that the minor was well informed concerning the abortion process and its consequences. The order states, in part:

"The petitioner has counseled with her gynecologist (a doctor), with her school counselor, with the employees of [a women's clinic.] She can recite the mantra of possible consequences of an abortion. She has been made aware of the options to abortion. While this Court normally has required a petitioner to counsel with Sav-A-Life, or a similar pro-life organization, to do so in this case would be redundant. Her doctor and her school counselor have told her what Sav-A-Life would tell her. She has seen the ultrasound of her child. The Court is satisfied that she is well-informed."

However, the court found that the minor was not sufficiently mature (1) because she wants to play sports in order to earn a full scholarship to college (rather than give birth); (2) because she engaged in sexual intercourse "with her scholarship on the line" and with knowledge of her parents' threat of "cutting her off" financially if she became pregnant; (3) because she has no work experience; (4) because she has never before had to make a "serious decision"; (5) because, seeing the difficulties encountered by friends who have become pregnant, she got "herself into the same situation"; and (6) because the minor will reach the age of majority shortly before the end of her first trimester or shortly after she enters her second trimester, it is "not an act of

(continues)

In re Anonymous (Continued)

maturity on her part to put the burden of the death of this child upon the conscience of the Court."

In regard to its finding that the minor is not sufficiently mature because she would rather participate in athletics in an attempt to maintain a scholarship than go through a pregnancy, the court states "that is not the only means by which she can obtain a college education even if her parents refuse to or are unable to pay for it." The court states that the minor's grades and extracurricular activities are sufficient for her to obtain financial aid and that if she is a talented athlete, then missing seasonal athletics would not hinder a scholarship. The court stated "[The minor] has not thought through her options in a manner that a mature minor would do." First, the trial court makes presumptions that are not supported by the record, such as whether the minor would be eligible for financial aid. Second, the trial court found that her scholarship would not be in jeopardy even though this is in direct contrast to the minor's testimony. Further, it is abundantly clear from the record that the minor has thoughtfully considered her options to achieve her goal of attending college.

The trial court determined that the minor was not sufficiently mature because, it says, a mature minor would not have engaged in sexual activities if she wanted to keep her scholarship or continue to be supported financially by her parents. This does not indicate that she lacks the maturity to make the decision to terminate a pregnancy. See Ex parte Anonymous, supra, 810 So.2d at 796 (Lyons, J., concurring in the result)(quoting from an Ohio case that noted "'that although the fact that appellant, an unemancipated minor, is pregnant indicates a certain level of immaturity, the legislature has envisioned that, notwithstanding this fact, she may be sufficiently mature to make the decision to terminate the pregnancy'").

The trial court determined that the minor was not sufficiently mature because she has not had any work experience. However, the record does not indicate that she has never had a job. Instead, the record indicates that the minor's parents currently pay for her financial needs. Additionally, the lack of work experience would not be indicative of immaturity where a minor is heavily involved in sports and extracurricular activities and maintains good grades.

The trial court also determined that the minor was not sufficiently mature because she had not made any "serious decisions" in her life. Our supreme court has stated:

> *"In every case where a minor female is involved, we would not find the experience to be expected of an adult female. Hence, the trial judge's preoccupation with the experience of this minor is misplaced; no minor female would be able to pass the experience test if adult-level experience were a criterion."*

The trial court concluded that the minor was not sufficiently mature because she chose to engage in sexual intercourse in spite of seeing her friends who have become pregnant out of wedlock encounter hardships. The court stated, "[The minor] has a [friend] who has had an abortion with no apparent negative results (except to that child). She has two other friends who have borne children out of wedlock and are struggling to get by. Simply put, she wants out of the situation that she has created." Again, having sexual intercourse does not mean that the minor lacks the maturity to make the abortion decision. Further, the minor did use a method of birth control in an attempt to prevent pregnancy.

Last, the trial court determined that the minor was not sufficiently mature because she could wait

(continues)

In re Anonymous (Continued)

several weeks and have an abortion without the necessity of a judicial bypass and without burdening this particular trial judge's conscience with granting a waiver of parental consent.

In summary, none of the facts set out by the trial court support a finding that the minor was not sufficiently mature. In direct contrast to the indicia of maturity the trial court relied on, the courts of this state have found academic performance, participation in extracurricular activities, plans for the future (including college), and understanding the procedures and consequences of an abortion to indicate maturity.

The trial judge in his order subjected the minor to demeaning and sarcastic remarks, as follows:

> "[T] he legislature, in its infinite wisdom, has determined that an unborn child who never has had even the ability to do any wrong, could be put to death so that his mother can play [sports].
>
> "Ah, but this young woman has more ambition than to play [sports]. Her possible . . . scholarship is but the means to the end of her becoming a [health-care provider]. But what is the duty of a [health-care provider]? To save lives. Should her child die so that, possibly, she might later save other lives?
>
> "There may be physical complications to an abortion. There may be psychological complications or consequences. She said that she does not believe that abortion is wrong, so, apparently, in spite of her church attendance, there won't be spiritual consequences, at least for the present."

As an elected official, the trial judge has a duty to uphold the United States Constitution, the Alabama Constitution, and the laws of this state. In 1987, the Alabama Legislature enacted the Parental Consent Act, requiring the written consent of one parent or legal guardian before a minor may obtain an abortion. As required by Bellotti v. Baird, 443 U.S. 622, 99 S.Ct. 3035, 61 L.Ed.2d 797 (1979), Alabama's Parental Consent Act also provides for a judicial-bypass procedure through which a minor may petition for a waiver of parental consent.

The judge states in his order, "This is a capital case. It involves the question whether [the minor's] unborn child should live or die." A review of the record and of the trial judge's comments lead us to question his objectivity in a judicial-bypass case. The record is replete with evidence that the minor in this case is mature and well informed and that the abortion would be in her best interest. Our supreme court has stated:

> "[I] t is not the [trial] court's responsibility to superimpose its judgment or its moral convictions on the minor in regard to what course of action she should take with reference to her own body. It is not a question of whether she is making a decision that we would approve of, but whether she is making a mature decision or one in her best interest."

Accordingly, we hold that the trial court was plainly and palpably wrong in determining that the minor was not sufficiently mature and that having an abortion would not be in her best interest. The other issues raised by the minor on appeal are pretermitted. The judgment denying the waiver is reversed and the case is remanded. Because of the importance of time, the trial court is directed to enter a judgment granting the waiver, not later than 12:00 noon, January 6, 2005. If the trial court does not enter a judgment granting the waiver by that time, then effective at 12:01 p.m. on that date a judgment granting the statutory waiver is rendered by this court. REVERSED AND REMANDED WITH INSTRUCTIONS OR REVERSED AND JUDGMENT RENDERED.

The Complainant Was a Victim of Physical or Sexual Abuse

Many of the states that have parental notification of abortion statutes have exceptions for victims of sexual abuse where the pregnancy was the result of incest or rape, and physical abuse where the young woman is the victim of child abuse. These exceptions apply in two ways. Either they can act as an exception to the requirement of consent from or notice to the parents, thus excusing the young woman from the prescripts of the law, or they can serve as independent grounds for granting a judicial bypass.

The burden is generally upon the young woman to prove sexual abuse. Some statutes require genetic testing to buttress the claim that the pregnancy is the result of incest. Many also require that if such claims are substantiated, the attending medical professional must report the abuse or send tissue samples of the aborted fetus to the proper state authorities, that are then compelled to prosecute the offender.

The girls must demonstrate that she is the victim of a pattern of physical abuse, such that she would suffer further abuse if she were to reveal her pregnancy to her parents or guardians.

The Bypass is in the Complainant's Best Interests

The best interests consideration accompanies all actions that take place in juvenile court. The court must determine in judicial bypass cases that the waiver of notice or consent will be in the best interests of the young woman. This is a catch-all provision.

APPEALS

Judicial bypass decisions are appealable. The appellate process, like the initial hearing, must be fast, confidential, anonymous, and free. The court must immediately notify the girl of her right to appeal and provide her with all necessary records, transcripts of the hearing and whatever assistance in properly filing the appeal.

The appellate court cannot assess any filing fees or other costs against the girl. Oral argument must take place within a certain number of days after docketing. If the appellate court fails to enter judgment by the fifth day, it will be deemed to have granted the appeal, overturning the trial court's decision to deny the minor's complaint. The entire process, from trial court decision to appellate ruling, must be completed within a set number of days.

CASE PROBLEM

An unmarried and unemancipated minor petitioned for a waiver of parental consent for an abortion.

The minor, who is 14 years old, testified that she believes her pregnancy resulted from sexual abuse practiced upon her by her father. She has consulted an obstetrician/gynecologist, who informed her of the medical and physical ramifications of the procedure, and she is aware of the risks involved. A letter from the doctor regarding the consultation states: "[During] the discussion [the minor] asked excellent questions regarding procedure, recovery, risks, [and] time she may miss from school. She was mature and thoughtful in her interaction with our clinic regarding the pregnancy." The minor testified in detail about the steps involved in the procedure as explained to her by her obstetrician. The minor is aware of the alternatives to abortion; she believes an abortion is in her best interests.

The minor's mother, who was present at the hearing, knows that the minor is pregnant, but she will not sign her consent to the abortion because of her "religious beliefs." The mother testified that, although she is unwilling to give written consent to the abortion, she will take the minor to a hospital where the procedure can be performed and that she will care for the minor while she recovers from the procedure.

The juvenile court denied the petition, stating:

> "[I]t was not within [the court's] jurisdiction to order the procedure sought in this matter which will result in the extinction of a four month old human life when the child's family is fully informed and able to make this decision. This court should not substitute its judgment for that of a child's family when that family is present and voicing objections to same."

The minor moved the court to reconsider its judgment. The court denied the motion stating: "[A] child who seeks a judicial bypass is in fact seeking an abortion. Given that circumstance, this court [would be] in fact ordering an abortion."

The minor appealed. What is the result?

ROLE-PLAY PROBLEM

The students in your class are legislators in the state of Sweet Haven, which currently has no parental notification of abortion laws. A coalition of parents groups, church groups, educators, and medical professionals has organized petition drives and protests calling upon the legislature to enact such a law.

Half of the legislature ranges from slightly to extremely pro-life. The other half ranges from slightly to extremely pro-choice. You must work together to craft legislation that will make it through the legislature, satisfy the governor so that he will sign it, satisfy your constituency, comport with your personal beliefs, and withstand constitutional attacks.

The exercise will be most beneficial all students take the opposite position of that which they actually hold.

HYPOTHETICAL PROBLEM

You are a law clerk working for a judge in Arizona who has just heard a judicial bypass case. These are the facts:

Rae is 15 years old. She and her boyfriend have been together for two years. They have been having sexual relations for about six months. They use condoms for birth control. It appears the condom malfunctioned, because they have never had relations without using one.

Rae gets average grades in school, but she is a star singer. She is a member of the school choir, the a cappella choir, her church choir, and sings in the school jazz band. She is hoping to get a scholarship to college for her singing.

Her mother is extremely religious and would never allow her daughter to get an abortion. Her father is equally religious and favors physical discipline. Rae is positive her father would beat her severely if he learned she was pregnant. In addition, he would withhold food from her for up to a full day, as he often does as a form of punishment.

Rae has a good relationship with her mother, and she fears that this would destroy that relationship. She also has a good relationship with her boyfriend's mother, who knows Rae is pregnant. She has offered to drive Rae to the clinic and to care for her afterwards.

Rae has a rather unrealistic view of the abortion process. She claims to understand how it works, but does not exhibit a true understanding of it. She told the judge she expected to have no doubts, regrets, or second thoughts. She does not want to consider adoption, but she will not or cannot say why.

The judge has asked you to prepare a memorandum outlining the arguments for and against Rae's petition for a judicial bypass. How will you define the arguments?

ETHICAL CONCERNS

An imposing ethical dilemma for practicing legal professionals occurs when they called upon to advocate for something that goes against their personal beliefs. The issue of abortion is not one about which many people feel neutral. Rather, most people have very strong opinions one way or the other. To many people, the issue of abortion is tied inextricably with religious beliefs that are not easily cast aside.

Professionalism, however, demands that legal practitioners cast aside their personal beliefs if they are representing a client who has asked them to perform a task that clashes with those beliefs.

The rules of professional conduct allow attorneys and other legal professionals, such as paralegals, to decline a case or to withdraw from a case under certain circumstances. One circumstance is where attorneys or paralegals believe they cannot zealously advocate on behalf of their clients.

It would be very difficult for a person to zealously advocate on the issue of abortion for a result that goes against their personal beliefs. It may be possible under those circumstances to decline or withdraw from a case.

DISCUSSION QUESTIONS

Consider the case of *In re Anonymous,* above.

1. Do you agree with the judge's opinion that the fact that the minor became pregnant is evidence of her lack of maturity, thus providing grounds for the denial of her petition?

2. Do you agree with the appellate court's response that the legislature did not intend for that to be the case?

3. If the trial court judge's reasoning were correct, then could any pregnant girl ever convince the court of her maturity?

4. Do you agree with the argument that it showed a lack of maturity on the part of the applicant to ask the court to approve the bypass, thus putting the "burden of the death of this child upon the conscience of the Court"?

5. Do you think a girl who has been impregnated by her father should have to ask her father to consent to her abortion?

Consider the State Law Chart on page 199.

Which state's laws most comport with your philosophy of parental notification of abortion? Why?

KEY TERMS

clear and convincing evidence
Jane Doe hearing
judicial bypass
minor

parental notification of abortion
  laws
properly redacted opinion

END NOTES

i Alabama, Alaska, Arizona, Arkansas, California, Colorado, Delaware, Florida, Georgia, Idaho, Illinois, Indiana, Iowa, Kansas, Kentucky, Louisiana, Maine, Maryland, Massachusetts, Michigan, Minnesota, Mississippi,

Missouri, Montana, Nebraska, Nevada, New Hampshire, New Jersey, New Mexico, North Carolina, North Dakota, Ohio, Oklahoma, Pennsylvania, Rhode Island, South Carolina, South Dakota, Tennessee, Texas, Utah, Virginia, West Virginia, Wisconsin, and Wyoming

ii Alaska, California, Florida, Idaho, Illinois, Montana, Nevada, New Hampshire, New Jersey, and New Mexico

iii Written notice to the mother is sufficient if the pregnancy is the result of sexual intercourse with the father, stepfather, or legal guardian.

iv The woman can obtain an abortion without consent if she certifies that the pregnancy resulted from sexual intercourse with a member of her immediate family. There is no exception for abuse.

v There is no exception for rape or incest, but there is an exception if the woman is a victim of child abuse.

vi There is an exception for incest, but not for child abuse.

vii The statute has an exception for rape or "felonious incest"; there is no exception for child abuse.

viii The statute does not define "minor."

ix There is an exception if the pregnancy is the result of incest; there is no exception for child abuse.

x The medical exception includes a provision allowing for such an exception if the threatened harm is psychological.

xi A state court has held that the law is unconstitutional and unenforceable because it violates the woman's right to privacy.

xii A state court has held this law is unconstitutional and unenforceable because it violates the woman's right to privacy.

xiii A state court has held that this law is unconstitutional and unenforceable because it violates the woman's right to privacy.

xiv A state court has held this law is unconstitutional and unenforceable because it contains an inadequate medical emergency exception.

xv A state court has issued a permanent injunction preventing enforcement of this law.

xvi A federal court has held that a provision requiring parental notice of the judicial bypass proceeding is unconstitutional; the bill is otherwise constitutional and enforceable.

xvii A state court has held this law is unconstitutional and unenforceable because it violates the woman's right to privacy.

xviii A state court has held this law is unconstitutional and unenforceable because it contains and inadequate judicial bypass procedure.

xix A state court has held that this law is unconstitutional and unenforceable because it does not contain an adequate exception to preserve the young woman's health or life.

xx A state court has held that this law in unconstitutional and unenforceable because it violates a young woman's fundamental right to an abortion.

xxi The state Attorney General has stated that this law is unconstitutional and unenforceable because it does not contain a judicial bypass procedure.

Chapter 13

MARRIAGE

OBJECTIVES

By the end of this chapter, the student should know:

- The nature of marriage as a contract and how contract laws apply to marriage
- The requirements of parties to a valid contract
- The definition of legal capacity
- The parameters of minors' contractual rights and obligations
- Which marriages are prohibited
- The marriage laws of the states and the District of Columbia
- The legal effects of marriage

INTRODUCTION

Marriage is a contract. The parties to the marriage contract, just as the parties to any contract, must have the capacity to contract and must contract voluntarily for the marriage to be valid.

REQUIREMENTS OF PARTIES TO A VALID CONTRACT

The requirements for parties to a valid contract are that the parties consent to the contract and that the parties have **capacity** to contract. The requirement of capacity to contract is the significant one that comes in cases involving marriages of minors.

Capacity

Capacity is the ability to enter legally binding relationships, incur legal obligations, and obtain legal rights. The law presumes that certain people—minors, people who are intoxicated, and people who are suffering from mental defects or mental illness—lack capacity to contract. It is possible for these people to enter contracts, but the resulting

211

capacity

The ability to enter legally binding relationships, incur legal obligations, and obtain legal rights

voidable contract

A contract that that one of the parties can disaffirm, without incurring legal liability or consequences

avoid

To disaffirm a contract without incurring legal liability

necessaries

Those things that person requires in order to survive, such as food, clothing, shelter, and transportation to a place of employment

contracts are **voidable.** A voidable contract is one that one of the parties can **avoid,** or disaffirm, without incurring legal liability or consequences.

If the party who has the ability to avoid the contract does not do so, the party has *affirmed,* or ratified, the contract. That means that the contract has become a valid, legally enforceable one, pursuant to which both parties incur legal obligations and acquire legal rights.

If a minor enters a contract, that contract is voidable. The minor has the opportunity to nullify the contract, cast off any legal obligations he has incurred, and surrender any legal rights he has acquired until he reaches the legal age of majority.

The exception is where minors contract for **necessaries.** Necessaries are those things that person requires in order to survive, such as food, clothing, shelter, and transportation to a place of employment. Minors' contracts for necessaries are not voidable. The law has made this exception in order to protect minors. If such contracts were not excluded from the general rule that minors' contracts are voidable, no merchants would be willing to contract with minors, and thus the minors would be deprived of those thing they need to survive.

Marriage Contracts

The law treats minors' marriage contracts the same as it does all minors' contracts. When minors marry below the legal age of consent, they may disaffirm, or avoid, the marriage contract until such time as they ratify it. They can ratify marriage contracts by remaining together as husband and wife, living together, and continuing the marital relationship, past the age of legal consent.

All state marriage statutes designate the age at which any party who is not otherwise prohibited from marrying can do so. If a person who is below the minimum age gets married, or enters into a contract for marriage, that contract will be voidable in most states and void in some states.

The following case involves a voidable marriage that the minor did not affirm, and demonstrates the consequences of such failure to affirm a marriage contract.

Mims v. Hardware Mut. Cas. Co.
60 S.E.2d 501 (Ga.App. 1950)

James Mims, an employee of M. G. Aldridge, was killed as a result of an accident arising out of and in the course of his employment. The employer, Aldridge, and his insurance carrier, Hardware Mutual Casualty Co., entered into an agreement with Frances King Mims, the alleged widow of the deceased, to pay

(continues)

Mims v. Hardware Mut. Cas. Co. (Continued)

compensation at the rate of $14.22 per week for a period of 300 weeks. Subsequently, a claim was entered by Frances Mims, the mother of the deceased, alleging that Frances King Mims was not the lawful widow of the deceased and that she, as the decedent's mother dependent upon him for support, was entitled to compensation.

The sole issue at hearing was the person entitled to benefits under the act. The mother claimant contended that the marriage between the widow claimant and the deceased was void because the alleged widow, at the time she entered into a marriage ceremony with James Mims, was in fact the undivorced wife of one Essick Exom. The testimony at the hearing revealed a comedy of errors involving the claimant and her predecessors in the affections of the deceased substantially as follows: that in September, 1924, one Wimberly Hughes married a girl named Annie Bell Slappy who was at that time between 12 and 13 years of age, her exact age being unknown; that he lived with her, according to his testimony, for a period of time between 18 months and 3 years; that after their separation Annie Bell married one Essick Exom without first being divorced from Hughes and lived with him for about 9 months; that Exom, without bothering to obtain a divorce from Annie Bell, then married the claimant, Frances King, on June 17, 1928, and lived with her about 6 years. Thereafter, Exom married another woman and Frances King, on July 10, 1938, married James Mims, the deceased employee.

Marriage certificates properly authenticated were introduced in evidence to show the marriage of Frances King to Essick Exom and also to James Mims. Both Exom and Frances King Mims testified at the hearing. Neither one stated whether or not a divorce had been obtained between them, nor was it established whether Exom had resided solely in Twiggs County between the date of their separation and the date of the accident out of which this claim arose. There was evidence that the widow claimant had lived in Bibb County for several years prior to the bringing of this action.

The deputy Director entered an award finding that the marriage between Wimberly Hughes and Annie Bell Slappy, the first knot in this matrimonial tangle, was a valid marriage; that in consequence the marriage between the deceased and Frances King Mims was invalid and that she was not entitled to compensation. This decision was affirmed on appeal by the judge of the Superior Court of Bibb County, and this judgment is assigned as error in the bill of exceptions.

TOWNSEND, Judge (after stating the foregoing facts).

To be able to contract a valid marriage, the girl must be at least 14 years of age. If she contracts a marriage which is invalid because she is under the age of consent, but, on arriving at this age, ratifies the marriage by continued cohabitation, the marriage is thereafter valid. "Such marriages partake more of the nature of voidable than void marriages. They are imperfect marriages which the party may affirm or disaffirm after reaching the age of consent."

The burden of proof is upon the person seeking to prove that the marriage was in fact affirmed by the acts of the parties thereto after the removal of the disability, since otherwise it remains completely lifeless. Where such evidence is in conflict, the ruling of the court thereon is conclusive provided such ruling is based upon competent evidence.

Here the only evidence as to whether or not the marriage was ratified was the testimony of Wimberly Hughes. Hughes married the girl when she was between the age of 12 and 13. He did not

(continues)

Mims v. Hardware Mut. Cas. Co. (Continued)

know what her exact age was. He did not know how long he lived with her. He did not know at exactly what time they separated, and he did not know whether or not she had reached the age of 14 at that time. His testimony on this subject was without probative value one way or the other, and, there being no other evidence on this subject, the claimant failed to carry the burden of proving that this marriage was in fact ratified, since the only result to be reached from Hughes' testimony was that she was either a few months under or a few months over 14 at the time they finally separated.

No ratification of this marriage having been proved, this marriage must be taken as void. In consequence it offered no disability to the marriage of Annie Bell Slappy to Essick Exom. Assuming that none of the parties obtained divorces, it follows by process of elimination that Exom, at the time he married the claimant Frances King Mims, was laboring under the disability of his marriage to Annie Bell, in consequence of which his marriage to the claimant was void. Under this state of facts the claimant could not possibly have contracted a valid marriage to Exom, and labored under no disability at the time she married

the deceased employee. She would therefore be entitled to compensation as his widow.

Upon the hearing, duly authenticated certificates were introduced in evidence of the marriage between Frances King and Essick Exom, and of the marriage between Frances King and James Mims. Upon the introduction of the latter, the presumption arose that the subsequent marriage was valid, which presumption was not defeated merely by introduction of proof of the former marriage.

The burden was not upon the alleged widow to prove that her marriage was valid, but was upon the other claimant to prove it invalid, and she had the right to rely upon the presumption of validity until it was negatived by disproving every other reasonable possibility save that of its invalidity. The plaintiff did not carry this burden, and for this additional reason she was entitled to compensation as the widow of the deceased employee.

The judge of the superior court erred in affirming the award of the Board of Workmen's Compensation and disallowing death benefits to the widow claimant.

Reversed.

SIDEBAR

PROHIBITED MARRIAGES

States generally prohibit marriage between close relatives—brothers and sisters, parents and children, grandparents and grandchildren, aunts and nephews, nieces and uncles, first and second cousins. All states prohibit marriages where one of the parties already has another spouse.

The states have declared that these marriage contracts are **void.** That is, they are considered null, or nonexistent, from their very inception.

void contract

A contract that is null, or nonexistent, from its very inception

(continues)

All states except Massachusetts currently prohibit or do not sanction marriages between members of the same sex. Vermont, the District of Columbia, and Alaska recognize civil unions between two members of the same sex. The issue is a controversial and polarizing one; many observers view same sex marriage as one of the deciding issues of the 2004 presidential election.

Juveniles below the statutory age may marry with their parents' or the court's consent. Some states require the consent of the parent or guardian *and* the court in certain circumstances. Many states make an exception in cases where the female is pregnant or where she has already had a child. Alaska makes an exception for pregnancy and for members of the armed forces.

In some states a juvenile who marries below the sanctioned age can be adjudged an **unruly child**—a minor who engages in dangerous or potentially harmful behavior, or a **status offender**—a minor who has committed an offense that is only an offense when a minor commits it, such as consumption of alcohol, or getting married. This will not cause the marriage to be void but will allow the court to acquire jurisdiction over the juvenile. Once the court has acquired jurisdiction, it can compel the juvenile to comply with certain directions.

The Georgia statute is a typical marriage statute. It contains a minimum age requirement, exceptions for those with the consent of their parent or guardian, an exception for pregnancy and a reference to prohibited marriages.

Exhibit 13-1 shows the states' marriage laws.

unruly child

A minor who engages in dangerous or potentially harmful behavior

status offender

A minor who has committed an offense that is only an offense when a minor commits it, such as consumption of alcohol, or getting married

GEORGIA STATUTES § 19-3-2 PERSONS ABLE TO CONTRACT

To be able to contract marriage, a person must:

(1) Be of sound mind;

(2) Be at least 16 years of age. If either applicant is under the age of majority, parental consent shall be required, as provided in Code Section 19-3-37. However, the age limitations contained in this paragraph shall not apply upon proof of pregnancy on the part of the female or in instances in which both applicants are the parents of a living child born out of wedlock, in which case the parties may contract marriage regardless of age;

(3) Have no living spouse of a previous undissolved marriage. The dissolution of a previous marriage in divorce proceedings must be affirmatively established and will not be presumed. Nothing in this paragraph shall be construed to affect the legitimacy of children; and

(4) Not be related to the prospective spouse by blood or marriage within the prohibited degrees.

EXHIBIT 13-1 State Marriage Laws

State	Age Without Parental Consent or Judicial Order		With Parental Consent		With Judicial Order		Notes
	Male	Female	Male	Female	Male	Female	
Alabama	14	14					
Alaska	18	18	16	16	14	14	*
Arizona	18	18	16	16	16	16	
Arkansas	18	18	17	16	16	16	†
California	18	18	<18	<18	<18	<18	
Colorado	18	18	<16	<16			
Connecticut	18	18	<18	<18	<16	<16	
Delaware	18	16	<18	<16			*
District of Columbia	18	18	<18	<18			
Florida	18	18	16	16			*
Georgia	18	18	16	16			*
Hawaii	16	16			15	15	
Idaho	18	18	<18	<16	<16	<16	
Illinois	18	18	16	16	<18	<18	
Indiana	18	18					
Iowa	18	18					
Kansas	18	18	<18	<18	<18	<18	
Kentucky	18	18	16–18	16–18	<16	<16	
Louisiana	18	18	18	18	16	16	‡
Maine	18	18	<18	<18	<16	<16	
Massachusetts	18	18	<18	<18	<18	<18	
Michigan	16	16					§
Minnesota	18	18	16	16	16	16	
Mississippi	21	21	17	15	<17	<15	
Missouri	18	18	15	15	<15	<15	
Montana	18	18	<18	<18	16–17	16–17	
Nebraska	19	19	17	17			

EXHIBIT 13-1 (Continued)

State	Age Without Parental Consent or Judicial Order		With Parental Consent		With Judicial Order		Notes
	Male	Female	Male	Female	Male	Female	
Nevada	18	18	16	16			
New Hampshire	18	18					⋊
New Jersey	18	18	16	16	<16	<16	
New Mexico	18	18	16	16	<16	<16	
New York	18	18					¥
North Carolina	18	18	16	16	14	14	*
North Dakota	18	18	16	16			
Ohio	18	18	18	16			*
Oklahoma	18	18	17	17	<18	<18	*
Oregon	18	18	17	17	<18	<18	
Pennsylvania	18	18	<18	<18	<16	<16	
Rhode Island	18	18	18	16	18	16	
South Carolina	16	16					
South Dakota	18	18	16	16			
Tennessee	18	18	16	16			
Texas	18	18	14	14	<18	<18	
Utah	18	18	<18	<18	15	15	
Vermont	18	18					
Virginia	18	18	16	16	<16	<16	*
Washington	18	18	17	17	<17	<17	
West Virginia	18	18	16	16	<16	<16	
Wisconsin	18	18	16	16			
Wyoming	18	18	16	16	<16	<16	

* Exception for members of the armed forces
† Exception for pregnancy or delivered children
‡ Violation of these age limits does not make the marriage void or even voidable. Rather, the clerk issuing the license is subject to censure.
§ A marriage between people below the age of 16 is void.
⋊ A marriage involving a male younger than 14 and/or a female younger than 13 is voidable.
¥ All other marriages are voidable.

LEGAL EFFECTS OF MARRIAGE

Minors becomes emancipated, or adult in the eyes of the law, when they marry and the marriage is valid or affirmed. A married person can enter other contracts; work; consent to medical treatments and procedures, including abortions; and prosecute lawsuits and other legal actions.

Statutes of limitations, or the legally prescribed time within which people must bring legal actions following the occurrence of an event, normally are **tolled,** or suspended, when a person is a minor. In other words, if someone injured a 15-year-old, and the statute of limitations on the action is one year, the one-year period will not begin to run until the injured person's 18th birthday.

statute of limitations
The legally prescribed amount of time a party has in which to file a legal action based upon an event

toll
To suspend the running of time in calculating the statutes of limitations on an action

CASE PROBLEM

A woman filed an action on March 2, 1989, against the county, claiming that a deputy jailer raped her while she was incarcerated. The county responded that the court should dismiss the action because the one-year statute of limitations had run out.

The woman was born on March 6, 1970. The incident she complained of took place on June 24, 1986. She married an adult man in a civil ceremony on June 12, 1987, by misrepresenting her age. The county recorded the marriage license on June 15, 1987. The two lived apart, but saw each other once a month and had sexual relations at those times. In the summer of 1988, she remarried her husband in another civil ceremony.

The county argued that the woman became an emancipated minor at the time of her marriage in June of 1987. Therefore, the statute of limitations began to run on that day, and expired on June 15, 1988.

Does the court grant or deny the defendants' motion for summary judgment?

ROLE-PLAY PROBLEM

The county is prosecuting a man for endangering the welfare of a child by active participation in arranging the child's voidable marriage.

The man is a recent convert to Islam. He claims that it is part of his religious faith that early marriage is preferable to fornication or adultery. Therefore, he has ordered the marriage of his 12-year-old daughter to a 20-year-old man. The father claims that the daughter has long had a sexual interest in the man, and he arranged the marriage to protect her honor.

The girl denies that she had an interest in the man, and asserts that she barely knows him. Further, she states that she did not wish to marry the man, and does not want to be married to him now. However, she is pregnant.

The man is seeking a dismissal of the charges against him.

1. You are the lawyer for the father. How will you defend him?

2. You are the prosecutor? How will you seek to prosecute this father?

3. You are the judge? How will you rule?

HYPOTHETICAL PROBLEM

Sonya, who is a resident of Arizona, went to Las Vegas and married her 18-year-old boyfriend, Jake, when she was 15 years old. She signed a statement that represented she was 18 years old. She produced a false driver's license to prove her age.

Sonya and Jake returned to Arizona, where they lived sometimes together, sometimes apart for three years. Jake worked for a construction company. When Sonya turned 18, she and Jake were living apart. A few weeks after Sonya turned 18, she and Jake moved back in together. The next day, Jake died in an accident at work.

Sonya filed a worker's compensation claim as Jake's spouse. The state denied the claim on the grounds that Jake and Sonya were not legally married.

Sonya appealed the decision to the state court. What will the court rule?

ETHICAL CONCERNS

Ethical concerns may arise in cases where a minor's parents wish to allow the minor to marry, even though it may not be in the minor's best interests. There are many cases where parents, for religious, cultural, or selfish reasons, wish to see their young children married. The courts will declare such marriages void, or even sustain criminal charges against parents or the adult spouses of very young minors who marry with their parents' consent.

Lawyers must weigh their duty to advocate zealously on behalf of their clients against the possibility that the client may face charges of contributing to the delinquency of a minor, endangering the welfare of a child, or other charges when they assist a client in seeking the marriage of their minor children.

DISCUSSION QUESTIONS

1. Do you agree with the minimum age requirements for minor marriage? If not, how would you change them?

2. Do you believe that, as children are maturing physically at younger and younger ages, the minimum age to marry should also decline?

3. How would you deal with parents who consent to their minor children's marriages just so that they can stop supporting their children?

4. How would you deal with parents who consent to their minor children's marriage because of religious or cultural beliefs?

5. Do you think it is right that there are, in many states, different minimum ages for males and females?

6. Should the laws concerning minimum age to marry be different for minors who are in the military?

Mathew Koso and Crystal Guyer, who live in Nebraska, met when Crystal was 8 and Matthew was 16. They began to date four years later. When Crystal's mother found out about the relationship, she filed a restraining order against Matthew, stating, "He needs to hang around with girls his own age."

Matthew and Crystal kept dating nonetheless, and soon Crystal became pregnant. She hid the pregnancy until her seventh month. By the time the families found out, they had few options. Crystal was too far along in her pregnancy for an abortion and adoption was "out of the question," according to Matthew's mother.

Matthew and Crystal traveled to Kansas, where girls as young as 12 can marry with their parents' consent, and married with the consent of Crystal's parents. A few days after the marriage, Crystal's mother revoked the restraining order because, "Matthew and Crystal Guyer are married now."

State Attorney General Jon Bruning found out about the marriage "from outraged Falls City citizens" and charged Matthew with sexual assault, a felony that carries a possible sentence of 50 years in jail. "I'm not going to stand by while a grown man has a sexual relationship with a 13-year-old," he stated.

Crystal's and Matthew's parents support the couple now that they are married and have a daughter. "People don't believe a 14-year-old girl can be in love, but she is," said Matthew's mother. The state of Nebraska recognizes legal marriages from another state, and so recognizes this marriage.

7. Was the attorney generally legally correct in filing charges against Matthew?

8. Was he morally correct?

9. What will a conviction accomplish?

KEY TERMS

avoid	toll
capacity	unruly child
necessaries	void contract
status offender	voidable contract
statutes of limitations	

Chapter 14

YOUTH GANGS

OBJECTIVES

By the end of this chapter, the student should know:

- How gang members use names, colors, insignias, tattoos, and hand signs to identify themselves, communicate with one another, and wage war on rival gangs
- The extent of current gang membership
- The correlation between gang membership and criminal behavior
- The risk factors for gang membership
- The legal ramifications of gang membership
- The methods police and state legislatures use to control gang activity, such as loitering and gathering statutes, injunctions, and requiring juveniles to register as gang members, and how those methods withstand constitutional challenges

INTRODUCTION

A **youth gang** is a loose or formal collection of individuals, aged 12 to 24, who identify themselves as part of a common group; have a group name; display visual identifiers involving clothing, jewelry, hairstyle, or hand signs; occupy a certain territory; and engage in delinquent activities. Sociological definitions for street gangs differ somewhat from legal definitions, but the majority of sociological opinions emphasize the same characteristics as do the legal definitions.

There are old, well-established youth gangs that are part of larger criminal gangs, such as the Crips and the Bloods, both of which originated in Los Angeles and now have branches all over the United States. There are also numerous variants of the established gangs. These are smaller, independent gangs that call themselves Crips, Bloods, or other well-known gang names, but that are not actually part of those

youth gang

A loose or formal collection of individuals who identify themselves as part of a common group; have a group name; display visual identifiers involving clothing, jewelry, hairstyle, or hand signs; occupy a certain territory; and engage in delinquent behavior

gangs. There are small, independent gangs throughout the United States whose identities or characteristics are based upon older, established gangs. The most significant new gang is Mara Salvatrucha, known alternatively as MS 13. This violent Salvadoran gang began in Los Angeles in the 1980's and quickly spread throughout North, Central, and South America. Many major American cities now have a significant Mara Salvatrucha presence.

Most states have statutes that attempt to define and regulate gangs. The Alabama statutes, for example, states a "'streetgang' means any combination, confederation, alliance, network, conspiracy, understanding, or other similar arrangement in law or in fact, of three or more persons that, through its membership or through the agency of any member, engages in a course or pattern of criminal activity."

Alaska law states that a "'criminal street gang' means a group of three or more persons "(A) who have in common a name or identifying sign, symbol, tattoo or other physical marking, style of dress, or use of hand signs; and (B) who, individually, jointly, or in combination, have committed or attempted to commit, within the preceding three years, for the benefit of, at the direction of, or in association with the group, [a criminal offense]."

The Office of Juvenile Justice and Delinquency Prevention (OJJDP), a branch of the United States Department of Justice, states that an "accepted definition of a youth gang is a self-formed association of peers having the following characteristics: three or more members, generally ages 12 to 24; a gang name and some sense of identity, generally indicated by such symbols as style of clothing, graffiti, and hand signs; some degree of permanence and organization; and an elevated level of involvement in delinquent or criminal activity."

FEMALE GANGS

A survey by the National Youth Gang Center (NYGC) reveals that there tend to be more female gang members in small cities and rural areas than in large cities. This survey and other field studies reveal that female gang members are involved in fewer violent crimes than their male counterparts, and in more property offenses and status offenses.

Tallying female gang members has been difficult because many jurisdictions do not count female gang members separately. They either count them among the general gang population or fail to acknowledge them at all. Another reason females are harder to track is that many females do not register as gang members because they drop out at a younger age than the males, often due to pregnancy.

Many females associate with male gangs, going to their parties, fighting alongside them, aiding in drug sales and the commission of other crimes, but do not consider themselves to be in the gang. An outsider, however, would view them as gang members.

A popular Web site created by, for, and about street gangs, www.gangstyle.com, has a "Girls and Gangs" section dedicated to gang life "from the ladies' perspective." The poetry, short stories, and essays in that section reveal a life of pain, shame, regret, domestic violence, rape, child abuse, drug addiction, self-mutilation, prostitution, and loneliness. Many of the writings are warnings to get out of the gang life, to stay away from gangsters. Very few, if any, of the writings glamourize gang life.

NAMES, COLORS, TATTOOS, INSIGNIAS, AND HAND SIGNS

Identifying regalia is of key importance to gang culture. It not only allows gang members to distinguish fellow gang members from the enemy, but it also adds to the allure and glamour of the gang.

Many statutory definitions of gangs refer to names, **colors,** which are certain combinations of colors associated with a particular gang, tattoos, insignias, and **hand signs,** which are certain gestures made with the fingers and hands that indicate membership in a gang, demonstrate disrespect toward another gang, or convey messages within the gang. Such outward indicia of gang identity are not required to prove gang membership, but their presence suggests it.

colors
Certain combinations of colors associated with a particular gang; a gang's identifying clothing

hand signs
Certain gestures made with the fingers and hands that indicate membership in a gang, demonstrate disrespect toward another gang, or convey messages within the gang

SIDEBAR

GANG REGALIA AND IDENTIFIERS

Colors (Red is associated with the Bloods; blue is associated with the Crips. Other gangs use other colors such as purple, black, white, or green.)

Bandanas (The colors of the bandanas and the way the members wear them)

(continues)

Hats and baseball caps (Gangs use team names, wear caps backwards or at a certain tilt, or wear a certain style or color. New York Yankees caps are especially popular.)

Right side–left side (Gangs associate with certain sides. For example, Gangster Disciples and Folk Nations wear their hats, belt buckles, earrings, and other articles of clothing to the right; Vice Lords and Bloods wear their gang items to the left.)

Brands of clothing (Dickey brand work pants, Adidas shoes or shirts)

Hair and facial hair (Shaved heads, symbols shaved into the hair)

Hairstyles

Combs (Placement in hair)

Professional sports team jackets

Baggy clothing

Combat-style clothing

Sweatshirts (The style of layering or the colors)

Sweaters (Gangs have two similar sweaters, one with their main gang color for social events, such as funerals; the other one for war.)

T-shirts (T-shirts can be custom printed, airbrushed, or embroidered with gang names, symbols, messages, or a pro sports team with the same name, initials, or symbols.)

Gloves (Worn on a certain hand or with fingers cut out)

Belt buckles (The symbol on the buckle or the side they are worn on)

Pant legs rolled up, shirt cuffs (The leg or arm that is rolled up indicates gang affiliation.)

Inside pants pockets (The pockets can bear the gang's colors.)

Gym shoes (The name of the shoe can indicate a gang slogan. [See Gang Slang, On page 229])

Eyebrows (The way they are shaved)

Fingernails (Whether they are painted, which ones are painted, and the color they are painted)

Tattoos and branding

Jewelry (Rings, pins, pendants, nose rings, and earrings in a specific ear, in a specific color, or a specific number)

GANG COMMUNICATION

Gang members communicate verbally via gang slang and visually via hand signs and graffiti. The list below identifies several of these methods.

Graffiti (Words, symbols, pictures, letters, or a combination thereof that demonstrates the dominance of a gang in a certain neighborhood, or *turf*. Graffiti also indicates disrespect toward another gang, declares war upon another gang, or communicates messages within the gang. Graffiti that is upside down indicates disrespect toward another gang.)

Hand signals

Writing in a certain fashion (Crips substitute the letter "C" for "B" in written communication.)

Having nicknames for members of the gang (Crips refer to one another as "Cuzz"; Bloods refer to one another as "Blood.")

graffiti

Words, symbols, pictures, letters, or a combination thereof that demonstrates the dominance of a gang in a certain neighborhood, or *turf*. Graffiti also indicates disrespect toward another gang, declares war upon another gang, or communicates messages within the gang. Graffiti that is upside down indicates disrespect toward another gang

Gang Slang

Slang is an important part of gang culture. It allows gang members to identify other members and provides those who use the slang with a sense of belonging. Feeling a sense of belonging is a primary reason many young people join gangs; consequently, slang has acquired a high level of importance.

Many gang education programs warn parents to note their children's use of gang slang as an indicator of gang involvement. This is not an easy task, however, as the breadth and extent of gang slang is staggering. It is continually changing and is unique to each gang. As with most youth slang, the moment the adults figure out, the youths change it. It is difficult to provide a completely accurate, current, and exhaustive list of slang. Following is a small sampling of some common terms in use at the writing of this book.

SIDEBAR

GANG SLANG

5 in the sky 6 must die—A People Nation member (represented by a five pointed star) was killed; the People Nation gang will retaliate against the Folks Nation gang (represented by a six-pointed star)

AB—Aryan Brotherhood

Adidas—Used by Crips; All Day I Destroy A Slob (Bloods)

All Is One—Term used by Folks Nation

(continues)

All Is Good—Term used by People Nation

Always and forever—Blood for life

Answer up—Respect your superiors' orders

BFL—Blood for life

BG—Baby gangster; very young member

B Queen—Female member of Bloods

B's Up C's Down—Disrespect of Crips by Bloods

Baby Gangster—Very young children (7–12 years) whom the gang uses as lookouts, and to hold drugs and guns

Bangin'—Gang fighting or violence; being in a gang

Be Down—Loyalty

Be Real—Prepare for war

Blob—Crips' derogatory term for Bloods

Bloods—Black street gang originated in Los Angeles

Blood In-Blood Out—A requirement to join some gangs; i.e., to join, you must kill someone; your death is the only way out of the gang

Brand—Tattoo

Brother—A fellow gang member

CAT—Crippin' all (the) time

CFL—Crip for life

CK—Crip killer; term used by Bloods

C Queen—Female Crips member

C's Up B's Down—Disrespect of Bloods by Crips

Carnal—Brother

Carnala—Sister

Colors—Item of clothing worn to signify gang membership

Crab—Derogatory name for Crips used by Bloods

Crew—Gang

Crips—Black street gang originating in Los Angeles

Double O.G.—Second-generation gang-banger

Dressed down—Wearing gang colors

Dropping the flag—Quitting the gang

Faded—Killed or dead

K-Swiss—Kill slobs when I see slobs

OG—Original gangster

Varrio—Neighborhood

GANG POETRY

FADED

The light has dimmed within my eyes

who among these war torn avenues hears my cries.

Flags of red and blue divide these streets

and the battle lines are drawn as i sneak among my enemies.

Your best friend could be a spy,

tomorrow you may die.

Bullets and chalk outline the dead

as thoughts of warfare burn in your head

this is no mans land

this is war among brothers and strangers and those who stalk in the night.

So i drop to my knees and pray

i won't be faded tonight.

Sledhead
www.gangstyle.com

CURRENT GANG MEMBERSHIP

All large cities, the vast majority of mid-sized cities, and a significant portion of small cities report the presence of gangs. The majority of those cities that reported the presence of gangs also reported a significant amount of violence and homicide associated with those gangs.

HIGHLIGHTS OF THE *2002 NATIONAL YOUTH GANG SURVEY* BY ARLEN EGLEY, JR., AND ALINE K. MAJOR

OJJDP created the NYGC as part of a comprehensive, coordinated response to what it perceived to be a worsening youth gang problem in the United States.

(continues)

NYGC began conducting annual surveys of police departments and sheriff's departments in all of the large and mid-sized cities and counties, and a random sampling of the smaller cities and counties in 1995.

The 2002 survey used a newly selected sample of law enforcement agencies based on updated data from the U.S. Census Bureau and the Federal Bureau of Investigation. The following local agencies were included in the nationally representative sample:

- All police departments (n = 627) serving cities with a population of 50,000 or more (larger cities).
- All suburban county police and sheriff's departments (n = 745) (suburban counties).
- A randomly selected sample (n = 699) of police departments serving cities with a population between 2,500 and 49,999 (smaller cities).
- A randomly selected sample (n = 492) of rural county police and sheriff's departments (rural counties).

The survey asked recipients to report information solely for youth gangs, defined as "a group of youths or young adults in your jurisdiction that you or other responsible persons in your agency or community are willing to identify as a 'gang.'" Motorcycle gangs, hate or ideology groups, prison gangs, and exclusively adult gangs were excluded from the survey. NYGC collected the survey data in 2003; they represent the prior calendar year.

SURVEY FINDINGS

Of the 2,563 survey recipients, 2,182 (85 percent) responded to the 2002 survey. All cities with a population of 250,000 or more reported youth gang problems in 2002, as did 87 percent of cities with a population between 100,000 and 249,999. Thirty-eight percent of responding suburban county agencies, 27 percent of responding smaller city agencies, and 12 percent of responding rural county agencies also reported youth gang problems in 2002. In general, smaller city agencies outnumber larger city agencies 10 to 1, and rural county agencies outnumber suburban county agencies 3 to 1.

Based on survey results, NYGC estimates that in 2002 youth gangs were active in more than 2,300 cities with a population of 2,500 or more and in more than 550 jurisdictions served by county law enforcement agencies. These results were comparable to those from recent NYGC surveys and provide preliminary evidence that the overall number of jurisdictions experiencing gang problems in a given year may be stabilizing.

NYGC also estimates that approximately 731,500 gang members and 21,500 gangs were active in the United States in 2002. The estimated number of gang members between 1996 and 2002 decreased 14 percent and the estimated number of jurisdictions experiencing gang problems decreased 32 percent. NYGC reports that this difference is largely a result of the decline

(continues)

in reported gang problems by smaller cities and rural counties that have also reported comparatively fewer gang members over survey years. Larger cities and suburban counties accounted for approximately 85 percent of the estimated number of gang members in 2002.

A total of 142 cities with a population of 100,000 or more reported both a gang problem and gang homicide data (i.e., the number of homicides involving a gang member) in 2002. Of these cities, 51 reported 0 gang-related homicides. Of the remaining 91 cities that reported 1 or more gang-related homicides, 89 reported a total of 577 gang-related homicides and 2 (Chicago and Los Angeles) reported a total of 655 gang-related homicides. When compared with the more than 1,300 total homicides recorded in Chicago and Los Angeles in 2002,1 these findings suggest that approximately half of the homicides in these 2 cities were gang related in that year.

Forty-two percent of respondents indicated their youth gang problem was "getting worse" in 2002 compared with 2001 and 16 percent indicated it was "getting better." In the 2001 survey, these statistics were 27 percent and 20 percent, respectively, indicating an appreciable increase in the proportion of respondents who regarded their gang problem as worsening.

GANG MEMBERSHIP AND CRIMINAL BEHAVIOR

There is a clear relationship between gang membership and delinquency. The spike in delinquency in youths who are gang members as opposed to high-risk youths who are not gang members is dramatic. The study outlined below details how that relationship appears in three cities.

SIDEBAR

COLORADO-FLORIDA-CLEVELAND STUDIES

The National Institute of Justice funded research in three communities—Aurora, Colorado; Denver, Colorado; and Broward County, Florida—and the Office of Juvenile Justice and Delinquency Prevention (OJJDP) funded research in Cleveland, Ohio, to answer three questions:

• What is the nature and magnitude of self-reported criminal behavior among youth gang members?

• What is the nature and magnitude of such behavior among at-risk youths—those who are not yet gang members?

• What is the effect of gang membership on criminal behavior?

(continues)

Also, as part of the OJJDP grant, researchers in Columbus, Ohio, tracked leaders of youth gangs to determine what happens to gang leaders over time.

The Colorado-Florida and Cleveland studies obtained self-reported data through one-time confidential interviews. Researchers in each community interviewed 50 gang members and 50 youths who were at risk of becoming gang members, developing as close a demographic match between the two groups as possible. They selected interviewees through referrals from local youth-serving organizations, rather than from police databases of arrestees. Questions focused on criminal and noncriminal activities of the youths and their peers.

The data on criminal activity showed differences between the behavior of gang members and at-risk youths. For example, individual gang members in both studies reported that they had stolen cars (Colorado-Florida, 58.3 percent; Cleveland, 44.7 percent); aggregate rates for auto theft—reflecting statements that members of their gang had stolen cars—were much higher (Colorado-Florida, 93.6 percent; Cleveland, 82.6). Auto theft rates among at-risk youths were markedly lower (Colorado-Florida, 12.5 percent; Cleveland, 4.1 percent). The researchers found similar contrasts when looking at violent crimes. About 40 percent of gang members in the Cleveland sample said they had participated in a drive-by shooting, compared with 2 percent of at-risk youths. In the Colorado-Florida study, 64.2 percent of gang members said that members of their gang had committed homicide, whereas 6.5 percent of at-risk youths said that their friends had done so.

Although both gang members and at-risk youths admitted significant involvement with guns, gang members were far likelier to own guns, and the guns they owned were larger caliber. More than 90 percent of gang members in both studies reported that their peers had carried concealed weapons; more than 80 percent reported that members of their gang had carried guns to school. In contrast, about one-half of at-risk youths in both studies had friends who had carried a concealed weapon; about one-third of at-risk youths said their friends had carried guns to school.

In both studies, gang members were more involved with selling drugs (Colorado-Florida, 76.9 percent; Cleveland, 72.3 percent) than were at-risk youths (Colorado-Florida, 6.4 percent; Cleveland, 9.1 percent). When asked what level of legitimate wages would induce them to stop selling drugs, about one-quarter of the young people in both studies cited an amount little higher than that earned in fast-food restaurants. Approximately half of the interviewees, both gang members and at-risk youths, said they had held jobs in the past year.

(continues)

The second component of the Ohio study focused on the criminal activity of identified gang leaders in Columbus. The researchers analyzed the arrest records of 83 gang leaders in the years 1980 to 1994. Membership of 78 of these leaders was distributed among five gangs; the rest belonged to other gangs.

During these 15 years, the 83 gang leaders accumulated 834 arrests, 37 percent of which were for violent crimes ranging from domestic violence to murder. Property crimes and drug-related offenses also figured prominently. The researchers identified a clear pattern of arrest charges in each of the five prominent gangs. A gang's peak arrest rate for property crimes occurred about 1.5 years before its peak arrest rate for violent crimes; the peak arrest rate for drug crimes followed about 3 months later. The researchers theorized that violent crimes increased as the gangs began engaging in drug activity and may have been connected to the establishment of the drug trade. The increasingly violent activities took their toll on the gangs: by the end of the period studied, a disproportionate number of the gang leaders had died.

RISK FACTORS FOR GANG MEMBERSHIP

Youths join gangs to obtain protection, a sense of belonging, money, fun, or glamour. Gangs actively recruit youths. Youths are desirable not only because they increase the gang's numbers, but also because they are ideally suited for carrying out criminal enterprises. Young people energetic, daring, and easily manipulated, and because of their youth, they are subject to less severe legal penalties when they are caught.

Individual characteristics, family conditions, school performance, peer group influences, and the community all influence whether a youth will join a gang. Risk factors predictive of gang membership include prior and/or early involvement in delinquency, especially violence and drug use; problematic parent-child relations; low school attachment and academic achievement; association with peers who engage in delinquency; and disorganized neighborhoods in which large numbers of youth are in trouble.

PENALTY ENHANCEMENT FOR GANG INVOLVEMENT

Not only does gang membership increase the likelihood that youths will participate in criminal activity, it also increases the penalties that the youths will suffer once they enter the court system as a result of that activity. Twenty-three states have statutes that enhance dispositional penalties in cases where the juvenile was a gang member, committed the offense pursuant to gang activity, or committed the offense as part of a pattern of gang activity.[i] Most states have statutes criminalizing graffiti. Recruiting into a gang is an offense, as is threatening or intimidating a person who attempts to leave a gang.

Statutes that prohibit membership in known gangs with known criminal activities generally require specific intent to further the criminal enterprise, or to aid, assist, or abet the commission of criminal acts. Without such a provision, the statutes would criminalize the act of being in a gang, and that would be a violation of the constitutionally protected right of association.

Membership in a youth gang can be a criterion for classification as a habitual juvenile offender. Indiana provides that its juvenile courts do not have jurisdiction over juveniles who are members of street gangs, thus providing for the automatic transfer of such juveniles into adult criminal court.

In some states, membership in youth gangs provides grounds to transfer juveniles to adult criminal court. Courts examine whether he has sought actively to further the criminal activities of the gang. Mere membership in the gang is not enough to sustain a transfer.

CONTROLLING GANGS

States have found it challenging to control gangs legislatively. Gangs are difficult to define and therefore difficult to regulate. The problem for the legislatures is in crafting laws that regulate the gangs without crossing constitutional boundaries. Legislatures attempt to control or eliminate the presence of gangs, restrict their operations, and penalize their activities through laws that prohibit gang graffiti, prohibit the wearing of gang colors or regalia in the schools, and prohibit gangs from occupying certain structures to the extent that they create a public nuisance.

Juveniles have attacked these provisions on the grounds that they are too vague, and they violate the juveniles' right to equal protection under the law, their right of association, and their right to due process.

The courts have Generally denied those appeals. They cite the courts' narrow interpretations of the statutes, as well as the particularities of the statutes, as staving off charges of vagueness. In answer to charges of a violation of equal protection, courts point out that the difference between gang membership and membership in other groups that may engage in criminal activity (for instance, college fraternities who engage in **hazing,** or the ritualized initiation into the organization, a process that often involves some level of pain, humiliation, or ordeal) is that the primary purpose of a youth criminal gang is to engage in criminal activity, whereas the criminal activity associated with

hazing
The ritualized initiation into the organization, a process that often involves some level of pain, humiliation, or ordeal

other enterprises (the college fraternity, for instance) is only incidental. Finally, the right to association in a criminal enterprise is not one that the Constitution seeks to protect.

The laws that have withstood constitutional challenges are those laws that have certain essential elements. These statutes prohibit:

- Joining a gang that the joiner *knows* to be engaged in criminal enterprise; *and*
- Aiding, abetting, assisting, or otherwise furthering the commission of some criminal enterprise within the gang; or
- *Actually committing a criminal or delinquent act* while a member of the gang; or
- *Actually committing a criminal or delinquent act*, such as battery, as part of the initiation into the gang.

The statutes that do not withstand legal scrutiny are those that simply prohibit membership in a gang, prohibit the gang from existing, or prohibit gang members from showing themselves in public.

The following case demonstrates the variety of legal issues that a defendant can raise in response to a gang-related penalty enhancement, and the court's response to those arguments.

Helton v. State
624 N.E.2d 499 (Ind. App. 1993)

Today we decide whether Indiana's Criminal Gang Activity Statute is constitutional under the United States and Indiana Constitutions.

Appellant-defendant James W. Helton, II, appeals his conviction for Participating in Criminal Gang Activity, a Class D felony.

ISSUES

Helton raises several issues for our review:

I. Whether Indiana's Criminal Gang Activity Statute (Gang Statute) is unconstitutional because:
   A. It is void for vagueness under the First and Fourteenth Amendments to the U.S. Constitution.
   B. It is unconstitutionally overbroad and impermissibly infringed upon Helton's right of association guaranteed under the First and Fourteenth Amendments to the U.S. Constitution.
   C. It deprived Helton of equal protection of the laws as guaranteed under the Fourteenth Amendment to the U.S. Constitution.

FACTS

The undisputed facts are that James Helton, a sixteen-year-old white male also know as G-Dog, is a member of the Imperial Gangster Disciples (IGD), a twelve

(continues)

member youth group.[3] In October 1991, while Helton was second in command or the number two G, he and other members initiated Scott Bullington into IGD. IGD members perform the initiation ritual, called "a 46," by striking the initiate forty times in the head and six times in the chest while standing in a circle around an ironing board with a blue bandana, a candle, and a handgun placed on top.

In February 1992, twelve to fourteen IGD members met to initiate Travis Hammons. Helton and two other IGD members initiated Hammons after number one G Charlie Moran recited the traditional initiation "prayer."[4] While four IGD members restrained Hammons, Helton delivered 20 bare-fisted, hard blows directly to Hammons' head while pronouncing "he was going to beat [Hammons'] ass into the ground."[5] Both Bullington and Hammons knew of the initiation rite and consented to "a 46" by Helton and other members in order to become IGD members themselves.

At Hammons' initiation, IGD members also discussed the need to travel in pairs, to be aggressive with others, to never back away from anyone or a fight, determined that anyone who missed an IGD meeting would "get violated" (receive six blows to the chest), and decided that anyone leaving IGD would

---

[3] IGD member Biff Kinnick testified that IGD stands for Insane Gangster Disciples. This may be a more appropriate name; however, all other IGD members who testified stated that IGD stands for Imperial Gangster Disciples. The IGD gang colors are black and blue.

[4] At initiations, IGD members circle around an ironing board while a leader recites the IGD "prayer." The "prayer" is: "Let it rain, let it pour, let a G [IGD member] kill a Lord [Vice-Lord, another gang]."

[5] Helton and another member held the gun briefly during the initiation, however, it remained on the ironing board most of the time.

be "eight-balled" (surrounded by eight members and then beaten by them).

The Morgan County court waived juvenile jurisdiction over then fifteen-year-old Helton, to the Morgan Superior Court. The State charged Helton by information with participating in criminal gang activity on or about February 12, 1992, for committing a battery on Hammons. Helton was released on bond.

The trial court determined the Gang Statute was constitutional and found Helton guilty of criminal gang activity. The trial court sentenced Helton to three years imprisonment, suspended so long as he complied with the terms of his probation. Helton now appeals.

DECISION AND DISCUSSION

I. Constitutionality

In considering constitutional challenges, we accord the statute with every reasonable presumption supporting its validity and place the burden upon the party challenging it to show unconstitutionality. To be constitutional, a statute must be carefully drafted or be authoritatively construed to punish only constitutionally unprotected conduct. We will assign a constitutional meaning to a statute if we can do so while remaining faithful to the legislative purpose. The language of a judicial opinion is as good as the language of the statute construed in the opinion.

A. Vagueness

Helton first contends the Gang Statute is void under the First and Fourteenth Amendments to the U.S. Constitution because it is unconstitutionally vague.

Under basic principles of due process, a law is void for vagueness if its prohibitions are not clearly defined. A statute is not void for vagueness if individuals of ordinary intelligence would comprehend it

(continues)

Helton v. State (Continued)

to fairly inform them of the generally proscribed conduct.[10] Statutes which threaten to inhibit the exercise of constitutional rights or which impose criminal penalties are subjected to greater scrutiny and less vagueness is tolerated in them than in other types of laws. However, the act of associating with compatriots in crime is not a protected associational right.

The Gang Statute provides: "A person who knowingly or intentionally actively participates in a criminal gang commits criminal gang activity, a Class D felony." A "criminal gang" is defined as:

. . . a group with at least five (5) members that specifically:

(1) either:

    (A) promotes, sponsors, or assists in; or

    (B) participates in; and

(2) requires as a condition of membership or continued membership; the commission of a felony or an act that would be a felony if committed by an adult or the offense of battery.

The Gang Statute clearly forbids a person from knowingly and actively participating in a group with five or more members which participates in and requires as a condition of membership the commission of a battery. When Helton beat Hammons, he actively participated in the IGD gang with knowledge that the IGD gang participates in and requires as a condition of membership the commission of a battery. Helton's conduct is clearly proscribed by the Gang Statute.

[10] Vague laws offend three important values: (1) the requirement that laws give a person of ordinary intelligence a reasonable opportunity to know what is prohibited, (2) by not providing explicit standards for those who apply them, vague laws lead to arbitrary and discriminatory enforcement and impermissibly delegate basic policy matters to police, judges and juries for resolution on an ad hoc basis, and (3) where a vague statute impinges upon sensitive areas of basic First Amendment freedoms, it inhibits the exercise of those freedoms.

Additionally, Helton claims the Gang Statute is void for vagueness because it vests unfettered discretion in the prosecutor allowing him to enforce it in an arbitrary and discriminatory manner to punish groups he alone deems undesirable.

A statute is also void for vagueness if its terms invite arbitrary or discriminatory enforcement. However, no statute need avoid all vagueness. Because statutes are condemned to the use of words, there will always be uncertainties for we cannot expect mathematical certainty from our language.

Obviously, the decision to prosecute for any type of criminal activity must reside somewhere. The prosecutor's decision to prosecute does not determine the final outcome. Moreover, courts have repeatedly held this type of procedure constitutional. Enforcement of laws always requires some degree of judgment on behalf of police and prosecutors, but, as confined, that degree of judgment is permissible here.

Furthermore, undesirable groups, the wrong type of crowd, or annoying conduct alone is not punishable under the Gang Statute. The Gang Statute does not permit five or more persons to associate only at the whim of a police officer or the prosecutor.

Rather the group must be one which both promotes, sponsors, assists in, or participates, and requires as a condition of membership the commission of a felony or battery and the person must actively participate in the group, with knowledge of the group's criminal conduct and a specific purpose to facilitate the group's criminal conduct before the prosecutor may charge the person with participating in criminal gang activity. The Gang Statute gives persons of ordinary intelligence fair warning of the proscribed, unprotected conduct and is thus not unconstitutionally vague.

Here, Helton contends that the Gang Statute infringes upon his right of association guaranteed under

(continues)

Helton v. State (Continued)

the First and Fourteenth Amendments of the U.S. Constitution. As the basis for this challenge, Helton asserts that he was, and can be at any time in the future, prosecuted for merely associating with a group of juveniles that has been labelled a criminal gang.

First, the Gang Statute does not prohibit the mere association of five or more persons as Helton contends.[12] Before a person may be charged with criminal gang activity, the Gang Statute expressly requires that the person actively participate in a group which promotes, sponsors, assists in, or participates in, and requires its members to commit felonies or batteries, with knowledge of the group's criminal advocacy.

Furthermore, we construe the Gang Statute to require that the active member with guilty knowledge also have a specific intent or purpose to further the group's criminal conduct before he may be prosecuted. Thus, the Gang Statute does not impermissibly establish guilt by association alone, but it requires that a defendant's association pose the threat feared by the legislature in proscribing it, that is, the threat of criminal gang activity which terrorizes peaceful citizens.

Therefore, members of a former "criminal gang" who adopt morals and policies of engaging in solely lawful conduct may associate freely without fear of prosecution under the Gang Statute. As discussed above, the Gang Statute does not unconstitutionally criminalize the mere status of gang membership.

A plain reading of the statutes dictate[s] that the Gang Statute clearly forbids a person from: (a) actively participating or being an "active" member in a group with five or more members which promotes, sponsors, assists in, or participates in the commission of a felony or an act that would be a felony if committed by an adult or a battery, and requires as a condition of membership the same criminal conduct, (b) with knowledge of the gang's illegal advocacy of felonies or batteries, and (c) with specific intent to further, facilitate, or accomplish the substantive criminal conduct, that is, the commission of a felony or an act that would be a felony if committed by an adult or a battery.

A person who merely becomes a member of an illegal organization, by this act alone, does nothing more than signify his assent to the group's purposes and conduct and provide moral encouragement and sympathy. It may be argued that such encouragement and assent fall short of the active participation required to permit the imposition of criminal sanctions. *Id.* A member, as distinguished from an active participant or a conspirator, may indicate his approval of a criminal gang by the fact of his membership without thereby necessarily committing himself to further the criminal gang's goals by any act or course of conduct whatever.

The Gang Statute requires that a person knowingly and "actively participates" in the criminal gang and have a specific intent to further the gang's unlawful goals before he may be prosecuted. "Actively participates" requires more than the mere voluntary listing of a person's name on the gang's roll. The mere presence of a person's name on a gang's roll is insufficient to impute to him the gang's illegal goals. Thus, the Gang Statute does not unconstitutionally establish guilt by association alone or unconstitutionally punish nominal, inactive, purely technical, or passive membership, even if accompanied by knowledge and intent.

Under the Gang Statute, IGD is an organization which engages in the targeted criminal conduct. Neither a person who actively and knowingly works in

---

[12] We also note that once a "criminal gang" under the Gang Statute, not always a criminal gang. If a criminal gang one day decides it will no longer promote, sponsor, assist in, or participate in, or require the commission of a felony or a battery for membership or continued membership, then the group will no longer fall within the statutory definition of a criminal gang.

(continues)

Helton v. State (Continued)

the ranks of the criminal gang, intending to contribute to the success of the gang's illegal activities, nor a member to whom the gang has assigned the task of carrying out the substantive criminal act, is immune from prosecution.

The Gang Statute does not cut deeper into the freedom of association than is necessary to deal with the substantive evil of gang violence and does not make criminal all association with an organization which has been shown to engage in illegal activity. The Gang Statute requires clear proof that a defendant actively participated in the gang with knowledge of its criminal advocacy and a specific intent to accomplish the gang's illegal aims. Thus the Gang Statute is not unconstitutionally vague or overbroad and does not unconstitutionally interfere with one's right to freedom of association.

C. Equal Protection Clause

Helton next contends that the Gang Statute deprived him of equal protection under the laws as guaranteed under § 1 of the Fourteenth Amendment to the U.S. Constitution. Specifically, Helton claims that the prosecutor has and will continue to apply the Gang Statute in a discriminatory manner to groups he alone deems undesirable, which tend to be poor, disadvantaged youths. Helton argues discriminatory prosecution for intra-group violence denies individual members of undesirable groups equal protection of the laws.

The purpose of the equal protection clauses is to prevent the distribution of extraordinary benefits or burdens to any group. A statute which does not discriminate on its face may nonetheless deny equal protection if it is enforced or applied in a discriminatory manner. The defendant bears the burden of establishing such discrimination.

Here, Helton does not contend that the Gang Statute facially violates his right to association, rather he baldly asserts, without any supporting evidence, that the prosecutor has applied and will continue to apply the Gang Statute in a discriminatory manner. "A defendant's constitutional right to equal protection of the laws is not violated by the prosecutor exercising discretion in deciding to prosecute or not to prosecute a violation of a criminal statute." Moreover, we held in *Issue I.A.* that the degree of discretion afforded the prosecutor under the Gang Statute is constitutional. Helton was not denied equal protection under the laws.

Additionally, Helton claims he was denied equal protection of the laws inasmuch as the prosecutor has discretion to prosecute gangs for criminal gang activity, a Class D felony, but to prosecute fraternities under Indiana's Hazing Statute, a Class B misdemeanor for the same conduct.

A statute which prescribes different punishments or different degrees of punishment for the same conduct committed under the same circumstances by persons similarly situated violates the equal protection clause. Therefore, the critical inquiry here is whether the elements of the Gang Statute and the Hazing Statute are the same or essentially similar; if not, then no equal protection issue is presented.

The Hazing Statute provides:

(a) As used in this section, "hazing" means forcing or requiring another person:
   (1) with or without the consent of the other person; and
   (2) as a condition of association with a group or organization; to perform an act that creates a substantial risk of bodily injury.

(b) A person who recklessly, knowingly, or intentionally performs:
   (1) an act that creates a substantial risk of bodily injury to another person; or

(continues)

Helton v. State (Continued)

(2) hazing; commits criminal recklessness, a Class B misdemeanor.

. . . (c) A person who recklessly, knowingly, or intentionally:

    (1) inflicts serious bodily injury on another person; or

    (2) performs hazing that results in serious bodily injury to a person; commits criminal recklessness, a Class D felony.

Hazing is a class B misdemeanor if the act involved creates only a risk of substantial bodily injury to another person. A person commits criminal recklessness, a class D felony, if the hazing act actually results in serious bodily injury to a person. A person may be prosecuted under the Gang Statute for a class D felony if, among other requirements, he is a member of a group which consists of five or more persons which requires the commission of a felony or an act that would be a felony if committed by an adult or a battery as a condition for membership or continued membership.

The elements of a class B misdemeanor under the Hazing Statute and a class D felony under the Gang Statute differ since the former applies to acts creating only a risk of bodily injury. Therefore, there are distinctions between the two offenses, and no equal protection question is presented. The statutes do not prescribe different punishment for the same conduct depending on the actor. Under each statute, an actor commits a class D felony if he engages in the same type of conduct.

The Gang Statute did not deprive Helton of equal protection of the laws or equal privileges or immunities.

The Gang Statute was not intended to interfere with the constitutional exercise of the protected rights of freedom of association and expression. The criminal activities proscribed, individually and collectively, present a clear and present danger to the public order and safety and are not constitutionally protected.

CONCLUSION

Indiana's Criminal Gang Activity Statute passes constitutional muster. Its prohibitions include a battery committed by one gang member on another consenting gang member.

Judgment affirmed.

Loitering and Gathering Statutes

The Illinois legislature conducted a series of public hearings after which it determined that the gang presence on the streets contributed to a continuing increase in the city's murder rate, an escalation of violent and drug-related crimes, and intimidation of city residents. They found that gang members established control over areas of the city by their presence, creating fear for the people and property in the area.

The state legislature passed a law that made it a criminal offense to loiter. The law defined loitering as "remain[ing] in any one place with no apparent purpose." The law required the police to first order the loiterers to disburse, and subjected the loiterers to arrest if they did not obey the police order.

The Supreme Court held that the statute was unconstitutionally vague on its face, in that it punished as criminal activity an activity that the Constitution allows, and that contains no element of *mens rea,* or criminal intent.

Other state statutes prohibit loitering with the intent or purpose of publicizing a criminal street gang's dominance of an area. Courts have upheld these statutes in the face of constitutional challenges, but have held that the state must demonstrate that the juvenile engaged in prohibited behavior. It is not enough for the state to demonstrate that the juvenile was a member of a gang, and that other members of the gang had engaged in prohibited behavior.

Enjoining Gang Activities

Some states have sought **injunctions,** or court orders, prohibiting gang members from engaging in gang-related activity, such as "throwing" gang signs, using gang phrases, displaying gang gestures, or wearing gang clothing or jewelry. The courts have granted these injunctions, and reviewing courts have upheld their validity where the state can prove that the defendants are actually gang members, and that as such they are responsible for the public nuisance that the injunction alleges.

For example, a municipality will ask a court to enjoin gang members from operating cell phones or pagers, possessing materials associated with graffiti (spray paint, markers, razors), creating graffiti, trespassing, urinating in public, or harassing or annoying residents within an area definable as the gang's turf.

The state can prove that individuals are gang members by demonstrating that they "participate in, or act in concert with, an ongoing organization, association, or group of three or more persons, whether formal or informal, having as one if its primary activities the commission of act constituting the enjoined public nuisance, having a common name or common identifying sign or symbol and whose embers individually or collectively engage in the acts constituting the enjoined public nuisance. The participating or acting must be more than nominal, passive, inactive or purely technical."[ii]

Courts have upheld these injunctions, holding that they do not violate the gang members' First Amendment right to freedom of association. They have held that the Constitution does not protect a generalized right of social association, but rather recognizes a limited right to associate and protects only two types of association: those with an "intrinsic or intimate value," characterized by personal and familial relationships, and those that are "instrumental to forms of religious and political expression," characterized by "a wide variety of political, social, economic, educational, religious, and cultural ends . . . closely aligned with freedom of speech."[iii]

mens rea
Criminal intent

injunction
A court order prohibiting a person or group from engaging in certain activities

Requiring Juveniles to Register as Gang Members

A California statute, the Street Terrorism Enforcement and Prevention Act (STEP) requires, among other things, that all juveniles against whom juvenile courts have sustained petitions for "any crime that the court finds is gang-related at the time of sentencing or disposition" to register as gang members with the chief of police or the sheriff of the city or county in which they reside within 10 days of their release from custody of their arrival in the city.

Courts have consistently upheld these laws against charges that they are unconstitutionally vague, they constitute **double jeopardy,** or two punishments for the same wrong act, they violate the defendants' right to counsel, they violate the defendants' privilege against self-incrimination, they constitute cruel or unusual punishment, or they punish gang members for their mere association with a gang.

double jeopardy

Being convicted or punished twice for the same wrong act

CASE PROBLEM

The state of Florida filed a petition in juvenile court charging O.C., a juvenile, with attempted aggravated battery to cause great bodily harm and misdemeanor battery. The state then filed a motion to have O.C. declared a gang member for disposition enhancement purposes pursuant to section 874.04, Florida Statutes. O.C. moved to dismiss the enhancement request asserting that section 874.04 is unconstitutional because it omits an intent requirement, violates free speech and freedom of association, and imputes guilt by association.

Chapter 874, the Criminal Street Gang Prevention Act of 1996, provides for enhanced criminal penalties for a convicted defendant who is a member of a criminal street gang: § 874.04 Criminal street gang activity; enhanced penalties— Upon a finding by the court at sentencing that the defendant is a member of a criminal street gang, the penalty for any felony or misdemeanor, or any delinquent act or violation of law which would be a felony or misdemeanor if committed by an adult, may be enhanced if the offender was a member of a criminal street gang at the time of the commission of such offense. Each of the findings required as a basis for such sentence shall be found by a preponderance of the evidence. The enhancement will be as follows:

(2)(a) A felony of the third degree may be punished as if it were a felony of the second degree.

Section 874.03, the definition section of the statute, defines a "criminal street gang" as an organization or group of three or more persons who have a common name or identifying signs colors or symbols, and have two or more members who, individually or collectively, engage in or have engaged in a pattern of criminal street gang activity. The statutes defines a criminal street gang member as someone who meets two or more of the following criteria:

(a) Admits to criminal street gang membership.

(b) Is identified as a criminal street gang member by a parent or guardian.

(c) Is identified as a criminal street gang member by a documented reliable informant.

(d) Resides in or frequents a particular criminal street gang's area a nd adopts their style of dress, their use of hand signs, or their tattoos, and associates with known criminal street gang members.

(e) Is identified as a criminal street gang member by an informant of previously untested reliability and such identification is corroborated by independent information.

(f) Has been arrested more than once in the company of identified criminal street gang members for offenses which are consistent with usual criminal street gang activity.

(g) Is identified as a criminal street gang member by physical evidence such as photographs or other documentation.

(h) Has been stopped in the company of known criminal street gang members four or more times.

The court sustained the petition, then heard the motion for gang enhancement and disposition. A sheriff's deputy involved in gang surveillance testified that O.C. is a member of an Orlando gang known as Universal Mafia Crew (UMC) and identified additional members. The deputy testified that O. C. told him while on the street that she was a member of UMC and in fact was the leader.

Another deputy sheriff who specializes in gangs testified that UMC has a hierarchy consisting of a godfather, godmother, bosses, and foot soldiers. O.C. was the godmother. The gang had colors, met monthly, and was implicated in other crimes. Local police had taken into custody several members of the gang on felony charges including armed burglary, aggravated battery with a knife, possession of a short barrel shotgun, and grand theft auto. At least three of the arrests had occurred within the past year.

The trial court denied O.C.'s constitutional challenge to the statute. The court found UMC to be a criminal street gang as that term is defined in section 874.03(1), that O.C. was a criminal street gang member and that under section 874.04 the two convictions would be enhanced upward one degree (to a second degree felony and third degree felony). The court sentenced O.C. as though it were a felony of the second degree.

On appeal O.C. argued that the trial court erred (1) in finding the enhancement penalty provided in section 874.04, Florida Statutes, to be facially constitutional in that it punishes lawful activity without requiring criminal intent and it limits freedom of association.

What did the appeals court rule?

ROLE-PLAY PROBLEM

You are a legislator in a mid-sized city that has recently seen an explosion of gang activity. In the past two years, your town has gone from having no gang problem to having several well-established, violent, and growing gangs.

One particular gang, the OG's, has been especially troublesome. They are heavily involved in drug trafficking, an enterprise they carry out in the open at the corner of 33rd and Main streets, in the city center. Residents in the four-block area the OGs now occupy are terrorized, afraid to leave their homes during the day or night. The OGs have covered their houses, garages, fences, and vehicles with graffiti. They play loud music, swear, fight, shoot guns, litter, and harass passersby.

Housing prices have dropped 40 percent in the two years since the OGs' arrival. Almost a quarter of the local business have closed, and many more are on their way to closing. The school enrollment has dropped, dropout rates have risen, and test scores have fallen. The number of homicides, other violent crimes, and property crimes in the area has risen 25 percent.

Devise a plan to control or eliminate this activity. Draft a piece of legislation, outline a social program, enlist the help of the courts, and use any other means you can think of.

HYPOTHETICAL PROBLEM

You work for a defense attorney. The state has filed a petition against your client, a juvenile, alleging he is delinquent because he spray painted gang graffiti on the walls of a government building—a naval base. This is a serious offense because the vandalism took place on federal government property. Your client has a substantial juvenile record, so if the court sustains this petition your client is facing commitment.

You have examined pictures of the graffiti. It consists of the Crips' names and symbols written upside down. You know this to be a symbol of disrespect to the Crips at the very least, and possibly a declaration of war or a specific threat to the Crips in general or to a member in particular. You also know that your client is a member of the Crips, and as such, would never create that graffiti.

Do you proffer your client's Crips membership as evidence that he would not create the graffiti in question, thus subjecting him to possible other consequences?

ETHICAL CONCERNS

When defending juveniles the biggest ethical concern most attorneys and paralegals experience is the tension between advocating to win a dismissal of the charges against your client, and advocating for what is in your client's best interests, which may not be a dismissal. It is difficult to represent a youth who is in a gang, and is caught in a cycle of committing crimes, victimizing others, being a victim, and spiraling downward.

Attorneys and paralegals must always remember that when acting as a defender rather than a guardian ad litem, they must work for their client's desires, rather than the attorney's or paralegal's perception of what is in the client's best interests.

DISCUSSION QUESTIONS

1. What are the competing interests in trying to control gang activity?

2. Is it more important to preserve the integrity of individual freedoms and civil liberties under the Constitution or to preserve and maintain order and safety on the public streets?

3. Is it possible for people to be gang members and do no harm either to themselves or to society?

4. The great majority of female gang members are victims of sexual or physical abuse at home, and joined the gang for protection from life on the streets. Should these females be subject to legal penalties for their gang involvement under these circumstances?

5. Should there be some sort of penalty or consequence for a person who is an active gang member and has young children? Should such a parent be allowed to keep their children?

6. Which do you believe is the most effective way to control gangs—legal mechanisms, or educational programs?

KEY TERMS

colors   hazing
double jeopardy   injunction
graffiti   *mens rea*
hand signs   youth gang

END NOTES

[i] Alaska, Arizona, Arkansas, California, Florida, Georgia, Illinois, Indiana, Kansas, Louisiana, Maryland, Minnesota, Mississippi, Missouri, Nevada, New Jersey, North Dakota, Ohio, South Dakota, Tennessee, Texas, Utah, and Wisconsin
[ii] *People v. Englebrecht*, 106 Cal.Rptr.2d 738 (Cal.App. 4 Dist., 2001)
[iii] *People v. Lopez,* 78 Cal.Rptr.2d 66 (1998)

MARYLAND LAWYER'S RULES OF PROFESSIONAL CONDUCT

The Maryland Lawyer's Rules of Professional Conduct are typical of such rules throughout the United States, and are based upon the Model Rules of Professional Conduct.

MARYLAND LAWYER'S RULES OF PROFESSIONAL CONDUCT (EXCERPT)

Rule 1.6 Confidentiality of Information

(a) A lawyer shall not reveal information relating to representation of a client unless the client consents after consultation, except for disclosures that are impliedly authorized in order to carry out the representation, and except as stated in paragraph (b).

(b) A lawyer may reveal such information to the extent the lawyer reasonably believes necessary:

(1) to prevent the client from committing a criminal or fraudulent act that the lawyer believes is likely to result in death or substantial bodily harm or in substantial injury to the financial interests or property of another;

(2) to rectify the consequences of a client's criminal or fraudulent act in the furtherance of which the lawyer's services were used;

(3) to establish a claim or defense on behalf of the lawyer in a controversy between the lawyer and the client, or to establish a defense to a criminal charge, civil claim, or disciplinary complaint against the lawyer based upon conduct in which the client was involved or to respond to allegations in any proceeding concerning the lawyer's representation of a client; and

(4) to comply with these Rules, a court order or other law.

Rule 1.14 Client Under a Disability

(a) When a client's ability to make adequately considered decisions in connection with the representation is impaired, whether because of minority, mental disability, or for some other reason, the lawyer shall, as far as reasonably possible, maintain a normal client-lawyer relationship with the client.

(b) A lawyer may seek the appointment of a guardian or take other protective action with respect to a client only when the lawyer reasonably believes that the client cannot adequately act in the client's own interest.

Rule 5.3 Responsibilities Regarding Nonlawyer Assistants

With respect to a nonlawyer employed or retained by or associated with a lawyer:

(a) a partner in a law firm shall make reasonable efforts to ensure that the firm has in effect measures giving reasonable assurance that the person's conduct is compatible with the professional obligations of the lawyer;

(b) a lawyer having direct supervisory authority over the nonlawyer shall make reasonable efforts to ensure that the person's conduct is compatible with the professional obligations of the lawyer; and

(c) a lawyer shall be responsible for conduct of such a person that would be a violation of the Rules of Professional Conduct if engaged in by a lawyer if:

(1) the lawyer orders or, with the knowledge of the specific conduct, ratifies the conduct involved; or

(2) the lawyer is a partner in the law firm in which the person is employed, or has direct supervisory authority over the person, and knows of the conduct at a time when its consequences can be avoided or mitigated but fails to take reasonable remedial action.

RESOURCES FOR CHILDREN AND FAMILIES

National Runaway Switchboard
www.nrscrisisline.org
30810 N. Lincoln Ave.
Chicago, IL 60657
800.621.4000
　The National Runaway Switchboard's mission is to facilitate relationships that ensure youth and families have access to resources in their communities.

CHILDREN'S LEGAL RIGHTS

American Bar Association (ABA)
www.abanet.org
Center on Children and the Law
740 15th St., NW
Washington, DC 20005
202.662.1720
　Consultation, technical assistance, and training for professionals in using the legal system to protect children.

American Civil Liberties Union
www.aclu.org
Children's Rights Project
132 W. 43rd St.
New York, NY 10036
212.549.2500
　A national program of litigation, advocacy, and education.

National Association of Counsel for Children (NACC)
www.naccchildlaw.org
1825 Marion St., Suite 340
Denver, CO 80218

888.82-NACC
　Professional organization for lawyers and other practitioners who represent children in court.

FAMILY RESOURCES

Grandparent Information Center
www.aarp.org
601 E St., NW, Room B5436
Washington, DC 20049
800.424.3410
　For grandparents raising grandchildren, professionals, support groups, researchers, and policy makers.

Family Support America
www.frca.org
20 N. Wacker Dr., Ste. 1100
Chicago, IL 60606
312.338.0900
　A membership organization of social service agencies concerned with strengthening families through preventive services.

MEDICAL RESOURCES

American Academy of Pediatrics
www.aap.org
141 NW Point Blvd.
Elk Grove Village, IL 60007
847.434.4000
　Provides numerous materials for professionals working in the child abuse prevention field.

PARENT RESOURCES

Big Brothers/Big Sisters of America
www.bbsa.org
230 N. 13th St.
Philadelphia, PA 19107
215.567.7000
Volunteers support families under stress and single parents by working with children in need of additional attention and friendship.

Center for the Improvement of Child Caring
www.ciccparenting.org
11331 Ventura Blvd., Suite 103
Studio City, CA 91604
818.980.0903
Provides training for parents and training of parenting instructors nationwide. Offers a wide variety of workshops nationwide.

SUPPORT FOR NEW PARENTS

Birth to Three
www.efn.org
86 Centennial Loop
Eugene, OR 97401
541.484.5316
Programs are for parents of infants, toddlers, and teenage parents.

Healthy Families America® (HFA)
www.healthyfamiliesamerica.org
200 S. Michigan Ave.
17th Floo
Chicago, IL 60604
312.663.3520
An innovative initiative designed to support and educate new parents through voluntary home visitation.

ASSOCIATIONS/ORGANIZATIONS

American Professional Society on the Abuse of Children (APSAC)
www.apsac.org
407 S. Dearborn St., Suite 1300
Chicago, IL 60605
312.554.0166
A multidisciplinary membership society promoting support among professionals who work with victims of child abuse.

American Public Human Services Association
www.aphsa.org
810 First St., NE, Suite 500
Washington, DC 20002-4267
202.682.0100
Concerned with effective administration of publicly funded human services.

National Council on Child Abuse and Family Violence
www.nccafv.org
800.222.2000

National Center for Victims of Crime
2000 M Street, NW, Suite 480
Washington DC 20036
800.FYI.CALL
800.394.2255

National CASA
www.nationalcasa.org
100 West Harrison—North Tower, Suite 500
Seattle WA 98119
800.628.3233
The national organization of Court Appointed Special Advocate (CASA) associations, which advocate for abused and neglected children.

This information is reprinted courtesy of Prevent Child Abuse America, 2003. For more information on preventing child abuse and neglect, please visit www.preventchildabuse.org.

APPENDIX C

CHILD ABUSE HOTLINES

Most states have toll-free 24-hour child abuse hotlines. If your state does not have such a hotline or if you have trouble getting through to a phone number listed below call Childhelp® USA National Child Abuse Hotline at 1-800-4-A-CHILD® (1-800-422-4453), TDD: 1-800-2-A-CHILD. This line operates 24 hours a day, seven days a week, and offers crisis intervention, information, literature, and referrals.

This information is reprinted courtesy of Prevent Child Abuse America, 2003. For more information on preventing child abuse and neglect, please visit www. preventchildabuse.org.

Call the police or 911 immediately if:

- You witness an assault
- You witness or become aware of extreme or serious abuse
- You confront an emergency situation

Alabama
  334.242.9500
Alaska
  800.478.4444
Arizona
  888.SOS.CHILD
  (888.767.2445)
Arkansas
  800.482.5964

California
  800.540.4000
  800.272.6699 (TDD/Hearing
    Impaired)
  213.283.1960 (from outside California)
Colorado
  303.866.3003
Connecticut
  800.842.2288
  800.624.5518 (TDD/Hearing Impaired)
Delaware
  800.292.9582
District of Columbia
  202.671.7233
Florida
  800.96.ABUSE
  (800.962.2873)
Georgia
  800.843.5200
Hawaii
  808.832.5300
Idaho
  800.600.6474
Illinois
  800.252.2873
Indiana
  800.800.5556
Iowa
  800.362.2178

Kansas
    800.922.5330
Kentucky
    800.752.6200
Louisiana
    225.925.4571
Maine
    800.452.1999
Maryland
    800.332.6347
Massachusetts
    800.792.5200
Michigan
    800.942.4357
Minnesota
    651.296.8337
    (after hours, call 911)
Mississippi
    800.222.8000
Missouri
    800.392.3738
Montana
    866.820.KIDS
    (866.820.5437)
Nebraska
    800.652.1999
Nevada
    800.992.5757
New Hampshire
    800.894.5533
New Jersey
    800.792.8610
    800.835.5510 (TDD/Hearing
        Impaired)
New Mexico
    800.797.3260
New York
    800.342.3720

North Carolina
    800.662.7030
North Dakota
    800.245.3736
Ohio
    614.466.9274
Oklahoma
    800.522.3511
Oregon
    800.854.3508
Pennsylvania
    800.932.0313
Rhode Island
    800.RI.CHILD
    (800.742.4453)
South Carolina
    803.734-0220
South Dakota
    800.227.3020
Tennessee
    615.742.9192
Texas
    800.252.5400
Utah
    800.678.9399
Vermont
    800.649.5285
Virginia
    800.552.7096
Washington
    800.562.5624
West Virginia
    800.352.6513
Wisconsin
    800.CHILDREN
    (800.241.5373)
Wyoming
    800.457.3659

TOLL-FREE CRISIS HOTLINE NUMBERS CONTACT INFORMATION FOR RELATED ORGANIZATIONS

CHILD ABUSE

Childhelp USA
Phone: 800.4.A.CHILD (800.422.4453)
Who They Help: Child abuse victims, parents, concerned individuals

Youth Crisis Hotline
Phone: 800.HIT.HOME (800.448.4663)
Who They Help: Individuals reporting child abuse, youth ages 12 to 18

CHILD SEXUAL ABUSE

Stop It Now!
Phone: 888.PREVENT (888.773.8368)
Who They Help: Child sexual abuse victims, parents, offenders, concerned individuals

FAMILY VIOLENCE

National Domestic Violence Hotline
Phone: 800.799.SAFE (800.799.7233)
Who They Help: Children, parents, friends, offenders

MISSING/ABDUCTED CHILDREN

Child Find of America
Phone: 800.I.AM.LOST (800.426.5678)
Who They Help: Parents reporting lost or abducted children

Child Find of America—Mediation
Phone: 800.A.WAY.OUT (800.292.9688)
Who They Help: Parents, with abduction prevention and child custody issues

Child Quest International Sighting Line
Phone: 888.818.HOPE (888.818.4673)
Who They Help: Individuals with missing child emergencies and/or sighting information; victims of abduction

National Center for Missing and Exploited Children
Phone: 800.THE.LOST (800.843.5678)
Who They Help: Families and professionals, social services, law enforcement

Operation Lookout National Center for Missing Youth
Phone: 800.LOOKOUT (800.566.5688)
Who They Help: Individuals with missing child emergencies and/or sighting information for children ages 18 and under

RAPE/INCEST

Rape and Incest National Network
Phone: 800.656.HOPE, Ext. 1 (800.656.4673, Ext. 1)
Who They Help: Rape and incest victims, media, policy makers, concerned individuals

RELIEF FOR CAREGIVERS

National Respite Locator Service
Phone: 800.677.1116
Who They Help: Parents, caregivers, and professionals caring for children and adults with disabilities, terminal illnesses, or those at risk of abuse or neglect

YOUTH IN TROUBLE/RUNAWAYS

Girls and Boys Town
Phone: 800.448.3000
Who They Help: Abused, abandoned, and neglected girls and boys; parents; family members

Covenant House Hotline
Phone: 800.999.9999
Who They Help: Problem teens and homeless runaways ages 21 and under, family members, youth substance abusers

National Referral Network for Kids in Crisis
Phone: 800.KID.SAVE (800.543.7283)
Who They Help: Professionals, parents, adolescents

National Runaway Switchboard
Phone: 800.621.4000
Who They Help: Runaway and homeless youth, families

National Youth Crisis Hotline Youth Development International
Phone: 800.HIT.HOME (800.448.4663)
Who They Help: Individuals wishing to obtain help for runaways; youth ages 12 to 18 experiencing drug abuse, teen pregnancy, homelessness, prostitution, or physical, emotional, or sexual abuse

CRIME VICTIMS

National Center for Victims of Crime
Phone: 800.FYI.CALL (800.394.2255)
Who They Help: Families, communities, and individuals harmed by crime

Source: National Clearinghouse on Child Abuse and Neglect Information

NÚMEROS TELEFÓNICOS GRATUITOS SOBRE LAS CRISIS

MALTRATO DE MENORES/ ABUSO INFANTIL

Childhelp USA
Teléfono: 800.4.A.CHILD (800.422.4453)
A quienes ayudan: Víctimas de maltrato de menores, padres, individuos preocupados

ABUSO SEXUAL DE MENORES

Stop It Now!
Teléfono: 888.PREVENT (888.773.8368)
A quienes ayudan: Víctimas del abuso sexual, padres, infractores, individuos preocupados

VIOLENCIA EN LA FAMILIA

National Domestic Violence Hotline
Teléfono: 800.799.SAFE (800.799.7233)
A quienes ayudan: Niños, padres, amigos, infractores o delincuentes

NIÑOS DESAPARECIDOS/ SECUESTRADOS

Child Quest International Sighting Line
Teléfono: 888.818.HOPE (888.818.4673)
A quienes ayudan: Individuos con emergencias de niños perdidos/o información sobre si se han visto a los niños perdidos o secuestrados; víctimas de secuestro

National Center for Missing and Exploited Children
Teléfono: 800.THE.LOST (800.843.5678)
A quienes ayudan: Familias y profesionales servicios sociales, agencias policiales

VIOLACIÓN/INCESTO

Rape and Incest National Network
Teléfono: 800.656.HOPE, Ext. 1 (800.656.4673, Ext. 1)
A quienes ayudan: Víctimas de violación y incesto, los medios de comunicación, personas encargadas de formular la política de un comité o partido, individuos preocupados

ALIVIO PARA LOS CUIDADORES DE NIÑOS

National Respite Locator Service
Teléfono: 800.677.1116
A quienes ayudan: Padres, personas que tienen a su cuidado a un incapacitado sin recibir por ello renumeración, y profesionales que tienen a su cuidado a niños o adultos discapacitados, con enfermedades terminales o personas que están en riesgo de abuso o negligencia Asistencia en Español—9:00 a.m.–5:00 p.m.

JÓVENES CON PROBLEMAS/O QUE SE FUERON DE LA CASA

Girls and Boys Town
Teléfono: 800.448.3000
A quienes ayudan: Niños y niñas abusados, abandonados, y descuidados; padres; miembros de familia

Covenant House Hotline
Teléfono: 800.999.9999
A quienes ayudan: Jóvenes con problemas y jóvenes sin hogar que se escapan de la casa de 21 años y menor, miembros familiares, jóvenes que abusan de los estupefacientes

National Runaway Switchboard
Teléfono: 800.621.4000
A quienes ayudan: Niños que se fueron de la casa y jóvenes sin hogar, familias

VÍCTIMAS DE CRIMEN

National Center for Victims of Crime
Teléfono: 800.FYI.CALL (800.394.2255)
A quienes ayudan: Familias, comunidades, y individuos que fueron afectados por algún crimen

Source: *The National Clearinghouse on Child Abuse and Neglect Information*

HELPFUL WEB LINKS

www.thomas.lovc.gov . . . . (Federal government resources)

www.findlaw.com . . . . (Legal resources)

www.law.cornell.edu . . . . (Legal resources)

www.medlineplus.gov . . . . (National Institutes of Health and United States National Library of Medicine—children's health issues)

nccanch.acf.hhs.gov . . . . (National Clearinghouse on Child Abuse and Neglect)

www.nrscrisisline.org . . . . (National Runaway Switchboard)

www.abanet.org . . . . (American Bar Association)

www.aclu.org . . . . (American Civil Liberties Union)

www.naccchildlaw.org . . . . (National Association of Counsel for Children [NACC])

www.aarp.org . . . . (Grandparent Information Center, American Association of Retired Persons)

www.frca.org . . . . (Family Support America)

www.aap.org . . . . (American Academy of Pediatrics)

www.bbsa.org . . . . (Big Brothers/Big Sisters of America)

www.ciccparenting.org . . . . (Center for the Improvement of Child Caring)

www.efn.org . . . . (Birth to Three)

www.healthyfamiliesamerica.org . . . . (Healthy Families America® [HFA])

www.apsac.org . . . . (American Professional Society on the Abuse of Children [APSAC])

www.aphsa.org . . . . (American Public Human Services Association)

www.nccafv.org . . . . (National Council on Child Abuse and Family Violence)

www.ciccparenting.org . . . . (Center for the Improvement of Child Caring)

www.casanet.org . . . . (Court Appointed Special Advocates)

www.acenet.edu/calec/ged/ . . . . (GED—General Educational Development)

www.ncjrs.org/html/ojjdp/
   nationalreport99/chapter6.pdf . . . . (Probation statistics from OJJDP-NCJRS)

www.jbutts.com . . . . (Evaluation of Teen Courts Project)
www.acenet.edu . . . . (American Council on Education)
www.nrlc.org . . . . (Pro-life organization)
www.plannedparenthood.org . . . . (Pro-choice organization)
www.gangstyle.com . . . . (Information by, for, and about gang members, including outreach and counseling services)
www.youthcourt.net . . . . (National Youth Court Center)

GLOSSARY

42 USC § 1983—A federal statute that allows citizens to sue the federal government for constitutional violations

abuse-neglect-dependency actions—Actions involving children who have been victims of intentional, negligent, or innocent mistreatment, inattention, abandonment, or relinquishment

adjudicatory hearing or phase—The phase of a juvenile hearing where the court determines whether the facts the state has alleged are true

admissions—A statement against one's interest

adult judge model—A youth court in which an adult acts as the judge; youths play all other roles

amenability hearing—The portion of a juvenile transfer hearing that is devoted to determining whether a juvenile can benefit from treatment or rehabilitation within the juvenile court system

arraignment—A proceeding at which accused criminal offenders enter their pleas of guilty or not guilty to charges against them, or delinquent offenders admit or deny the truth of the charges against them, and the magistrate sets bail for the defendants

attorney general—The head of the state's justice department; the state's chief law enforcement attorney

attorney-client privilege—The legal doctrine that prevents lawyers from disclosing anything that their clients tell them about crimes they have committed

authentication of records—The process by which a party seeking to introduced written records into

evidence demonstrates that the records are genuine, trustworthy, and what they purport to be

avoid—To disaffirm a contract without incurring legal liability

bail—The release of a defendant prior to the hearing in exchange for the payment of a sum of money

bail bondsman—A person who is in the business of posting bond for defendants in exchange for fees

Bill of Particulars—A document that the prosecution produces during the discovery phase of a criminal trial specifying the time, place, manner, and means of commission of a criminal or delinquent act

bond—The sum of money that secures the release of criminal or juvenile defendants

burden of persuasion or burden of proof—The obligation to convince the court of the truth of the matter at hand or of the existence of certain facts or conditions

capacity—The ability to enter legally binding relationships, incur legal obligations, and obtain legal rights

case plan—A document that social services agency workers devise in conjunction with the parents

certify—To send a case from one court to another

chain of custody—A detailed and accurate accounting of where evidence has been and what precautions the parties holding the evidence have taken to prevent tampering, alteration, loss, or removal of it, from the moment of its discovery until the moment of its introduction in court

citation in lieu of arrest—An order to appear in court before a magistrate or judge at a later date

clear and convincing evidence—A standard of proof that lies above **preponderance of the evidence** and below **proof beyond a reasonable doubt;** most legal practitioners quantify preponderance of the evidence as 51 percent certainty, proof beyond a reasonable doubt as approximately 90 percent certainty, and clear and convincing evidence as somewhere between those two degrees

colors—Certain combinations of colors associated with a particular gang; a gang's identifying clothing

concurrent jurisdiction—The doctrine that, like prosecutorial discretion, mandates that jurisdiction over certain offenses lies in both the adult criminal court and the juvenile court and leaves it to prosecutors to decide in which court they will try cases

confidentiality—The doctrine that prevents divulging information

constructive emancipation—The conferring of adult status upon minors by means of a change in the minors' positions in the eyes of society, in most instances through marriage or joining the military

criminal intent (or *mens rea*)—"Guilty mind." Desiring to do something illegal or malicious. Wanting to bring about a certain result and working to bring about that result.

declaratory judgment—A binding adjudication of the rights and status of litigants. The court grants no consequential relief other than a declaration of the petitioner's rights.

delinquency—Committing an act that would be a crime if an adult committed it

dependent children—Children over whom the court assumes jurisdiction because they are in need of care through no fault of their parents

discretionary transfer—Statutes that allow the juvenile court judge to decide whether to transfer a case to adult court or keep it in juvenile court

dispositional hearing or phase—The phase of a juvenile hearing where the court determines which course of action will be in the children's best interests

diversion—The process by which a juvenile offender can avoid facing charges in the traditional court system by agreeing to participate in an alternative forum

double jeopardy—Standing trial in the same forum more than once for the same act

due process—The correct and proper way of carrying on a legal action; prescribed by the Fifth and Fourteenth Amendments to the Constitution.

element—One of the constituent parts of a crime. For example, the constituent parts of the crime of robbery would be (1) the taking (2) by force (3) of the property of another (4) from the person of the victim. If any of these is missing, a robbery has not occurred, although another crime may have occurred.

emancipation—The legal recognition that a child is mature enough to have the legal status of adult. Emancipation removes many of the legal disabilities attendant to minority. The process by which a minor attains majority, or adult, status in the eyes of the law.

emotional or mental abuse—Berating, humiliating, denigrating, or otherwise purposely inflicting psychological pain upon a child

exclusion—Statutes that proscribe the juvenile court from having jurisdiction over certain offenses or offenders

exclusive jurisdiction—The sole power to hear an action. Those courts possessing exclusive jurisdiction are the only courts empowered to hear cases falling within that jurisdiction.

express emancipation—The conferring of majority status upon a minor by means of the parents' spoken or written consent

fetal alcohol syndrome—A condition where a child displays symptoms known to be associated with the mother's having consumed intoxicating substances while she was pregnant with that child

findings of fact and conclusions of law—The findings of fact are those things that the court adjudges the parties to have proven. The conclusions of law are the legal conclusions that the court has drawn from applying the statutes and case law to the facts at hand.

graffiti—Words, symbols, pictures, letters, or a combination thereof that demonstrates the dominance of a gang in a certain neighborhood, or **turf.** Graffiti also indicates disrespect toward another gang, declares war upon another gang, or communicates messages within the gang. Graffiti that is upside down indicates disrespect toward another gang.

guardian ad litem—"Guardian for the case." A person, often a lawyer, whom the court appoints to advocate for the best interest of the child. Courts appoint guardian ad litems for the duration of the delinquency proceedings where there is no parent or legal guardian present. Guardian ad litems also serve in abuse-neglect-dependency cases.

habeas corpus—"You have the body." The name given to a class of writs whose primary objective is releasing petitioners from confinement.

hand signs—Gestures made with the fingers and hands that indicate membership in a gang, demonstrate disrespect toward another gang, or convey messages within the gang

hazing—The ritualized initiation into an organization, a process that often involves some level of pain, humiliation, or ordeal

hearsay—An out-of-court statement that a party offers to prove the truth of the matter stated therein

hostile or adverse witness—A person who testifies against the interests of the person who is examining or questioning him in court, and who is thus subject to cross examination

illegal (or unreasonable) search and seizure—A situation where a state agent takes possession of a person or property belonging to a person in a way that is inconsistent with the mandates of the United States Constitution

implied emancipation—The conferring of majority status upon minors by means of unspoken parental consent to the minors living separately and apart from their parents without the parents' or the minors' objection

Indivisible Day Rule—The rule that a person is a certain age at the start of the day on that person's birthday regardless of the person's actual time of birth

injunction—A court order prohibiting a person or group from engaging in certain activities

intake worker—A social worker who initiates a child abuse case or other juvenile action, taking physical custody of the child if necessary, starting a file for the child, and initiating legal proceedings

interrogation—The formal questioning of a suspected offender by the police while the offender is in custody

Jane Doe hearing—A colloquial name for a judicial bypass hearing. The name comes from the fact that in order to preserve the anonymity of the applicant, court personnel and records refer to the minor girl as "Jane Doe."

judicial bypass—A device that allows a pregnant, unemancipated minor to petition the court to allow her to obtain an abortion without having notifying or obtaining the permission of her parent or guardian in states that have parental notification of, or consent to, abortion statutes

judicial waiver—The process whereby a juvenile court gives up its jurisdiction over a case and transfers that case to the adult criminal court

jurisdiction—The authority by which courts and judicial officers take charge of and decide cases

legal custody—A disposition where the court places children with a person who assumes daily rights and responsibilities for the children, while the parents retain some parental rights

limitation statutes—Laws that prescribe the maximum amount of time that may pass between certain events, such as the filing of the complaint and the hearing

long-term foster care and **planned permanent living arrangement**—A disposition where the parents retain their residual rights, while the social services agency places children into foster homes or institutions on a long-term or permanent basis

magistrate—A judicial officer who performs many of the functions that a judge performs, but who has less authority than a judge has. The magistrate makes recommendations that do not become binding upon the parties until the judge signs them.

malice aforethought—Wishing to bring about the death of another human being and acting to do so

mandatory transfer—Statutes that prescribe that certain offenses must come under the jurisdiction of the adult criminal court even if a juvenile commits the offense

manslaughter—The unintentional killing of a human being through negligence

master—A judicial officer whom the court appoints to assist in performing judicial duties in a specific case. Like a magistrate, the master can perform judicial functions but the master's recommendations are not binding upon the parties until a judge signs them.

mens rea—Criminal or malicious intent to commit a crime

minor—In the context of parental notification of abortion laws, an unemancipated girl ranging from 16 to 18 years of age, who has not been married, and is not a member of the armed services

Miranda warnings—The set of cautions and instructions that police must provide to criminal suspects when they are in custody before the police may ask any questions of the suspect

mitigating factors—Those facts and circumstances that do not excuse or justify an offense, but which a court or jury in fairness and mercy may consider as extenuating or reducing the degree of moral culpability

murder—The intentional killing of a human being with **malice aforethought**

necessaries—Those things that person requires in order to survive, such as food, clothing, shelter, and transportation to a place of employment

neglect—Failing to provide necessary care in the form of supervision, clothing, food, shelter, medical care, education, or guidance

nolle prosequi—"I will no further prosecute." It means that the prosecutor will drop the charges against the defendant.

opening statement—A nonargumentative narrative of the chronology of a case, including which witnesses will appear and an outline of the testimony they will offer

parens patriae—"Parent of his country." It is the power of the state to act on behalf of, or for the good of, its citizens, especially children.

parentage proceedings—Proceedings involving such issues as paternity, custody, child support, and visitation that take place in juvenile or domestic relations court

parental notification of abortion laws—Laws that require minor girls to either notify or obtain the consent of one or both of their parents before they can obtain abortions

peer jury model—A youth court in which an adult presents the case to a jury of youths

penal—A legal action that carries with it the possibility of punishment or loss of liberty as its consequence

petition—A formal, written document that begins a delinquency proceeding

physical abuse—Hitting, shaking, burning, cutting, throwing, or otherwise purposely or recklessly inflicting pain or injury upon a child

praecipe—A request to issue a subpoena

preliminary injunction—An order temporarily barring a party from carrying out a certain action

pretrial—An informal meeting among the parties to a case that occurs before the scheduled trial date

privacy—The state of keeping proceedings out of the public eye

privilege—A class of communications that society values enough to grant it special protection or legal status

probable cause—A level of certainty sufficient to sustain the initiation of a criminal or delinquency proceeding; more than a hunch but less than total or even near-total certainty; a reasonable ground for belief in the existence of facts warranting an action. Probable cause is a relatively low-level burden of proof.

probable cause hearing—A hearing to determine whether probable cause exists to find whether someone committed a crime and whether a complaint or delinquency petition should follow

procedural due process—The part of due process that deals specifically with the manner in which things proceed; for example, when, how, and to whom the state must give notice of a delinquency proceeding; the processes the courts and the state must follow in order to preserve the constitutional rights of detainees and defendants.

properly redacted opinion—An opinion in which court personnel have blacked out any language that would tend to identify the participants

prosecute—To file and follow through on criminal or delinquency charges against a person with the aim of gaining a conviction

prosecutorial discretion—A doctrine that grants the prosecutor the right to make a decision whether to try a juvenile in juvenile or adult court

protective supervision—A disposition that allows parents to retain legal and physical custody of their children while they work on their case plan

right to a speedy trial—A constitutional mandate that criminal and juvenile defendants must stand trial within a prescribed time

seizure—To take possession of the property or person of another

serious youthful offender statutes—A new category of delinquency statutes that allow blended sentences in delinquency cases that are serious, but not serious enough to warrant transfer to criminal court

sexual abuse—Causing a child to perform, submit to, or view a sexual act

social service record—Written accounts of social services agencies' involvement with juveniles and their families

social services agency—A county organization charged with overseeing issues involving the health and welfare of its constituents

standard of proof—The degree of certainty that a party must establish in a particular case

status offender—A minor who has committed an offense that is only an offense when a minor commits it, such as consumption of alcohol or getting married

stop and frisk—Where police officers briefly detain a person and pats down the person to look for weapons; a quick and relatively unobtrusive search.

subpoena—A command to appear at a certain time and place and give certain testimony. It can include a command to produce documents or other physical evidence. The sheriff will execute a subpoena by force if necessary.

substantive due process—The content of the constitutional rights that due process protects

temporary custody—A disposition that removes children from their parents' custody and keeps the children under the juvenile court's jurisdiction for a discrete period with a view toward reunification of the family within a relatively short time

termination of parental rights—A disposition the completely and permanently deprives parents of custody and all rights and responsibilities attendant to raising their children

Terry stop—A brief stop predicated upon a reasonable suspicion by the police that criminal activity might be afoot. *See* **stop and frisk.**

unruly child—A minor who engages in dangerous or potentially harmful behavior

void contract—A contract that is null, or nonexistent, from its very inception

voidable contract—A contract that that one of the parties can disaffirm without incurring legal liability or consequences

waiver—The voluntary giving up of rights or privileges

warrant—A written order commanding the sheriff or the police to take custody of a certain person and bring that person before the court

youth courts, teen courts, or **peer courts**—Legal forums that are an alternative to traditional juvenile courts

youth gang—A loose or formal collection of individuals who identify themselves as part of a common group; have a group name; display visual identifiers involving clothing, jewelry, hairstyle, or hand signs; occupy a certain territory; and engage in delinquent behavior

youth judge model—A youth court in which youths play all roles, including that of judge

youth tribunal model—A youth court in which youths play all roles; there is a multi-person panel rather than a single judge

INDEX

Note: Key terms are indicated by page numbers in bold type. Page numbers in italic type indicate figures or tables.